Financ

Finance for BTEC National

John Hopkins

PITMAN

PITMAN PUBLISHING
128 Long Acre, London WC2E 9AN

First published in Great Britain in 1988

British Library Cataloguing in Publication Data

Hopkins, John
Finance for BTEC National.
1. Finance
I. Title
332

ISBN 0 273 02877 4

Note The assignment material on pages 137–146 is copyright-free and may be photocopied by the teacher and student in carrying out the integrative assignments.

Printed and bound in Great Britain at The Bath Press, Avon

Contents

Preface

The BTEC National Diploma/Certificate core unit *Finance* is not intended to be a traditional book-keeping/accounting course. Indeed, it is the intention of those who wrote the unit specification and the moderators who have overseen its implementation and development, to guide lecturers responsible for the teaching of the unit away from the traditional material that was used in the forerunner of this unit *Numeracy and Accounting*.

The objective of *Finance* is to communicate and develop the financial skills that students need for their personal experience and for their understanding of the broad field of business and its management. *Finance* should not, therefore, be seen as a self-contained unit – it needs to be integrated with the other core units and options in the course.

The approach has been to view this book as a study of an information system with an emphasis on information sources, particularly in the personal finance sections, information recording and information uses.

This book has been written with students studying BTEC National Diploma/Certificate core unit *Finance* specifically in mind. The contents have been structured so as to move through the General Objectives in the order set out in the Unit Specification, as there are obvious developmental steps involved; therefore it is advisable to progress through the chapters in chronological order.

Furthermore, the tasks provided at the end of the chapters may draw upon knowledge developed in previous chapters in order to reinforce that material and provide further applications for its use.

As a contribution towards unit integration and skills development, a number of assignments with these factors included are to be found in Chapter 20 at the end of the book. These integrative assignments (pages 137–146) are copyright-free and you may photocopy them for exercise use.

As the philosophy of BTEC National is to provide students with practical activities related to the business, Chapter 20 covers assignments linked with core units such as *People in Organisations* and *The Organisation in its Environment*.

Acknowledgements

The author wishes to acknowledge the part played in the production of this book by friends and colleagues, in particular Mrs Molly Potton for word processing and Mr Brian Farmbough FCA for contributions towards the assignments.

Permission to use copyright material has been granted by the following organisations, for which the author is most grateful:

Cheshunt Building Society
The Controller of Her Majesty's Stationery Office
The Financial Times
The M & G Group
National Giro Bank
New Forest District Council
Trustee Savings Bank (TSB)

1
Personal Income

INTRODUCTION

We all need money to live on, there are certain basic needs that have to be met, like food and shelter, and in our society the satisfaction of these needs must be paid for. Hence the degree to which life's needs can be satisfied depends upon the money available.

There are two types of money available, *capital* and *income*. Capital is the accumulated wealth of an individual, it may either be invested to provide for the individuals needs, e.g. purchase of a house to provide shelter, or it may be invested to provide income. Income is an inflow of money over a period of time. Most individuals adapt their various needs to match the capital and income available to them. Capital is used to acquire durable assets, e.g. a house, a car, furniture; income is used to pay for day-to-day consumption. Unless income is insufficient to satisfy the requirements of everyday expenditure, it would be unwise to use capital for this purpose. Surplus income can be used to increase capital through savings or the repayment of borrowed capital. This is, for the majority, the main way of accumulating capital. Income, then, is of considerable importance to all of us. We will consider your main sources of income, along with the effects of taxation and other deductions on your incomes.

TYPES OF INCOME

The main forms of income available to us are grants, interest from investments, benefits, earnings and pensions. Pensions are considered because you are likely to have some pension rights, if not now then in the future, as part of your conditions of service.

Student grants

The amount and type of grant available to you depend upon a number of factors, the most significant of these being parents' income. The higher your parents' income the lower will be your grant; this is known as a 'means tested' grant. Students who have been self-supporting for at least two years before making a grant application may find that they do not have parental income taken into consideration when their grants are assessed. Full details on the grants available in your circumstances can be obtained from your local education authority or you can contact your student advisor.

The important thing about student grants from the point of our studies is that they are non-taxable. This has implications for the other forms of income available to students which we will consider later.

If you are a student *over* eighteen and your grant is less than the full student grant because of means testing of parental income, your parents can pay you the difference.

Students who are concerned about the level of their grant should seek advice as previously indicated; do not be afraid to be persistent if you believe that your entitlement to a grant has not been fairly assessed.

For general information about students and income tax obtain Leaflet IR 60 from your local Inland Revenue office.

Income from investments

Income is provided from investments through the purchase of shares, government stocks and the depositing of funds with an institution that will pay interest on these funds. It should be noted that income from investments is subject to fluctuation because of interest rate changes and company dividends are not fixed.

This is a complicated subject and an individual who obtains a significant part of their income from investments should seek professional advice. However, all students of finance should inform themselves about the main sources of investment income. This topic is closely linked with that of savings (*see* Chapter 4).

When looking for income from investments you should remember the general rule that low-risk investments provide only low returns, the higher the risk the greater the potential return. The broad options available are:

Banks and building societies

These provide a very safe investment and offer a wide range of accounts, paying a variety of rates of interest dependent upon the sum deposited (Fig. 1.1.). There is a lot of competition in the High Street for your investment so look around for the best investment for your particular circumstances. The majority of this type of investment are designed for capital growth, i.e. the interest earned is periodically added to the original investment. It is important therefore to ensure that, if income is your requirement, interest can be withdrawn regularly.

Students should note that the interest on bank and building society deposits is paid net of income tax, i.e. with the income tax deducted. This income cannot be recovered. If you are not a taxpayer then depositing your funds in this type of institution will probably be the wrong form of investment – you should look at National Savings.

National Savings

National savings schemes are available at post offices. A competitive rate of interest is paid but income tax is not deducted; your interest is paid in full. Income from national savings is available through *deposit bonds* which, despite television advertising aimed at retired persons, are a suitable investment for non-taxpayers requiring a regular income from their investments.

Stock market investments

Companies pay a dividend to their shareholders (*see* Chapter 4) and the government pays interest on its stock, thus income is obtained. Both stocks and shares are usually purchased through the Stock Market. There is an element of risk attached to this form of investment; not only is the income from the investment subject to greater fluctuation than that based on High Street investment rates, but the value of your investment can fall. See the list of share prices in *The Financial Times* (Fig. 1.2) and note that the price of shares both rose and fell in a day's trading.

Buying stocks and shares is quite straightforward, but it is best to seek professional advice before risking your capital. The most obvious way to obtain advice is to approach a *stockbroker* and discuss your financial needs. Other professional advisors may assist you with your investments but they will probably charge a fee for that advice on top of the stockbroker commission, so the direct approach to a stockbroker is likely to be the least costly route to this form of investment.

In order to reduce the risk of this type of investment, it is usual to purchase a 'portfolio' of stocks and shares – that is a number of different types of share so that the fall in value of one does not mean a dramatic fall in the value of the total investment. The risk that income could be severely reduced is also mitigated. To

Fig. 1.1 Building society advert

Notice is hereby given in accordance with the Society's Rules that as from 5th December 1987 the rates of interest payable per annum on investment and deposit accounts will be as follows:

	NET *paid half-yearly + paid yearly	GROSS EQUIVALENT for tax payers at the basic rate of 27%
Investment Shares	4.00% *	5.48%
7 Day Notice Account (Silver Shares)	5.50% *	7.53%
1 Month Notice Account (Gold Shares)	5.75% *	7.88%
Cheshuntcash Instant Access Account		
£1,000 – £4,999	6.25% +	8.56%
£5,000 – £19,999	6.80% +	9.32%
£20,000 – £250,000 (inc)	7.05% +	9.66%
Monthly Income Option		
£1,000 – £4,999	6.08%	8.33%
£5,000 – £19,999	6.60%	9.04%
£20,000 – £250,000 (inc)	6.83%	9.36%
Special 4 Term Shares		
£500 – £4,999	6.50% +	8.90%
£5,000 – £19,999	7.00% +	9.59%
£20,000 – £250,000 (inc)	7.75% +	10.62%
Regular Monthly Savings	5.50% *	7.53%
Deposits (personal)	3.75% *	5.14%

The rate of interest on all other personal investment accounts will be decreased by 1% from 5th December 1987 with the exception of S.A.Y.E. accounts which remain unchanged.

Full details from:
Cheshunt Building Society, FREEPOST, Waltham Cross, Herts EN8 7BR

Cheshunt BUILDING SOCIETY

A member of the Building Societies' Association. Assets exceed £220m.
Shares and Deposits in this Society are Trustee investments.

Fig. 1.2 Share prices in *The Financial Times*

BANKS, HP & LEASING

1987/88 High	Low	Stock	Price	+ or –	Div Net	C'vr	Y'ld Gr's	P/E
259	128	ANZ $A1	136	....	Q21c	3.1	6.1	5.4
*273	175	Allied Irish	215	....	†Q61.6%	2.8	5.3	9.3
*£16 7/16	£10½	Algemene Fl.10	£11	....	Q2.7%	2.1	7.4	6.4
*128	53	Anglo Irish	70	....	Q19.69%	1.2	5.2	24.8
108	67	Ansbacher (H.) 1p	68	+1	N2.0	–	4.0	–
£49⅛	£24¼	Banco de Bilbao S.A.	£36#	....	♦Q38%	3.0	2.7	12.3
£34½	£23½	Banco de Santander	£29⅛	+⅛	Q22%	Φ	1.9	Φ
*245	175	Bank Ireland Ir£1	215	....	KQ15.3%	2.9	5.2	9.2
£15	£11½	Bank Leumi	£15	....	–	–	–	–
350	240	Bk.Leumi (UK)£1	350	....	12.4	–	4.9	–
643	395	Bank Scotland £1	563	+1	†16.5	3.4	4.0	10.0
88	65	Bank of Wales	65	....	♦†a2.4	2.2	5.1	12.4
655	413	Barclays £1	495	+2	†21.0	3.8	5.8	5.6
*83	31	Benchmark 20p	32	....	1.63	1.6	7.0	12.6
620	410	Brown Shipley £1	425	....	†10.0	–	3.2	–
135	40	Business Mort Tst	58	–2	2.0	2.3	4.7	12.9
*480	290	Cater Allen £1	345	–3	20.15	–	8.0	–
433	137	✠Chancery Securities	190	....	†3.3	2.4	2.4	21.1
£26¾	£13½	Commerzbk DM10	£13½	....	Q18%	–	4.7	–
*£27	£18	C'hgn.Hbk.Kr100	£20	–¼	vQ15%	2.9	7.0	4.9
*£285½	£125½	Deutsche Bk DM50	£127¼	–⅝	Q24%	–	3.2	–
359	165	First Nat. Fin. 10p	237	+3	8.75	Φ	5.1	Φ
190	103	FNFC 6.3pc CvRedPref	128	....	6.3%	–	6.7	–
68½	14	♥First Pac. Hldg. 50c	19	....	Q2.31c	6.4	6.9	2.3
£17¼	£11½	Fuji Bank Y50	£14½	+7/32	Q15%	5.0	0.2	91.8
124	83	GPG	85	....	♦2.65	Φ	4.3	Φ
*418	298	Gerrard & National	313	....	17.0	–	7.4	–
270	110	Goode Durrant 5p	120xd	....	Ka2.5	–	2.9	–
386	222	Hambros 20p	265	–3	8.2	–	4.2	–
805	398	Hill Samuel	805	....	♦14.8	–	2.5	–
*87	46	HK & Shang. HK$2.50	54	+1	tQ37c	–	4.9	–
*565	411½	Joseph (Leo) £1	438	....	g13.33	–	4.2	–
194	134	King & Shaxson 20p	153	+2	8.75	–	7.8	–
*610	277	Kleinwort, Benson L.	337	–5	14.0	–	5.7	–
435	218	Lloyds £1	260	+1	†h12.0	4.5	6.3	4.5
57	36½	Lon. Scot. Bank 10p	54xc	....	1.8	Φ	4.7	Φ
763	120	MCorp $5	148	....	–	–	–	–
*567	308	Midland £1	408	+3	g20.1	4.5	6.7	4.5
[illegible]3	208	Morgan Grenfell £1	285	....	†10.5	–	5.0	–
*280	126½	Nat Aust. Bk. A$1	176xr	....	Q24.75c	Φ	5.6	Φ
*794	498	Nat. West. £1	588	+4	†20.5	4.6	4.8	6.3

obtain a portfolio implies a reasonably large sum available for investment, and this may not be possible for the majority. However, the risk of stock market investment may be spread by the purchase of shares in an *investment trust*, or units in a *unit trust*. Investment trusts are companies whose assets are shares in other companies. Unit trusts are funds managed by professional investors who use the pool of funds provided by those who subscribe to the trust for investment in stocks and shares. Investment in the Stock Market via a unit trust can commence with as little as £250, the units are bought from and resold to the unit trust. The press is full of advertisements from investment and unit trusts, their progress can also be watched in the listings given by the *Financial Times*.

Income from company shares and unit trusts is paid net of income tax at the standard rate, but the tax can be recovered by non-taxpayers.

For further information about stock market investments write to:

The Public Affairs Department, The Stock Exchange, Old Broad Street, London EC2 1HP.

The Unit Trust Association, Park House, 16 Finsbury Circus, London EC2M 7JP.

Fig. 1.3 Unit trust advert

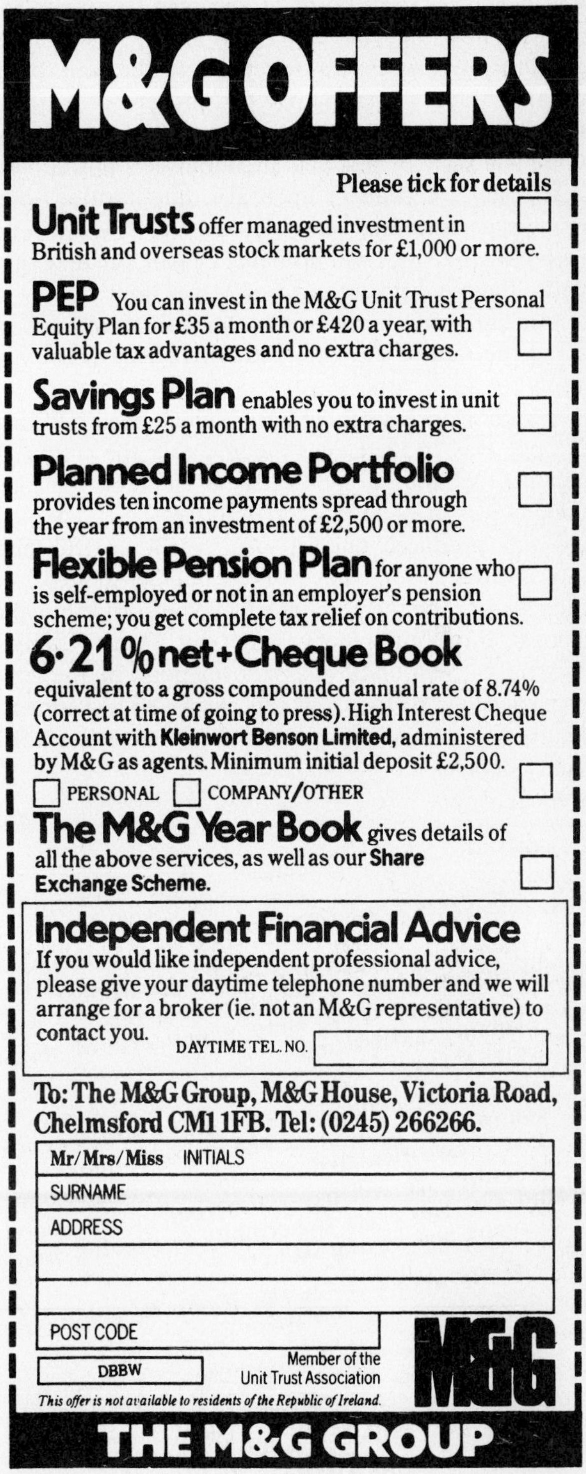

Income from benefits

Some students without parental support may be eligible for DHSS benefits. Booklet FB.2, available from the local social security office or post offices, will give a general guide to the benefits available and who qualifies for assistance.

It should be noted that some DHSS benefits are subject to income tax.

Income from earnings

Whether full- or part-time students, the majority of you will have some form of earnings from employment. Those of you employed in the managerial, administrative or clerical functions will be used to the usual methods of stating pay for this type of employment, i.e. a weekly wage or an annual salary. Often there is a scale of pay and an employee's position on that scale is dependent upon age, qualification, previous experience and length of service. Those of you with part-time jobs will probably be paid on an hourly basis, the pay being stated as £'x' per hour.

It is important to make sure that you clearly understand the rate of pay that is being offered when you apply for a job, otherwise you could be in for a shock! The author once accepted a job having been told that the pay was 1250. It was thought that the employer meant £1250 p.a., a good salary at the time – in fact the pay was £12.50 per week, only £650 p.a. The first pay day produced quite a surprise! Be careful with salary scales as some have a large number of steps, or *increments*, and the point at which you start can make a considerable difference to your pay. Try to establish how the calculation of your starting point on the scale is carried out so that you can check the assessment. Figure 1.4 shows a selection of job adverts stating salary details.

Total earnings can be made up of a variety of payments, basic pay can be increased by overtime, bonus, commission and other payments. The basis for these payments can be time- and output-related.

Earnings related to time

These can be stated in a number of ways, e.g. £2.50 per hour or £65 per week. In both cases payment is directly related to the time committed by you to an employer.

Variations on the basic rate may exist, this particularly refers to *overtime*. Overtime rates are usually paid after a certain number of 'normal' hours have been worked and the extra time worked is outside of the normal working hours, e.g. after 6.00 pm payment will be at $1\frac{1}{2}$ times the hourly rate. Some forms of employment have 'unsocial hours' payments for working outside the normal working day; this may also be known as a *shift allowance*.

Example

As a full-time student you are looking for part-time work to provide some income to supplement your meagre grant. The following options are open – which one offers the highest gross pay?

Fig. 1.4 Selection of job adverts

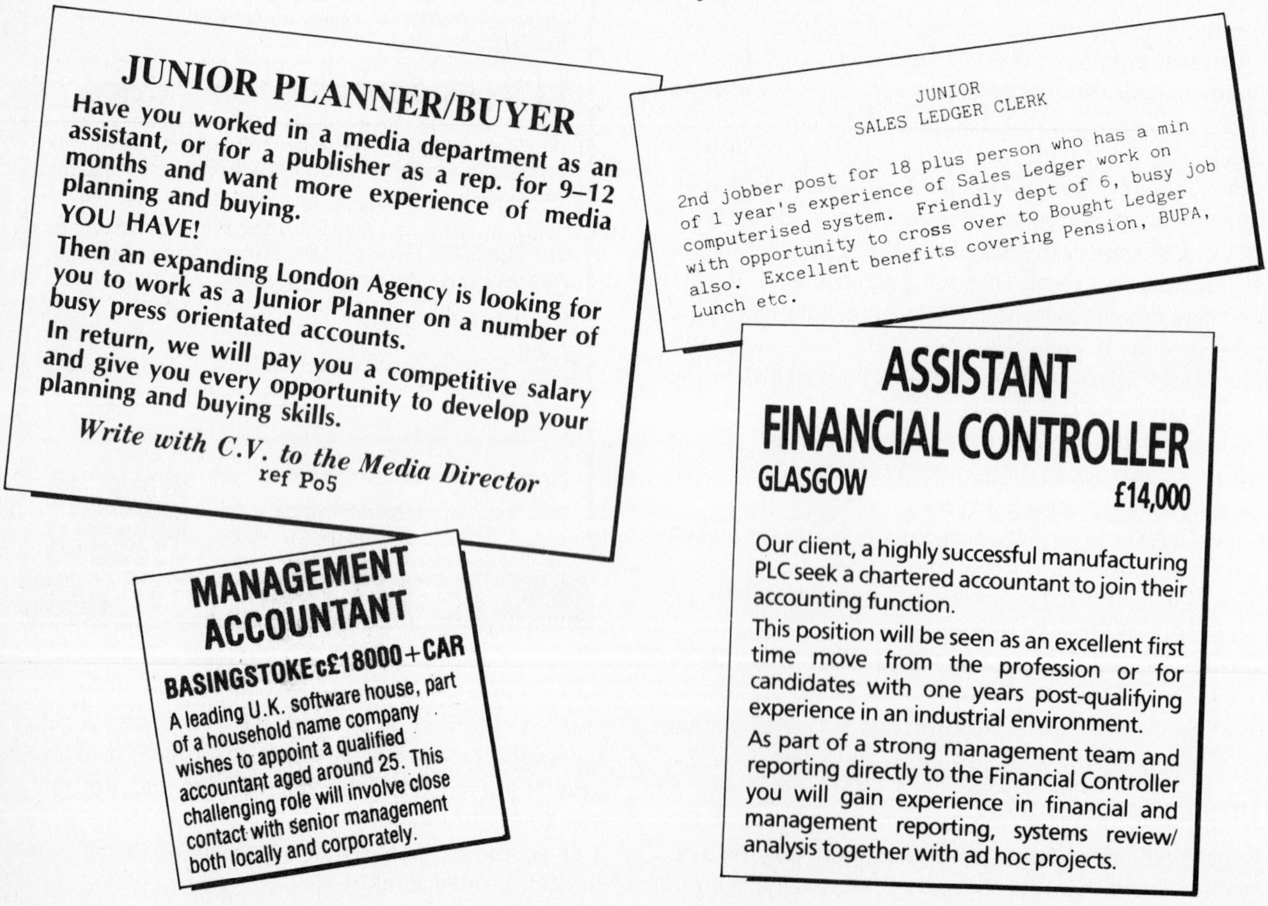

A *Stockroom assistant in a supermarket*
Hours: Friday 5.30 pm to 10.00 pm
Saturday 8.30 am to 5.30 pm
with one hour for lunch, unpaid.
Rate of pay £1.80 per hour plus time and one half for working after 6.00 pm and on Saturday.

B *Week-end bar staff at a local hotel*
Hours: Friday 7.30 pm to 11.30 pm
Saturday 11.00 am to 3.00 pm
and 7.30 pm to 11.30 pm
Sunday 8.00 pm to 11.00 pm
Rates of pay £2.00 per hour.

C *Nursing auxiliary at a private nursing home*
Hours: Friday night 8.30 pm to 8.30 am the next morning, with a half-hour unpaid break.
Rate of pay £2.50 per hour plus 40% unsocial hours enhancement.

Calculations

A *Stockroom assistant*

	£
Friday	
$\frac{1}{2}$ hour (5.30–6.00 pm) at £1.80 per hour	0.90
4 hours (6.00–10.00 pm) at £1.80 × $1\frac{1}{2}$	10.80
Saturday	
8 hours at £1.80 × $1\frac{1}{2}$	21.60
Total	33.30

Notice that the majority of the hours are paid at $1\frac{1}{2}$ times normal rate and that the unpaid lunch break has been taken into consideration in the calculation of Saturday's hours.

B *Bar staff*

Friday	4 hours	
Saturday	8 hours	
Sunday	3 hours	
Total	15 hours at £2.00 per hour	£30.00

Notice that there is only a basic hourly rate paid.

C *Nursing auxiliary*

Friday night	
11 hours at £2.50 per hour	27.50
Unsocial hours enhancement 40%	11.00
Total	38.50

On financial grounds only, the nursing auxiliary job would seem the best. However, we do not always choose on financial criteria alone – free time, type of work and working environment are all taken into consideration and a compromise may be taken. The stockroom assistant's job seems to offer the best combination of pay, free time at the week-end and a good night's sleep!

Earnings related to output

The simplest form of output related payment is *piece work*. Payment is made for each completed task. This type of payment is common with 'outworkers' or 'homeworkers', e.g. sewing up soft toys, in the worker's own home, from materials supplied in exchange for a payment per completed toy.

Bonus payments are also related to output, but are paid in addition to an hourly wage rate. The bonus is paid when a predetermined output target is achieved, e.g. a bonus of 25p each is paid for production over 100 units per day. A worker achieves 120 units and therefore receives, in addition to any time related payment, a bonus of (120 – 100) × 25p = 20 × 25p = £5.00. Bonus systems can be complex but the basis of all of them is an attempt to encourage output at a greater rate than the normal work rate.

Example

The management of your organisation wish to change the method of payment. The existing and proposed systems are set out below. If you were a union official would you advise acceptance of the change?

Existing system: piece work at £0.90 per unit.

Proposed system: basic pay of £2 per hour for a 35-hour week, above this overtime at $1\frac{1}{2}$ times normal rate, furthermore a bonus will be paid of 50p per unit for output that exceeds an average of 2 units per hour on a weekly basis.

In recent weeks the workers who would be affected have worked a 5-day 40-hour week and each has achieved an average output of 120 units per week.

Calculations (based upon recent work levels)

Existing system, weekly wage	
120 units at £0.90 per unit	£108

	£
Proposed system, weekly wage	
basic rate: 35 hours at £2 per hour	70
overtime : 5 hours at £2 per hour × $1\frac{1}{2}$	15
bonus : 120 units less (40 hrs × 2 units)	
at 50p per unit = 40 units × 50p	20
Total payment	105

i.e. £3 per week less than the current system.

Thus the existing system appears to be best for the workers under current circumstances. However, circumstances may change. Assuming the current output is near to maximum let us look at the situation if sales are halved and overtime working is no longer required.

Existing system, weekly wage	
60 units at £0.90 per unit	£54

Proposed system, weekly wage	
35 hours at £2 per hour	£70

No bonus is paid as output at 60 units is less than the average 2 per hour (2 units × 35 hrs = 70 units) required before bonus is paid.

Earnings related to financial performance

Two forms of payment need to be considered: profit and commission.

Profit sharing is simply a payment to employees related to the organisations profits: the method and timing of the payment will depend upon the individual company's scheme. The objective of this type of payment is of course to encourage behaviour that increases company profits. Workers who receive substantial profit-related payments might think twice before taking industrial action which would adversely affect the organisation's profit.

Fig. 1.5 Sales staff job adverts

Commission is a proportion of the proceeds of a transaction that the individual was responsible for. It may be a percentage of profit or sales value. The difference between commission and profit sharing is that commission is paid to an individual in proportion to that individual's revenue or profit earning activities; but company profits, the basis of profit sharing, are not dependent on an individual but are the result of collective efforts.

Sales staff often receive commission as part of their wages, in most cases a basic wage is paid plus commission. If only commission is paid then the rate of commission will be high.

Example

A car salesman is paid a basic wage of £50 per week plus a commission of 20% of the profit in a sale. He makes the following sales in a week. What are his earnings for the week?

		£
Ford Escort Mk II	profit	100
Austin Metro	profit	50
Austin Maxi	profit	nil
Vauxhall Cavalier	profit	200
Ford Escort XR2	profit	350
BMW 316	profit	500
Total profit on sales		1200

Calculation of a week's earnings

	£
Basic pay	50
Commission £1200 × 20%	240
Total earnings	290

Note: next week's earnings could be only £50 if no profitable sales are made. Therefore this type of payment can be subject to considerable fluctuation.

Note: Wages or salaries are often made up from a number of payments and it is possible to receive all three types of payment, time-related, output-related and financial performance related. Because of the need to gather information before calculating pay there is often a delay between payment of the basic wage and any extra earnings, typically the extra earnings are paid one pay period (week or month) after the basic pay. Hence January's overtime is paid with February's basic. Commission may take longer for payment made particularly if the transaction was a credit sale, then the commission may not be paid until the account has been settled.

Pensions

Assuming sufficient National Insurance contributions have been paid by or credited to an individual, that individual will receive the basic state pension upon retirement. Currently the normal retirement ages are at 60 years old for women and 65 years old for men.

Pensions above the level of the basic state pension are normally achievable through a State Earnings Related Pension Scheme (SERPS) or an employer-organised scheme.

BTEC National students may consider that pensions are of no immediate concern but your actions while working can have a serious effect on your eventual pension entitlement if you are a member of an employer-organised scheme. Unless the pension rights are transferable between different employers' schemes, changing your employment will reduce your eventual pension because pension rights are 'frozen' at the level of payments you were entitled to at the time of leaving.

Most pension schemes have the following features:

(a) a contribution from the employee of, say, 5% to 7% of earnings;

(b) a contribution from the employer which is often twice the employee's contribution;

(c) a pension paid on retirement that is calculated by a formula such as 1/60th times final salary times years of service;

(d) a lump sum on retirement that is calculated by a formula such as 3/60th times final salary times years of service.

Example

A 60-year old female employee on a salary of £12 000 per annum retires after 15 years of employment with the organisation. Employee pension contributions to the scheme are 5% of earnings.

Pension contribution by employee in final year
  £12 000 × 5% = £600

Pension paid upon retirement
  1/60 × £12 000 × 15 years = £3000 p.a.

Lump sum paid upon retirement
  3/60 × £12 000 × 15 years = £9000

The effect of job changes on final pensions if the pension rights accumulated are not transferable can be shown by considering two individuals. Both retire after working for 40 years and contributing to pension schemes that pay a pension based on the formula 1/80th times final earnings times years service.

Case 1

This person has worked for the same organisation for 40 years and retires from a post for which the salary is £8000 p.a.

Pension calculation:
  1/80 × £8000 × 40 years = £4000 p.a.

Case 2

A person who has changed employment for advance-

ment. The pattern of employment is given below.
10 years with company A, salary on leaving £500 p.a.
5 years with company B, salary on leaving £700 p.a.
15 years with company C, salary on leaving £5000 p.a.
10 years with company D, salary on retiring £16 000 p.a.

Pension calculation

Frozen pension from company
A 1/80 × £500 × 10 yrs = £62.50 p.a.
B 1/80 × £700 × 5 yrs = £43.75 p.a.
C 1/80 × £5000 × 15 yrs = £937.50 p.a.'
Pension from final employment
1/80 × £16 000 × 10 yrs = £2000.00 p.a.
Total of pension received from employment schemes:
£3043.75 p.a.

Notice that although the person in Case 2 retires from a post which paid a salary twice that of the person in Case 1, the pension received is approximately 25% less than the Case 1 pension. However, this does not take into consideration the benefits of high earnings while working; some of these earnings could have been invested to provide a further source of income on retirement.

Pensions are then an important part of the total income we will receive during our lifetimes. It is important to consider the effect of changes of employment on pension rights and investigate the term of a pension scheme as part of any evaluation of job opportunities.

2

Deductions from income

INTRODUCTION

In Chapter 1 we have looked at ways an income is obtained. We will now look at the effect of taxation and other deductions on income. In some situations deductions can be avoided or minimised and we will examine the main forms of income again and calculate the likely deductions in various situations that you may encounter.

DEDUCTIONS FROM EARNINGS

Earnings will be subject to various deductions before you receive any money. The amount earned is known as *gross income* and the amount you actually receive is known as *net income;* the latter is often called 'take home pay'.

Deductions fall into two broad areas:

(a) voluntary deductions – made by agreement between you and your employer;

(b) statutory deductions – taxation in its various forms.

Voluntary deductions

It is often adminstratively easier for the various payments, subscriptions, etc, associated with your employment to be deducted from earnings by the employer, who is then responsible for making the payments to the various organisations. These deductions may include:

(a) savings schemes – these can range from a simple transfer to National Savings through to a company share purchase scheme;

(b) sports and social club fees;

(c) union membership subscription;

(d) pension scheme contributions – these payments may not be voluntary in the true sense as it is often a condition of service that employees are members of the organisation's pension scheme and make contributions based on earnings. Six per cent of gross earnings is a typical pension scheme contribution, however tax is not paid on the contribution in most circumstances, thus reducing the overall tax liability of employees.

Statutory deductions

Assuming your gross wage/salary is above the appropriate minimum level, your employer is legally required to make the following deductions:

(a) Income Tax – this is done under the *Pay-As-You-Earn (PAYE) system,* so that your annual tax liability is spread over a year.

(b) National Insurance contributions – the proportion of earnings deducted will depend upon whether you are a member of an occupational pension scheme or not.

The rates of deduction are on two scales:

1 not contracted out contribution rates – for those who will depend entirely on the state scheme for a pension. This is the higher rate of contribution.
2 contracted out contribution rates – a lower scale of payments for those who are entitled to an occupational pension.

Income Tax

Tax is payable on all forms of income from employment. For the majority of us this is simply our wage or salary. However, other work-related payments and benefits received are taxable. These include bonuses, tips, expense allowances and 'benefits in kind' such as company cars. The tax due on the total income of an employee is paid through the PAYE system. The collecting government department is the Inland Revenue.

Personal allowances

Each year everybody has a certain amount of income that is free of taxation – the personal allowance. The

Fig. 2.1 Personal allowances for 1987/88

Chancellor of the Exchequer's Budget Proposals: 1987

Income Tax 1987-88

Rates of Tax

The basic rate of income tax is to be reduced to 27%. The higher rates of tax (40%-60%) are to remain unchanged. The starting point for the 40% rate is to be increased from £17201 to £17901 taxable income and for the 45% rate from £20201 to £20401. The other higher rate thresholds are to remain unchanged. The new bands compared with the 1986-87 bands will be as shown in the table:

		1986-87 Bands	1987-88 Bands
		£	£
Basic rate		1-17200	1-17900
Higher rates	40%	17201-20200	17901-20400
	45%	20201-25400	20401-25400
	50%	25401-33300	25401-33300
	55%	33301-41200	33301-41200
	60%	Over 41200	Over 41200

Personal allowances

The personal allowances are to be increased as shown in the following table:

Allowance	1986-87	*Increase*	1987-88
	£	£	£
Single person	2335	90	2425
Married man	3655	140	3795
Wife's earned income	2335	90	2425
Additional personal	1320	50	1370
Widow's bereavement	1320	50	1370
Blind person	360	180	540
Age-single person (Age 65-79)	2850	110	2960
*Age-Single person (Age 80 and over)		220	3070
Age-Married man (Age 65-79)	4505	170	4675
*Age-Married man (Age 80 and over)		340	4845

The income limit for the full age allowance will be increased to £9800 (previously £9400).

* From 1987-88 a new, higher level of age allowance for those aged 80 and over is being introduced. Subject to the income limit, you may be entitled to claim this for 1987-88 if you (or in the case of a married man, either you or your wife) will be aged 80 years or over on 5 April 1988.

amount depends upon a person's status and is set each year by the government in the 'Budget'. Figure 2.1 shows the allowances for 1987/8.

It should be noted that the *married man's allowance* may be claimed by whichever partner in a marriage would receive the most benefit from it. Additional allowances can be claimed in certain circumstances. For example for a single parent supporting a child or expenses wholly and necessarily incurred because of your employment. It is difficult to obtain allowance for expenses as an individual unless your employer, union or professional association has a specific agreement with the Inland Revenue.

Taxable pay

That proportion of income on which tax is due is known as taxable pay. It is found by:

Taxable pay = Total pay less allowances

Example 1

A job is advertised at £6720 per annum. How much of that pay will be taxable for (a) a married man, (b) a married woman and (c) a single person.

Using Fig. 2.1 we find that the personal allowance for a married man is £3795 per annum, a married woman and single person have the same personal allowance of £2425. The calculation is therefore:

Married man's taxable pay
£6720 – £3795 = £2925 p.a.
Married woman/single person's taxable pay
£6720 – £2925 = £4295 p.a.

It was assumed in the above example that contributions towards an occupational pension scheme were not required, i.e. they were *not contracted out.* It was noted in the section on voluntary deductions that occupational pension scheme contributions were tax free, so that if such payments were required the calculation would change to:

Taxable pay = Total pay *less* allowances *less* pension contributions.

Example 2

If the job advertised at £6720 per annum required a pension contribution of 5% of gross pay, what would the taxable pay be for the same groups of people?

Pension contribution is 5% of £6720 = £336. The calculation is therefore:

Married man's taxable pay
£6720 – £3795 – £336 = £2589 p.a.
Married woman/single person's taxable pay
£6720 – £2425 – £336 = £3959 p.a.

Tax payable

Having established the taxable pay, the tax payable on that sum is found by multiplying it by the tax rate. (*See* Fig. 2.1 for the rates.)

Note that the higher rates of tax are not payable on all of the taxable pay but only on the proportion of income that falls within the bands as specified.

The taxable pay in all the cases described in the examples above falls within the basic rate band, that is taxable pay up to £17 900, and is therefore taxed at 27%. The calculation for the married man, not contracted out is as shown:

Tax due = taxable pay £2925 × tax rate 27% = £789.75

The calculations for the other situations are carried out in a similar way and result in tax due for married woman/single person, not contracted out £1159.65; married man, contracted out £699.03; married woman/single person, contracted out £1068.93.

Do the calculation yourself to check the accuracy of these answers.

Example 3

Consider a person taking a senior post in local government administration, the salary will be £23 200, with pension contributions of 6% of salary. Calculate the tax payable on this level of earnings for a married man and a married woman/single person.

Pension contribution = £23 200 × 6%
= £1531.20 per annum

Remember:
Taxable pay = Total pay *less* allowances *less* pension contributions

Therefore, for a married man:
Taxable pay = £23 200 − £3795 − £1531.20 = £17 873.80
The tax due on this sum will be
£17873.80 × 27% = £4825.93

In the case of a married woman/single person the calculation becomes:

Taxable pay = £23 200 − £2425 − £1531.20 = £19 243.80

Note that this is more than the basic rate tax band (*see* Fig. 2.1). Therefore basic rate tax of 27% will be paid on the first £17 900 of taxable pay and the first of the higher rates will be paid on the balance of taxable pay as it falls in the band £17 901 to £20 400.

Calculations:
Tax due on the first £17 900 of taxable pay
= £17 900 × 27% = £4833.00 p.a.
Tax due on the balance
= (£19 243.80 − £17 900) × 40% = £537.52
Total tax due = £5370.52

Special situation

The married man's allowance can only be claimed for that proportion of a year that the person is married. *See* IR31. In the year of marriage the person claiming the married man's allowance will only be able to claim:

(a) the single person's allowance plus

(b) 1/12 of the difference between a single person's allowance and a married man's allowance for each month or part of a month that he/she was married in that tax year.

Example 4

If the marriage took place in July 19X7, three months after the start of the tax year, the personal allowance will be:

Single person's allowance £2425	
plus 9 months × 1/12 of the difference between the married man's allowance and a single person's allowance	
9/12 × (£3795 − £2425)	£1027.5
Total personal allowance for the year	£3452.5

Pay As You Earn (PAYE)

For the majority of us, our tax is collected weekly or monthly by deduction from our wages or salary by means of the PAYE system. The system works by taking a person's tax free pay allowance and dividing it by the number of pay periods in a year, e.g. by 52 for weekly paid employees and by 12 for monthly paid employees.

Therefore for each 1/12 of a monthly paid employee's annual salary that is received, 1/12 of the annual tax free allowance is given. Tax is paid on the balance each month and in this way the annual tax bill is spread evenly over the year.

Example 5

Annual salary	£12 000
less Personal allowance say	3 600
Taxable pay	8 400

Tax payable for the year = £8400 × 27% = £2268

Monthly calculation

Monthly earnings	12000/12 =	£1000
less Personal allowance p.m.	3600/12 =	300
Taxable pay p.m.		700

Tax payable for the month = 700 × 27% = £189

Note that 12 monthly tax payments total the amount due for the year: £189 × 12 = £2268

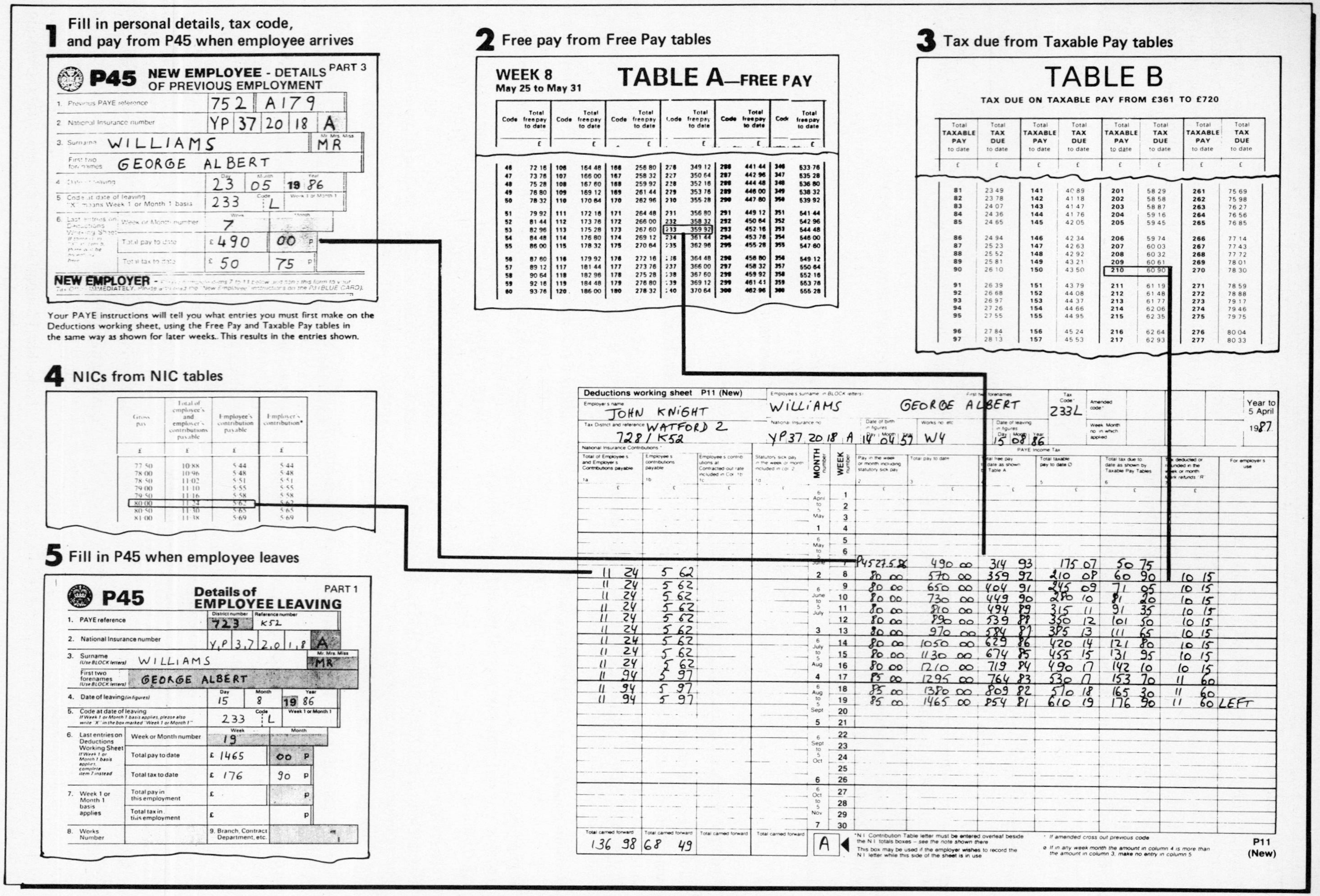

Fig. 2.2 How to use a deductions working sheet

PAYE in practice

Each person's tax free allowance is incorporated into a *code number*. You should receive a *Notice of Coding* each year from the Inland Revenue, if you are in paid employment. This code number is used with *tax tables* to calculate the tax due in a given pay period.

If you commence work you will be asked to fill in a tax return which will be used to establish your personal allowance and other allowances if any, and then set your code number.

Example 6

Single trainee accountant

Personal allowance	£2425
Professional association membership fees	£100
Total allowances	£2525

The tax code is found by removing the last digit, therefore in this case it will be 252.

The code will also include a letter which denotes the status of the tax payer. (*See* IR34 for explanation of letter, etc.)

Tax tables and deduction sheet

The Inland Revenue supply employers with the tables and forms to operate the PAYE system. (*See* Fig. 2.2.) The basic requirements are:

1 Table A: free pay tables. These are used to establish the tax free pay to date for a given code number.
2 Table B: tax due tables. Used to establish the tax due to date on a given taxable pay.
3 P11: deductions form. The working sheet on which the figures looked up in tables A and B are recorded and the subsequent calculations are shown.

This work will be carried out by the wages department and, unless you are employed in that department, you will not have access to these tables in order to check the accuracy of your own tax deductions. It is important, therefore, that you are able to estimate the tax deduction using the methods shown above.

Note: because of the effect of rounding in the tax tables any tax deduction estimate will not be exactly the same as the actual deduction, but will be sufficient to verify the magnitude of any deduction made.

National Insurance contributions

As previously discussed, the proportion of income paid in NI contributions depends upon whether an employee is *not contracted out* or *contracted out* of the State Earnings Related Pension Scheme (SERPS). The government require all persons in employment to make contributions towards a pension scheme that provides a pension that will be a proportion of earnings upon retirement. Employers can make the decision to set up their own scheme for employees to join and these employees are contracted out. If the employer does not have a scheme then employees will be in SERPS and hence are not contracted out. The levels of contribution are given in Fig. 2.3.

Note: once the threshold for payment of NI contribution has been reached then it is due on the gross earnings. This means that, unlike Income Tax where tax is only paid on the extra earnings, NI is payable on all earnings. This is of particular importance to part-time workers.

Example 7

Assume that National Insurance contributions are 5% of earnings and become payable when earnings reach £40 per week. Ignore Income Tax or other deductions.

Case 1

Earnings per week	£38.50
NI contributions at 5%	nil (earnings not £39 per week)
'Take home pay'	£38.50

Case 2

Earnings per week	£39.00
NI contributions at 5%	1.95
'Take home pay'	£37.05

So earning an extra 50p results in a £1.45 reduction in net pay.

National Insurance in practice

As with the PAYE system for income tax, NI contributions are calculated using tables. There are two basic sets:

1 contracted out contribution rate tables;
2 not contracted out contribution rate tables.

Using the appropriate table, the employer looks up the gross earnings for the pay period and deducts the amount shown in the table. The amount deducted is shown on the P11 form used for Income Tax. As with estimates of Income Tax, estimates of NI contribution will not be exact due to rounding in the use of the tables.

NI contributions are made on earnings during a week or month depending on the pay period, unlike Income Tax which is based upon the earnings in a tax year (PAYE is the method of spreading that liability over the year). The difference in assessment base means that NI contributions cannot be recovered once paid, i.e. a large payment on high earnings in one week cannot be refunded because of low or nil earnings in the next week.

Fig. 2.3 Extract from NI 208: NI contributions

Class 1 contributions

Most people who work for an employer have to pay a percentage of their earnings as Class 1 National Insurance contributions once their earnings reach the lower earnings limit. There is an upper earnings limit for contribution liability for employees only. The employer also has to pay contributions based on the employee's earnings. The total of the employee's and employer's contributions is normally paid along with PAYE tax. To find the total rate of National Insurance due add together the rates from the employee's and the employer's columns in the tables below.

Not contracted-out employment

Total earnings	Employee		Employer
	Standard	Reduced	
£ 39.00 to £ 64.99 weekly or £ 169.00 to £ 281.99 monthly or £2028.00 to £ 3379.99 yearly	5%	3.85%	5%
£ 65.00 to £ 99.99 weekly or £ 282.00 to £ 433.99 monthly or £3380.00 to £ 5199.99 yearly	7%	3.85%	7%
£ 100.00 to £ 149.99 weekly or £ 434.00 to £ 649.99 monthly or £5200.00 to £ 7799.99 yearly	9%	3.85%	9%
£ 150.00 to £ 295.00 weekly or £ 650.00 to £ 1279.00 monthly or £7800.00 to £15340.00 yearly	9%	3.85%	10.45%
over £ 295.00 weekly* or over £ 1279.00 monthly or over £15340.00 yearly	9% of £295.00 or equivalent	3.85% of £295.00 or equivalent	10.45%

Contracted-out employment

Total earnings	Employee				Employer	
	On first £39.00 or equivalent		On earnings over £39.00 or equivalent		On first £39.00 or equivalent	On earnings over £39.00 or equivalent
	Standard	Reduced	Standard	Reduced		
£ 39.00 to £ 64.99 weekly or £ 169.00 to £ 281.99 monthly or £2028.00 to £ 3379.99 yearly	5%	3.85%	2.85%	3.85%	5%	0.9%
£ 65.00 to £ 99.99 weekly or £ 282.00 to £ 433.99 monthly or £3380.00 to £ 5199.99 yearly	7%	3.85%	4.85%	3.85%	7%	2.9%
£ 100.00 to £ 149.99 weekly or £ 434.00 to £ 649.99 monthly or £5200.00 to £ 7799.99 yearly	9%	3.85%	6.85%	3.85%	9%	4.9%
£ 150.00 to £ 295.00 weekly or £ 650.00 to £ 1279.00 monthly or £7800.00 to £15340.00 yearly	9%	3.85%	6.85%	3.85%	10.45%	6.35%
over £ 295.00 weekly* or over £ 1279.00 monthly or over £15340.00 yearly	9%	3.85%	6.85% up to £295.00 or equivalent	3.85% up to £295.00 or equivalent	10.45%	6.35% up to £295.00 or equivalent and 10.45% thereafter

*Employees do not pay contributions on any earnings over £295.00 a week or the monthly or yearly equivalent

Example 8

In Example 1 we considered a job advertised at £6720 per annum. We will now calculate the National Insurance contributions payable on this salary. (*See* Fig. 2.3 for rates of contribution.)

(a) Calculation if *not contracted out*. The rate is 9% for earnings in the band £5200.00 to £7799.99 yearly, so the amount payable in the year is £6720 × 9% = £604.80

(b) Calculation if *contracted out*. The rate is divided, 9% on the equivalent of the first £39.00 per week (£2028 p.a.) and 6.85% on earnings over this level. (Both of these figures are taken from the £5200.00 to £7799.99 yearly band.)

The amount payable on an annual basis is

£2028 × 9%	= £182.52 p.a.
(£6720 − £2028) × 6.85%	= £321.40 p.a.
Annual national contribution payable	= £503.92

Estimation of Net Pay

We have seen how the statutory deductions are calculated and how accurate estimates of the amount to be deducted can be made; these estimates can now be brought together with voluntary deductions to enable us to establish an accurate assessment of *net pay*. Voluntary deductions tend to be fixed amounts, e.g. sports club £1 per week, or set percentages of earnings, e.g. company pension scheme contributions 6% of earnings. However, it is still necessary to be careful about the terms of these deductions as there may be some complexities, e.g. pension contributions may be 6% of normal earnings only, any overtime, bonus, etc. will not be counted as income for pension purposes.

Figure 2.4 gives the steps to take when estimating net pay.

Fig. 2.4 How to estimate net pay

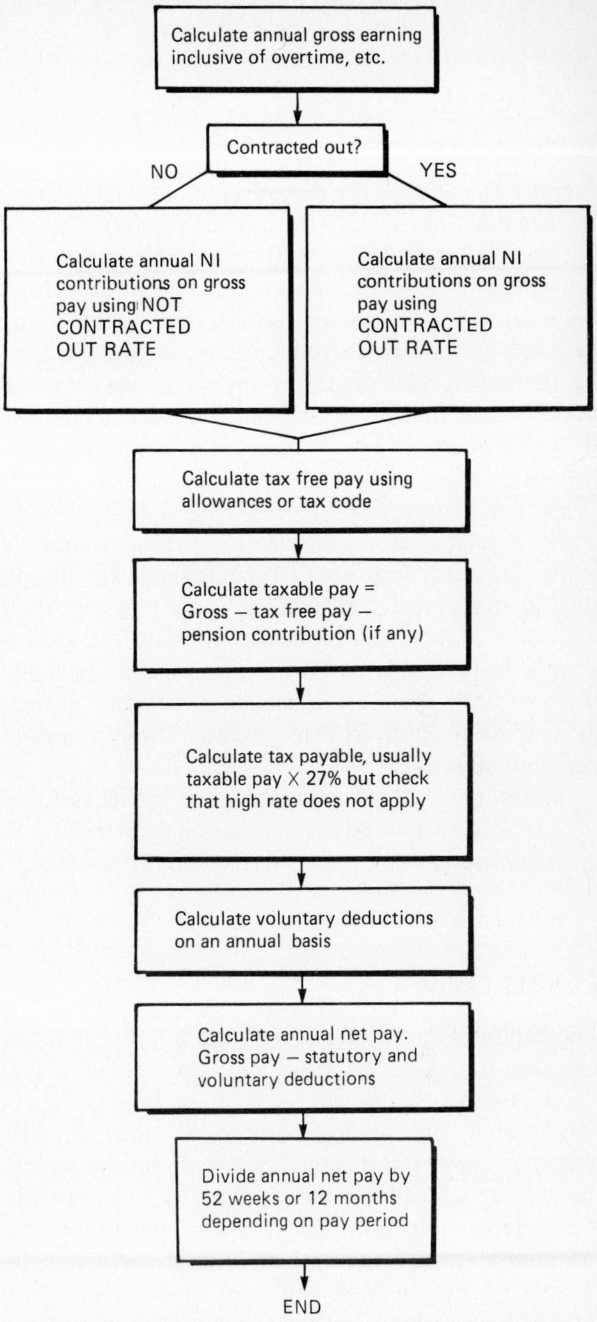

DEDUCTIONS FROM GRANTS

The usual local authority student grants are not subject to statutory deductions, nor are other educational awards like scholarships. If you receive a payment from a sponsor or employer for periods of further study at college, these again may be exempt from tax, however certain conditions must be met and you are advised to seek advice from your tax office on your particular circumstances.

Part-time work during term time and holiday jobs, even if with the organisation that gives you term time financial assistance, will be subject to the normal deductions as described in the previous sections. Do not forget to use form P38(S) if you think the income from this employment will not exceed your personal allowance.

Leaflet IR60 gives the broad details about students and taxation.

INVESTMENTS

Income Tax is usually payable on the interest received from investments and if the investment increases in value then when the funds are withdrawn there may be a liability for Capital Gains Tax.

Income Tax

Income Tax is, with the exception of national savings, deducted at source, i.e., the interest received has had Income Tax deducted at basic rate. This means that unless the investor is a higher rate taxpayer, no further liability for taxation will arise. This removes any taxation complications from investment for the majority. However, non taxpayers should be very careful about where they invest their money because the tax deducted at source by, for example a building society, cannot be recovered.

For non taxpayers, national savings is often the first choice as all interest is paid 'gross' – that is without tax being deducted. Individuals become liable for tax on their income if their personal allowance plus any other allowance is exceeded. Students may therefore receive income from this form of investment, and not be liable for tax until their total income (excluding grants) earned and from investments, exceeds the appropriate personal allowance.

Interest received on national savings certificates and the first £70 of interest from a national savings bank ordinary account are totally free of tax whatsoever.

Capital Gains Tax

The capital gains on an investment is the difference between the purchase price and the selling price. Calculation of the net capital gains on investments is complicated and involves indexation and tax free amounts. However, it should be noted that the rate of tax on capital gains is 30%, which is less than the higher rates of Income Tax. This can make investing for capital gains rather than interest attractive to persons paying the higher rates of Income Tax. This type of investment is, of course, more speculative as capital appreciation cannot be predetermined, unlike a stated interest rate.

DEDUCTIONS FROM BENEFITS

Some social security benefits, particularly those providing income support benefits, are taxable. The tax is not deducted when the benefit is paid but if total income exceeds the appropriate personal allowances then tax may become payable on this income. Housing benefit is not taxable. (*See* leaflet IR 41 for details.)

DEDUCTIONS FROM PENSIONS

Income Tax is payable on pensions as they form a person's income. If the person is over 65 then an extra personal allowance is available, known as *age allowance,* thus reducing the individual's tax liability. The amounts are shown in Fig. 2.1 (*See* IR 4 and IR 4a.)

Unfortunately the tax position of retired persons, who may receive income from a number of sources, can become more complicated than the situation that existed when employed and it may be worth consulting an accountant to ensure the most tax efficient structuring of their finances.

National Insurance contributions are not payable by persons over pensionable age (60 for a woman, 65 for a man).

SUMMARY

The number and complexity of deductions make it important that we can estimate them in order to ensure that any deductions claimed from our earnings have to be correctly assessed.

There is plenty of information available on statutory deductions and the latest editions of the publications relevant to your circumstances should always be to hand. Particularly NI 208 for National Insurance contributions and FA 1 for Income Tax rates and allowances, new editions are usually published shortly after the Budget giving the latest rates, which tend to change in April of each year.

Non tax payers should ensure that they are not paying tax by default because of investments which pay interest net of tax. This tax cannot be recovered.

TASKS

Data for Tasks 1–4, status of persons single unless stated otherwise:

(a) School leaver, taking up a clerical post at £55 per week;

(b) College leaver, starting as a management trainee on a salary of £4850 per annum;

(c) Married man, currently earning £9670 per annum as an administrator. He pays 5% of his salary into an occupational pension scheme;

(d) Single parent, with one child of 14, earns £145 per week as a retail store supervisor and is in receipt of child benefit at £7.25 per week plus one parent benefit at £4.10 per week;

(e) A married pensioner, aged 68, with income from an occupational pension of £4100 per annum and state retirement pension of £63.25 per week

You are advised to have available the following publications before attempting the tasks:

Inland Revenue
IR 4A Income Tax age allowance
IR 33 Income Tax and school leavers
IR 22 Income Tax personal allowance

DHSS
FB2 Which benefit – appropriate sections only

When completing the tasks, use the tax rates and bands as set out in Fig. 2.1 and the National Insurance contribution rates set out in Fig. 2.2.

Task 1

Establish the annual tax free pay for each person.

Task 2

Calculate the annual tax due in each case.

Task 3

Calculate the annual national insurance contributions payable in each case.

Task 4

Calculate the weekly net income in each case.

Task 5

A married woman has a part-time job working three nights per month as a night nurse. She receives £4.50 per hour for 11 hours work per night. The hospital have offered her an extra night's work this month. Estimate her additional net pay from this extra night's work. Employees of the hospital are paid monthly and part-time staff are not contracted out.

Task 6

You are looking for part-time work in the evenings and at week-ends while studying full-time at college. Your local paper has three advertisements for this type of work. Estimate the weekly take home pay for each of them and rank them in order of preference.

(a) Leaflet distribution, must be done on Friday night and on Saturday, pay £8 per 1000 and pro rata leaflets delivered with approximately 5000 to be delivered each week. Estimated time required: 12 hours.

(b) Shelf filling in a local supermarket, hours 6.30 pm to 11.30 pm three nights per week pay £2.20 per hour plus 39 p per hour unsocial hours bonus.

(c) Weekend care assistant at a local nursing home. 8.00 am to 5.30 pm with one hour for lunch, Saturday and Sunday. Rate of pay £1.975 per hour, enhanced to time and one half on Sunday.

Task 7

On leaving college in June you take up a job from 1 July paying £5600 per annum. Estimate your monthly take home pay in the first nine months of employment, that is in the period unit 31 March in the next year. Then estimate your net pay per month for the following twelve months, assuming no pay increase or change in tax rates etc., and that you remain single. What is the monthly difference between the two figures, and can you explain it?

Task 8

A friend is to be given promotion onto 'staff' grade by his employer. He is very pleased by this apparent recognition of his work for the company and asks you to estimate the increase in his take home pay. He has been paid weekly so state any increase in weekly terms. Your friend is a married man.

Current pay situation:
(a) £4 per hour for a $37\frac{1}{2}$ hour week:
(b) Regular overtime payments for four hours on a Saturday morning at time and one half;
(c) Branch sales bonus of 1% of turnover, which has averaged £3000 per week for a long time;
(d) Not contracted out.

Pay after promotion:
(a) Annual salary of £10 000 per annum,
(b) Hours: as required by management;
(c) £1000 bonus if annual turnover of branch exceeds £200 000 per annum paid three months after the end of the financial year, which is in two month's time;
(d) 5% of salary to be paid into a company pension scheme.

Task 9

David and Marian are getting married, they are both working and will continue to do so after marriage, David earns £8112 per annum as an accounts clerk, Marian is a local authority solicitor earning £12 200 per annum. Both are paid monthly and contribute to occupational pension schemes, David pays 5% of his salary and Marian 6%.

(a) Estimate their individual monthly net pay prior to marriage;

(b) Estimate their joint monthly net pay after marriage;

(c) David and Marian agree that it would be in their

mutual long-term interest if David were to become a professionally qualified accountant. This will mean David leaving employment and becoming a full-time student for three years. He expects to receive a grant of approximately £2500 per annum and has arranged two months summer holiday work with his old employer which will be paid at the same rate as his old salary. Estimate their average joint monthly net income under these arrangements.

Task 10

Brian Grant is to retire shortly at 65. He has contributed 5% of his salary to a company pension scheme and will receive a pension of 1/80th of his current salary, £7800 per annum, for each of his 17 years service with the company, plus 1/80 × 23 years of his leaving salary, £1000 p.a., from a previous employment. His wife Doris who is already retired, receives no pension from her former employment. They will receive a state pension of £62.25 per week. Both pension schemes will pay a lump sum of 3/80 times years service which can be invested at 6% p.a. net of tax to provide extra income. Estimate Brian and Doris's net monthly income before and after retirement.

Further practice at these tasks may be obtained by repeating them using the latest Income Tax and National Insurance rates, etc., if they have changed. Students may also check on the benefit rates quoted to ensure that they are up-to-date.

3 Personal expenditure

INTRODUCTION

Accountants draw a distinction between *capital* and *revenue* expenditure. Put simply and in domestic terms:

(a) Capital expenditure is spending on items of a permanent or semi-permanent nature, e.g. cars, electrical goods, houses.

(b) Revenue expenditure is meeting everyday living expenses, e.g. food, rent, transport.

This distinction is useful when deciding how to use one's income and making spending decisions. As a general rule, revenue expenditure must be met from income before any capital expenditure can be considered, i.e. pay the rent before buying a video!

FINANCING EXPENDITURE

For items of capital expenditure, it is often necessary to find a method of financing the purchase because the balance of income after meeting revenue expenditure is insufficient. The choice of finance is important, and three main points should be considered.

The finance term

In other words, how long it will take to repay the loan. The term should be appropriate to the life of the goods being purchased. For example, a 25-year mortgage is satisfactory on a house because the life of the house will usually far exceed this term and the benefit of the purchase will be enjoyed long after the loan has been repaid. However, a 3-year hire purchase (HP) agreement on a home computer may be too long a term because the machine will probably be obsolete within two years and need replacing before the payments have finished. The payments must continue but the benefits from the purchase have ceased.

The cost of finance

This is the charge made by the lender for the provision of finance. These charges vary between lenders and should of course be compared. Using the APR (annual percentage rate) is one of the ways of making an evaluation. The APR is the annual cost of the finance as a percentage of the amount borrowed; included in the calculation are all the charges for the finance, not just interest, e.g. arrangement fees, administration fees, settlement fees, etc. However, it is mainly because of the different methods of calculating interest charges that APR is required in order to make comparisons.

For example, flat rates of interest, as used in calculating HP interest, are charged on the total amount borrowed for the full term and may appear to be quite low when compared with an interest rate quoted on the outstanding balance. An HP rate quoted as 10% will give rise to an APR of just under twice the flat rate, say 19.5%, but an 18% bank interest rate charged on the balance outstanding will, after inclusion of charges, give an APR of only slightly more, say 18.5%. Therefore the 18% interest bank loan is cheaper than the 10% HP alternative.

Note that assuming no other charges, interest free finance will of course give an APR of 0% but the retail price of the goods may have been inflated. The interest charges are in effect hidden within the price charged. You must always compare the total credit price of goods.

For example a camera priced at £400 in a catalogue, which allows the payments to be spread over 38 weeks, may be purchased in a high street store for £260. The catalogue makes no charge for credit but the store could charge an APR of 70% on credit over the same period before matching the catalogue charge.

The repayment amount

You should always ensure that the weekly/monthly repayments can comfortably be met from your income after taking into consideration your 'revenue expenditure'. What will happen to the loan repayments if your income ceases through illness or redundancy? You will still have to make them, but it is possible to take out insurance cover against these events and avoid the possibility of repossession of the goods if the payments cannot be maintained.

SOURCES OF PERSONAL FINANCE

For the individual, the need for finance can be said to fall into one of two broad categories.

(a) Short-term finance to meet a general shortage of cash for general needs but over a well-defined time period, e.g. holidays, Christmas spending, unforeseen car repairs, etc.

(b) Medium- to long-term finance for the acquisition of a specific item, e.g. house, car, furniture, etc. Different types of finance are appropriate to both categories.

SHORT-TERM FINANCE

If the credit period required is less than one month, then it may be possible to obtain free credit by the use of:

(a) a monthly account, as offered by large department store chains like the John Lewis Partnership. All goods purchased in the store are charged to the account and a statement of account is sent to the customer at the end of the month. The total amount must then be settled in full.

(b) credit cards, which also allow purchases to be charged to the card holder's account. A monthly statement of account is sent to the card holder who is then offered a choice:

- settle in full by a specified date, thus obtaining up to six weeks free credit on purchases, or
- pay between the minimum specified amount, 5% of the statement balance, and the full amount.

Any unpaid balance will attract interest for the time that it is outstanding. The APR on this type of borrowing is moderately high, at the time of writing it is 23.8% (1.75% per month on the outstanding balance). Credit cards are issued by banks, Access by Lloyds, Midland and National Westminister; and Visa by Barclays, TSB and National GiroBank. The smaller banks and the regional banks also issue cards via these two organisations. These cards can be used in any retail establishments accepting them. Stores, like Marks & Spencer, also issue their own credit cards but, of course, their use is restricted to the issuing store.

Other forms of short-term borrowing attract interest as soon as the finance is used. Two types are considered:

Bank overdraft

To obtain a bank overdraft you must be a current account holder with a bank. In agreement with the bank, the account holder is allowed to write cheques for sums totalling more than the amount credited to the account, up to an agreed borrowing limit. There will usually be a specified time period during which the overdraft must be cleared. The interest charged on an overdraft will often be comparatively low, i.e. only 5–7% above the bank's base lending rate. However, as most personal customers of banks do not pay bank charges as their accounts are kept in credit, there may be a 'hidden cost' in the form of reimposed bank charges as the account becomes overdrawn. Some banks also charge an administration fee for setting up the overdraft. Straightforward overdrafts are becoming more difficult to obtain as the banks develop new forms of credit and different types of current account.

Revolving credit accounts

These accounts are a comparatively new form of credit provided by banks and stores. The account holder agrees to pay a set sum monthly into the account and can then spend up to, say, thirty times that amount. So for a payment of £20 per month goods to the value of £600 may be purchased. The interest charged on this type of account is often quite high; however, if the account is in credit interest may be given to the account holder, but the rate is unlikely to be very high.

Which form of credit is best? Let us compare the cost of various types in given situations.

Situation 1

It is half-way through January, your electric heater breaks down and a repair is not possible. A new one will cost £50 and after Christmas and New Year you have no spare cash. You will be able to afford one in February, but you are freezing now. How can you buy a new one?

1 *Store account* – the account will not be presented until the end of the month. Interest charge nil.

2 *Credit card* – again the account will not be presented until the end of the month and then you will have 21 days to pay; so again no interest will be paid. If you are lucky the date the account is presented, plus 21 days, will allow you to delay payment until March if it becomes necessary, without paying interest.

3 *Bank overdraft* – do not take an overdraft unless previously agreed because the bank will dishonour your cheque or charge you a very high rate of interest.

Assuming an agreement exists then borrowing £50 could cost:

Interest £50 × 15% p.a. × 2 weeks/52 weeks	= £0.29
Bank charges for the month in which you are overdrawn, say 10 transactions at 30p each	= £3.00
Total cost of overdraft	= £3.29

4 *Revolving credit* – if the transfer to the revolving credit account is £10 per month, it will take 5 months to pay off the £50 borrowed plus some time for the interest charged on the outstanding balance.

Balance outstanding at the end of month 1	50.00
plus Interest at say 30% p.a. (2.5% p.m.)	1.25
	51.25
less Payment for month 1	10.00
Balance at end of month 2	41.25
plus Interest at 2.5% per month	1.03
	42.28
less Payment for month 2	10.00
Balance at end of month 3	32.28
etc. until	
Balance at end of month 5	4.01
plus Interest	.10
	4.11

This outstanding balance, which will be cleared by the transfer of £10 during month 6, represents the total interest charged to the account for this transaction.

Clearly the store account or credit card should be used if they are available. Revolving credit gives the highest cost, and in most circumstances this will be true because of the high interest charges associated with these accounts and the inflexibility of the repayment amount and timing.

Situation 2

Your car requires repairs in order to pass the MoT test. These will cost £300, and as your surplus income after meeting all revenue expenditure is usually £100 per month, some form of credit is required. Only those forms of credit giving at least 4 months to repay can be considered (3 months at £100 to pay off the amount borrowed and the 4th month to pay the interest charges).

1 *Credit card*– the costs can be estimated as follows:

Note: no interest charge in first month

Month 1 balance outstanding	300.00
less Repayment	100.00
Month 2 balance outstanding	200.00
plus First interest charge at say 2% p.m.	4.00
	204.00
less repayment	100.00
Month 3 balance outstanding,	104.00
plus Second interest charge at 2%	2.00
	106.00
less Repayment of full amount	106.00
	NIL

Amount repaid 100 + 100 + 106	306
Amount borrowed	300
Interest charged	6

2 *Bank overdraft* – assume an overdraft has been agreed at 15% p.a. (1.25% p.m.) to be repaid within four months and a £5 administration charge is made. The cost can be estimated as above or alternatively if repayment is at approximately £100 per month

300 will be outstanding for 1 month costing 300 × 1.25% × 1 month	= 3.75
200 will be outstanding for 2 months costing 200 × 1.25% × 2 months	= 5.00
100 will be outstanding for 3 months costing 100 × 1.25% × 3 months	= 3.75
plus Administration fee	= 5.00
plus Bank charges incurred say 3 months at £3 per month	= 9.00
Total cost	= 26.50

3 *Revolving credit* – assume £10 per month transfer and an interest rate of 30% p.a. This means that it will take 30 months to repay the amount borrowed and as a consequence the interest charges will far exceed the cost of the other two methods.

A rough estimate of first year's interest can be made from:

Interest charged
= average amount outstanding × annual rate
= (£300 – £60*) × 30%
= £240 × 30%
= £72

* Amount borrowed *less* half of first year's repayments.

Short-term finance: a conclusion

Credit cards appear to be the most convenient way of obtaining short-term finance because:

(a) there is an interest free period of up to six weeks. Note that purchases using card only, cash advances pay interest from day one.

(b) flexible repayment terms, subject to minimum, allow you to choose the credit period.

(c) there are no 'hidden' charges.

(d) there is no need for approval for each new loan required.

Revolving credit accounts seem to be the least advantageous form of credit because:

(a) they tend to have the highest rates of interest for consumer credit.

(b) the inflexible repayment method which can extend short-term borrowing into medium-term finance with consequent increase in the total interest paid.

Fig. 3.1 Example of hire purchase conditions

On the Exclusive Ranger **309 XL**

*FINANCE EXAMPLE**
including FREE membership of RAC

Cash Price on Road	*£6995.00*
Less Deposit (min of 20%)	*£1500.00*
Balance Financed	*£5495.00*
Period of Loan	*36 months*
Interest Charge	*£1768.36*
Total Repayable	*£7263.36*
Equal Monthly Payments	*£201.76*
Approx. Weekly Equivalent	*£46.56*
Typical Annual APR	*20.9% variable*

**Subject to Status*

MEDIUM-TERM FINANCE

Medium term finance, say 1–5 years, tends to be provided by finance houses and banks and is intended for the purchase of specific goods or services. Since the tight controls on this type of lending were removed the number of sources have increased and their terms can vary considerably. Potential borrowers are therefore encouraged to compare a number of lenders for APR and other factors before making an agreement.

This type of finance can be obtained in three basic ways:

Hire Purchase (HP)

This is also known as *conditional sale*. Finance is normally arranged at the time of purchasing the goods, from a finance house via the organisation that sells you the goods. The usual method is for a deposit to be paid and the balance settled by regular instalments which will include interest payments.

Points to note about HP:

(a) interest is calculated on a flat rate basis (*see* p. 19);

(b) the ownership of the goods remains with the finance house, so you are not free to dispose of them. They are only 'hired' by you until the final instalment is paid.

(c) the goods may be repossessed by the finance house if you default on the instalments, although a court order is required before this can happen if over one third of the instalments have been made.

Hire purchase finance is provided by finance houses for goods which are likely to retain their value, so that if a repossession is necessary the goods may be resold to recover the amount outstanding. If a high retained value is unlikely, a *credit sale agreement* will be used.

Credit sale

Similar to hire purchase in most respects, except that the ownership of the goods passes to the purchaser. Therefore on default the purchaser is sued for the balance outstanding rather than repossession of the goods.

Bank personal loan

The high street banks all provide this type of finance in various forms and many building societies are now providing similar facilities to customers.

Unlike hire purchase, the borrowing does not have to be tied to the purchase of a particular item and subject to any legal restrictions; the full amount may be borrowed.

The repayment period can be set to suit an individual's circumstances, often from 12 to 60 months. The amounts lent under these schemes can range from £500 to £10 000.

Obtaining a personal loan from your bank usually only requires the completion of a simple form about your financial status. The bank will then quickly give you a decision (one bank advertises that it can take as little as 20 minutes to approve a loan!).

Because this source of finance is completely separate from the organisation supplying the goods you have the advantage of being a cash purchaser, which can often give the ability to negotiate over price.

Let us compare these various sources of finances.

Example – Buying a new car

Assuming you do not have sufficient savings for a large deposit or another car to part exchange in lieu of a deposit, then the following is not untypical for the HP terms offered by a garage in a local press advertisement:

Astra 1.3 Merit *Cash price £6155.42*
Deposit only £95 then 36 monthly instalments of £225.79
Total credit price £8223.36 (APR 27.3%)

Compare this with a bank loan for the full amount at rates quoted on the same day that the above advertisement appeared.

Reading from the tables in Fig. 3.3 and assuming £6100 is to be borrowed:

Loan amount £	*Monthly payment* £	*Total repaid* £
5000	180.55	6499.80
1100	39.72	1429.92
6100	220.27	7929.72

Having established the total credit price for both methods of financing the purchase it can be seen that the bank loan provides a saving of £8223.36 – £7929.72 = £293.64. This saving could be increased by the ability to negotiate a discount from list price because the bank loan enables you to act as a 'cash buyer'.

LONG-TERM FINANCE

Unlike the types of consumer credit considered so far, long-term credit will require security – *collateral* – that is a personal property that the lender can take and sell in order to recover any sum outstanding in the event of the borrower defaulting on repayments.

For most individuals, long-term finance takes the form of a mortgage. This is money borrowed to purchase a property and that property is then used as security for the loan. Terms vary but the majority of mortgages are for between 15 and 20 years. Mortgages are obtainable from banks, building societies, insurance companies and other institutions. There are two basic types: a *repayment mortgage* and *life insurance linked mortgages*.

Fig. 3.2 Extract from repayment tables

Note Interest 10% per annum flat (monthly repayments rounded down to nearest whole penny)

36 monthly repayments APR 19.4%

Without Protection Insurance

Monthly payment £	*Total amount payable* £	*Amount of loan* £
18.05	649.80	500
21.66	779.76	600
25.27	909.72	700
28.88	1039.68	800
32.50	1170.00	900
36.11	1299.96	1000
39.72	1429.92	1100
43.33	1559.88	1200
46.94	1689.84	1300
50.55	1819.80	1400
72.22	2599.92	2000
108.33	3899.88	3000
144.44	5199.84	4000
180.55	6499.80	5000
216.66	7799.76	6000
252.77	9099.72	7000
288.88	10399.68	8000
325.00	11700.00	9000
361.11	12999.86	10000

To use the tables
Look down the right-hand column to find the amount you wish to borrow, then look across to the column for the repayment. If the amount you wish to borrow is not shown just add two figures together to work out your repayments, e.g. for £2800, add the figures for £2000 and £800.

Repayment mortgage

The monthly repayments consist partly of interest and partly of capital. Interest is charged on the balance outstanding at the end of each year and the amount of interest charged decreases each year as the capital is repaid. This means that in the early stages of a repayment mortgage the majority of each monthly instalment is interest, and very little capital is repaid. The reverse is true towards the end of the mortage term.

Lenders provide repayment tables so that the cost can be established. (*See* Fig. 3.3.)

Mortgage costs

1 Interest 11.25% gross, net of tax relief at 27%, 8.2125% for mortgages up to £30 000, tax relief is available and so the lower rate applies; this is the *MIRAS rate* (*see* IR 63). The gross interest rate is payable for any sum borrowed above £30 000.
2 Various legal and survey charges when taking out the mortgage. (*See* Fig. 3.4.)
3 Life insurance, a mortgage protection policy, to repay the mortgage in the event of the borrower's death during the mortgage term.

Using Figs 3.3 and 3.4 we can establish that the cost of obtaining a £35 000 mortgage over 25 years on a house purchased for £50 000 will be:

1 Repayments £30 000 at MIRAS rate	230.41
£5000 at gross rate	49.48
Total monthly repayment	279.89

In addition, there will usually be a mortgage protection policy premium, but this will be a very small amount in comparison with the mortgage repayment. The actual insurance premium will depend upon the borrower's age, health, etc.
2 Legal and survey costs when taking out the mortgage:

Application fee for price band £45 001–£50 000	75.00
Legal fees for a mortgage of £35 000	76.25
Total	151.25

These are the lender's basic fees, which may increase depending upon special circumstances or if more extensive surveys of the property are undertaken.

There are other costs incurred when purchasing a house as a consequence of the drawing up of the contracts for purchase, but these are not associated with the mortgage.

Fig. 3.3 Monthly repayment table

Monthly repayment table

Basic mortgage rate 11.00%	MIRAS Rate 7.81%							
Amount borrowed	£1000	£3000	£5000	£10 000	£17 000	£20 000	£25 000	£30 000
15 YEARS APR 12.1%				REPAYMENT MORTGAGE				
MIRAS monthly payment	£9.62	£28.87	£48.12	£96.23	£163.59	£192.46	£240.58	£288.69
Gross monthly payment	£11.59	£34.77	£57.94	£115.89	£197.01	£231.78	£289.72	£347.66
Total amount payable (gross)	£2219	£6393	£10 569	£21 008	£35 632	£41 896	£52 338	£62 777
20 YEARS APR 11.9%				REPAYMENT MORTGAGE				
MIRAS monthly payment	£8.37	£25.10	£41.84	£83.68	£142.26	£167.36	£209.20	£251.04
Gross monthly payment	£10.47	£31.39	£52.32	£104.65	£177.90	£209.29	£261.62	£313.94
Total amount payable (gross)	£2642	£7673	£12 699	£25 266	£42 872	£50 415	£62 983	£75 553
25 YEARS APR 11.8%				REPAYMENT MORTGAGE				
MIRAS monthly payment	£7.68	£23.04	£38.40	£76.80	£130.56	£153.61	£192.01	£230.41
Gross monthly payment	£9.90	£29.69	£49.48	£98.95	£168.22	£197.90	£247.38	£296.85
Total amount payable (gross)	£3096	£9037	£14 978	£29 840	£50 639	£59 559	£74 410	£89 269
INTEREST ONLY PAYMENT FOR ENDOWMENT/PENSION MORTGAGES APR11.7%								
MIRAS monthly payment	£6.51	£19.53	£32.55	£65.09	£110.65	£130.17	£162.71	£195.25
Gross monthly payment	£9.17	£27.50	£45.84	£91.67	£155.84	£183.34	£229.17	£275.00
Total amount payable (gross)	£3883	£11 382	£18 884	£37 639	£63 904	£75 157	£93 912	£112 664

Fig. 3.4 Scales of charges

Legal fees

The table of legal fees may only be taken as a guide.

Amount of Mortgage	Legal Fee (excl. V.A.T.)
£10,000	£52.50
£15,000	£62.50
£20,000	£67.50
£25,000	£72.50
£30,000	£75.00
£35,000	£76.25
Exceeding £35,000	£76.25 plus a 50p for each £5000 or part thereof

Application fee

The application fee includes an initial inspection and one free re-inspection, if necessary, by the valuer and the scale of charges is shown below. If subsequent re-inspections are required then an additional charge of £20 will be made for each one.

Purchase Price or Valuation	Applic. Fee	Purchase Price or Valuation	Applic. Fee
Up to £7,500	£35	£40,001–£45,000	£70
£7,501–£15,000	£40	£45,001–£50,000	£75
£15,001–£20,000	£45	£50,001–£60,000	£80
£20,001–£25,000	£50	£60,001–£70,000	£85
£25,001–£30,000	£55	£70,001–£80,000	£90
£30,001–£35,000	£60	£80,001–£90,000	£95
£35,001–£40,000	£65	£90,001–£100,000	£100
	continued	over £100,000	on applic.

Life insurance linked mortgage

Under this scheme, the mortgage is not repaid until the end of the full term; only interest payments are made to the lender. In order to repay the capital the borrower takes out a with-profits life insurance policy which will guarantee repayment of the mortgage on death of the policy holder or when the policy matures at the end of the mortgage term. The borrower, of course pays life insurance premiums as well as mortgage interest. There are various schemes but the most popular has been a *low cost endowment mortgage*.

The advantage of this type of mortgage is in the long term. For a similar monthly outlay, the net cost of the mortgage may be reduced by a 'terminal bonus' at the end of the mortgage period. The terminal bonus is found by estimating the value of the accrued profits when the policy matures; if these profits exceed the capital repayment required the policy holder will be left with a lump sum, the terminal bonus.

Comparison of costs, repayment v. low cost endowment mortgage

For example:

Loan £20 000 over 25 years at 8.2125% (MIRAS rate)
Borrowers: male age 35, female age 32

Monthly outgoings	*Repayment mortgage* £	*Monthly outgoings*	*Low cost endowment* £
Mortgage repayment	158.98	Mortgage interest	136.88
Mortgage protection policy premium	7.00	Life insurance premium	28.20
Total monthly cost	165.98		167.08
Total cost of mortgage over 25 years	49 794		50 124
		less Estimated terminal bonus	14 029
		Net cost of mortgage	36 095

Note: life insurance premiums vary considerably with age.

In general, lenders limit the amount that can be borrowed by two factors:
1 Income of the applicant, terms and conditions vary considerably, but typically the maximum allowed is: three times main income plus $1\frac{1}{2}$ times second income.
2 Type and age of property: again policies vary considerably but lenders will often advance 95% or more of the value of modern property but less on older property, in some cases only 80% on pre-1945 houses.

For example

A married couple with savings of £5000 and income of husband £9000 p.a. (teacher), wife £15000 p.a. (accountant) might be able to afford:

	£
Savings	5 000
Three times main income (£15000)	45 000
$1\frac{1}{2}$ times second income (£9000)	13 500
Maximum value of property that can be purchased	63 500

This calculation is fine for a modern property where their savings of £5000 will be ample contribution for that value of property.

Deposit would be £5000/£63 500 = 8% leaving 92% to be borrowed.

Note that if an older property is desired and the lender requires a 20% investment in the property from the purchaser, then their limit will be £25 000 maximum value of property because the £5000 they have to invest is 20% of £25 000.

SUMMARY

1 The type of credit used should be appropriate to the planned expenditure.
2 Credit invariably has a cost and the least cost alternative must be found by using APR and/or total credit price.
3 Ensure that the repayments can be met from income surplus to your 'revenue expenditure' requirements.

TASKS

Task 1

Allen has started his first job after leaving school as a retail management trainee. His take home pay is £49.50 per week. As he will continue to live at home, he has agreed to give his mother £15 per week, and his other living expenses are:

1 Travel to work – £1.80 return fare each day;
2 Lunch and breaks, etc. – £2.00 per day;
3 Spending money – Allen estimates that he needs at least £15 per week;
4 Clothing, etc. – he has opened a revolving credit account with a menswear chain store for £10 per month to cover this need.

Make an estimate of Allen's weekly revenue expenditure and establish if he has any surplus income so that he can save for, or make repayments on a loan for, a motor bike.

Task 2

Julie has been offered a job with a large insurance company and she has been fortunate enough to find a room in a flat shared with three other girls, near the office. The girls each contribute £150 per month to a 'kitty' which pays for the flat rent, heating, lighting, etc. Julie's other expenses will be:

1 Food – subsidised meals from the company restaurant will keep costs down to an estimated £25 per week;
2 Clothing, etc. – Julie estimates that she could survive on a minimum of £50 per month;

Julie also hopes to save at least £30 per month to pay for her holiday.

Advise Julie if her plans are possible on an annual salary of £7210 per annum. Assume that Julie will be entitled to a single person's allowance and that she will be in a *non contributory* company pension scheme (i.e. contracted out but no contribution paid by employee to company scheme).

Task 3

Your local electrical goods store has a compact disc player on offer at £300. You would like it and there are two ways of financing the purchase open to you. You normally have £60 of surplus income each month, after paying for revenue expenditure, and this is now available.

1 Use the store's special low cost HP terms of 20% deposit, then the balance in 12 equal instalments over 12 months at 5% Flat Rate;
2 Use your credit card to pay for it outright, interest is currently 2% per month on any outstanding balance.

Which is the lowest cost method of financing the purchase?

Task 4

After looking at adverts in the local paper, you find that the compact disc player referred to in Task 3 is available in other shops at different prices and with different finance terms attached. Do the following advertisements change your decision to buy the player at your local shop?

1 Price £285, credit terms: revolving credit with no deposit, payment £10 per month, APR 30% per annum.
2 Price £310, free credit for 6 months. Deposit £58 and the balance in 6 equal instalments with APR 0% per annum.

Task 5

Jack wishes to change his car. He has been offered £3000 for it as a part exchange with a new car costing, on the road, £6240. The garage are offering two attractive ways of financing the balance.

1 0% HP for settlement of the balance with 12 equal monthly instalments;
2 5% HP for settlement of the balance with 24 equal monthly instalments.

Jack's bank would provide the balance by way of a personal loan. The appropriate section of the repayment tables is shown below.

Advise Jack on the best course of action, bearing in mind that he can afford a maximum of £225 per month for repayments.

Task 6

An advertisement for a new car appeared in a newspaper offering a low deposit and HP interest at 10.5% p.a. flat rate. Other details have been extracted and are shown below:

	£ .
Cash price on the road	4854.00
Deposit (minimum 10%)	485.40

Repayments over 3 years in 36 equal monthly instalments.

If you wish to buy the car, and had the deposit available, which finance method would you prefer: HP as offered or a bank personal loan?

Use the repayment table for bank loans shown below.

Task 7

A building society will provide mortgages of $2\frac{1}{2}$ times the main income, plus $1\frac{1}{2}$ times the second income, to married couples. The maximum advance is 90% of the property value. Estimate the maximum mortgage available and maximum value of property the following first time buyers can purchase.

	Main income	*Second income*	*Savings available for deposit*
(a)	David £8500 p.a.	Jenny £9600	£2500
(b)	John £10 200 p.a.	Alice £6800	£6000
(c)	Liz £13 000 p.a.		£4000

Monthly table of repayments Interest 10% per annum flat (monthly repayments rounded down to nearest whole penny)

	12 monthly repayments APR 19.5%		*18 monthly repayments APR 19.7%*		*24 monthly repayments APR 19.7%*		*30 monthly repayments APR 19.6%*		*36 monthly repayments APR 19.4%*		
Amount of loan £	*Monthly payment £*	*Total amount payable £*	*Monthly payment £*	*Total amount payable £*	*Monthly payment £*	*Total amount payable £*	*Monthly payment £*	*Total amount payable £*	*Monthly payment £*	*Total amount payable £*	*Amount of loan £*
500	45.83	549.96	31.94	574.92	25.00	600.00	20.83	624.90	18.05	649.80	500
600	55.00	660.00	38.33	689.94	30.00	720.00	25.00	750.00	21.66	779.76	600
700	64.16	769.92	44.72	804.96	35.00	840.00	29.16	874.80	25.27	909.72	700
800	73.33	879.96	51.11	919.98	40.00	960.00	33.33	999.90	28.88	1039.68	800
900	82.50	990.00	57.50	1035.00	45.00	1080.00	37.50	1125.00	32.50	1170.00	900
1000	91.66	1099.92	63.88	1149.84	50.00	1200.00	41.66	1249.80	36.11	1299.96	1000
1100	100.83	1209.96	70.27	1264.86	55.00	1320.00	45.83	1374.90	39.72	1429.92	1100
1200	110.00	1320.00	76.66	1379.88	60.00	1440.00	50.00	1500.00	43.33	1559.88	1200
1300	119.16	1429.92	83.05	1494.90	65.00	1560.00	54.16	1624.80	46.94	1689.84	1300
1400	128.33	1539.96	89.44	1609.92	70.00	1680.00	58.33	1749.90	50.55	1819.80	1400
2000	183.33	2199.96	127.77	2299.86	100.00	2400.00	83.33	2499.90	72.22	2599.92	2000
3000	275.00	3300.00	191.66	3449.88	150.00	3600.00	125.00	3750.00	108.33	3899.88	3000
4000	366.66	4399.92	255.55	4599.90	200.00	4800.00	166.66	4999.80	144.44	5199.84	4000
5000	458.33	5499.96	319.44	5749.92	250.00	6000.00	208.33	6249.90	180.55	6499.80	5000
6000	550.00	6600.00	383.33	6899.94	300.00	7200.00	250.00	7500.00	216.66	7799.76	6000
7000	641.66	7699.92	447.22	8049.96	350.00	8400.00	291.66	8749.80	252.77	9099.72	7000
8000	733.33	8799.96	511.11	9199.98	400.00	9600.00	333.33	9999.90	288.88	10399.68	8000
9000	825.00	9900.00	575.00	10350.00	450.00	10800.00	375.00	11250.00	325.00	11700.00	9000
10000	916.66	10999.92	838.88	11499.84	500.00	12000.00	416.66	12499.80	361.11	12999.96	10000

To use the tables

Look down the left-hand column to find the amount you wish to borrow, then look across to the column for the repayment period you prefer. This will then give you the amount of your monthly repayments. If the amount you wish to borrow is not shown just add two figures together to work out your repayments e.g. for £2800, add the figures for £2000 and £800.

If the building society's policy changed so that first-time buyers could borrow 100% of the property valuation, would any of the above be able to purchase a house of greater value than is possible under the existing rules?

Task 8

A building society has the following policy on lending.

1 maximum advance $2\frac{1}{2}$ times gross income and $2\frac{1}{2}$ times joint income for married couples.
2 maximum lending as a proportion of property value
(a) 95% of the value of property built since 1950;
(b) 80% of the value of property built prior to 1950.

Consider the following persons who all live in the same block of flats and are currently offering their flats for sale at £35 000

1 Angela, existing mortgage on the flat £15 000. Current salary £11 500 p.a. She would like to move to a new development nearer to her office. The asking price for the new flat is £45 500.
2 Brian and Janet, a married couple, current mortgage £20 000. Brian earns £9500 p.a. and Janet £7400 p.a. They would like to move to an old country property on offer at £60 000.
3 Ian and Valerie are a married couple with two children who would like to move to a property with a garden for the children to play in. They have seen a suitable property on a recently completed estate at £48 250. Only Ian works, he earns £165 per week. They have a mortgage of £8000 on the flat.

Taking into consideration their income and the capital retained by the sale of their flats, advise them if their plans are possible. Ignore transaction costs.

Task 9

Bill lives in a flat which he shares with two other people. His contribution towards the rent is £75 per month and another £25 per month is required to cover his share of the gas, electricity, rates, etc. He has decided he would rather buy his own house or flat. His income is £150 per week gross, £110 per week net. Other expenses incurred are:

1 Food and housekeeping expenses – £40 per week;
2 Travel to work – £5 per week;
3 General expenses – £20 per week;
4 Monthly credit accounts payments to a clothing store £20;
5 HP payments on his car, which will end in six months' time, £45 per month.

Bill has investments of £5000 which he has always intended to be used for house purchase.

(a) Calculate the maximum value of property he can purchase if the building society will allow mortgages of three times annual salary.

(b) Using the repayment mortgage table in Fig. 3.3, estimate the monthly cost of this level of mortgage.

(c) Taking into consideration Bill's expenses, estimate the maximum repayments and mortgage he can afford.

Task 10

Assume that you are a single person earning £8000 p.a. and paying 5% of that into a company pension scheme. You wish to buy a house which will cost you £40 000. You have received a legacy of £25 000 which will be invested in the property, the balance will be borrowed from your building society who will advance you up to three times your annual salary. You have no other savings. The transaction costs are likely to be:

1 Building society survey and legal fees, *see* Fig 3.5;
2 Your solicitor's fees of approximately £250 plus various search fees, etc., of say £100;
3 Stamp duty at 1% of value of property;
4 Removal costs say £250.

Estimate:

(a) The mortgage required.

(b) The monthly cost of that mortgage, repayment method. *See* table in Fig. 3.3.

(c) The monthly balance of net income after making the mortgage repayment.

4
Personal financial planning

INTRODUCTION

Successful handling of personal finances must start with *planning*, and these plans need to be based upon realistic information about income and expenditure. The information required can be obtained in two ways:

1 by investigating the cost of proposed actions in reasonable detail;
2 from personal records held on the documentation from similar transactions in the past.

The second element in the handling of personal finances leads from this, that is the need for a *record system*. Details of past expenditure can be a reliable basis for planning future expenditure, and having set down a plan, it is necessary to record the actual income and expenditure for comparison with the plan.

When the comparison between actual and planned is made, the third element comes in to play, that is *control*. If the plan and reality coincide then all is well, however in practice this is not often the case and at least minor controlling action will need to be taken. This action can take two forms:

1 adjust the plan because a part of it has proved to be unrealistic;
2 adjust income or expenditure to conform to the previously planned levels.

We can see in Fig. 4.1 that maintaining control over personal finances is a cyclical process.

Fig. 4.1 The cyclical process of controlling personal finance

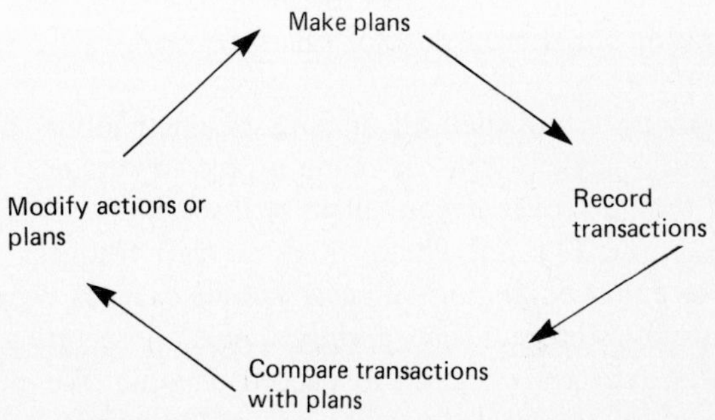

PLANNING AND BUDGETING

Budgeting is expressing plans in money terms and is therefore the best method of establishing if income will meet expenditure in a given period. Budgets are usually set out for twelve months on a month by month basis. This is a good compromise between the need for reasonable detail and uncertainty about the future. Those whose income is not received on the usual monthly basis may wish to adjust at least the early parts of the budget on to the same pattern as their income receipts. Events taking place after one year cannot usually have an accurate cost placed on them and are therefore excluded. The budget can of course be updated regularly so that it is always looking twelve months ahead, this is known as a *rolling budget*.

Preparing a budget

Your budget will be a statement of your financial *inputs* and *outputs* for the stated period. Inputs are usually easy to establish as you will be aware of your net income, or can estimate it accurately after working through Chapter 2. If budgeting for a family, do not forget income such as child benefit. Outputs break down into three areas:

Revenue expenditure

Here past experience and any records held will be used. The more documentation about past expenditure that can be found the better because it can be used as a basis for sensible estimates of future costs.

Remember that revenue expenditure is for the regular necessities of life and must be met out of income before any other spending. It is important to make realistic estimate of revenue expenditure and probably wise to make an allowance above the estimated level, say ten per cent, to cover unexpected increases in consumption and inflation.

Capital expenditure

You will need to establish your priorities for capital expenditure and the costs associated with alternative methods of financing this spending.

Savings

These must be considered as an output in the short term as you are deliberately reducing your current ability to spend. Savings will be discussed in more detail later but we can view them as part of long-term planning for the purpose of this section.

Having established all of your planned inputs and outputs they can now be made up into a budget. We will then discover if your plans will work!

Examine Fig. 4.2 which shows a Draft Budget.

Note that on an annual basis income exceeds expenditure by £160, but that in March, plus the second and fourth quarters, expenditure exceeds income. We must now check to see if this will cause an overdraft at the bank. This can be done by adding to the bottom of the budget a *Cash Budget* (*see* Fig. 4.3).

The balance carried forward at the end of each month/quarter is the balance brought forward for the next month/quarter. In our example the balance carried forward at the end of each period is positive, therefore a bank overdraft is avoided. Notice that the balance carried forward at the end of quarter 4, £160, is the same as the difference between total income and total expenditure.

Note: There are various alternative layouts and terms for this form of budget all of which will follow the same basic principles.

Decision making using a budget

Figures 4.2 and 4.3 showed a straightforward budget where income comfortably exceeded expenditure and an overdraft was not required to meet an income shortfall in any period. However, if £100 cannot be raised by selling the old computer and the estimates for Gas, Electricity, Rates and Telephones are too low then the picture will change to one of expenditure exceeding income.

Task

You may like to try this and examine the result, by removing the £100 income from the sale of the old computer and increasing Rates, Gas, Electricity and Telephone by 10% on the quoted figures, rounded up to the nearest whole pound. You will find that the budget shows an overdraft at the end of quarters 2 and 4, of £41 and £21 respectively

Decisions will now have to be made about the plan.

1 Is the overdraft acceptable? If so, it must be arranged. It should be remembered that overdrafts have a cost; interest charged, bank charges for the period in which the overdraft occurs and any arrange-

Fig. 4.2 Draft Budget

This is a twelve month budget but the last nine months have only been shown on a quarterly basis.

	Jan	*Feb*	*Mar*	*Apr / Jun*	*Jul / Sep*	*Oct / Dec*	*Total*
	£	£	£	£	£	£	£
Income							
1 Salary/wages net	490	490	490	1470	1470	1470	5880
2 Sale of surplus equipment, etc. (old computer)	100						100
3 **Other income**							
Total income	590	490	490	1470	1470	1470	5980
Expenditure							
1 Rent	150	150	150	450	450	450	1800
2 Rates				120		120	240
3 Electricity (light/cook)			35	35	35	35	140
4 Gas (heating)			70	40	40	60	210
5 House-keeping	120	120	120	360	360	360	1440
6 Travel expenses	40	40	40	120	120	120	480
7 House insurance			50				50
8 Telephone		50		50	50	50	200
9 HP (new computer system)	45	45	45	135	135	135	540
10 Savings	60	60	60	180	180	180	720
Total expenditure	415	465	570	1490	1370	1510	5820

Fig. 4.3 Cash Budget

	Jan	*Feb*	*Mar*	*Apr / Jun*	*Jul / Sep*	*Oct / Dec*
	£	£	£	£	£	£
Balance brought forward	*nil*	175	200	120	100	200
Add total income	590	490	490	1470	1470	1470
	590	665	690	1590	1570	1670
less total expenditure	415	465	570	1490	1370	1510
Balance carried forward	175	200	120	100	200	160

ment fee; these costs need to be incorporated into the budget.
2 If the overdraft is to be avoided, then the budget must be adjusted where possible.

The budget in Fig. 4.2 has two areas where it may be changed to ensure that an overdraft does not occur if the situation described above proves to be correct. The most obvious is savings; these could be reduced during the periods where the overdraft would occur. However, many savings schemes are of a contractual nature and the monthly payments are made by standing order. If this is the case there will not be any flexibility in the budget with savings except to reduce the planned monthly saving by an amount sufficient to ensure that an overdraft is not required. Capital expenditure can be financed in a variety of ways and so perhaps the new computer could be financed in a way that extend the term or has a lower interest rate; in both cases the monthly cost could be reduced. Let us assume that a saving of £5 per month interest could be made by taking a bank personal loan at 18% APR rather than use the store's own credit at 30% APR. This means that the annual cost of this expenditure will be reduced by $12 \times £5 = £60$, sufficient to remove the need for an overdraft of £21 at the end of the year. This may not be sufficient to remove the need for an overdraft at the end of quarter 2, so other budget items need investigation.

As the annual income now exceeds annual expenditure no further cuts in expenditure need take place. What is required is a way of spreading the cost of one or a number of items evenly to avoid peaks of expenditure. During quarter 2 rates of £120 are paid. This causes a peak of expenditure and hence the need for an overdraft. Many household costs, including rates can be spread over the year, usually by taking the annual payment, then dividing by 12 to give a monthly payment. Rates can often be paid by taking 10 monthly payments starting in May and ending in February of the following year. An arrangement of this nature would remove the cost of rates from quarter 2 and replace it by:

*£264 ÷ 10 = say £27 per month from May
(£81 per quarter)

The overdraft will be avoided and two monthly payments will be moved into the next year. They should not be forgotten!
*Total rates per year originally £240 now plus 10% = £264

Task

The budget may now be re-written to take these items into consideration and the period end balances checked. Summary of changes in both tasks:

1 No income from sale of old computer;
2 Rates, Gas, Electricity and Telephone cost increased by 10%;
3 New computer financed in a less costly way and interest charges reduced by £5 per month;
4 Rates switched to 10 monthly instalments of £24 commencing in May.

Result, no overdraft requirement and a balance of £87 carried forward at the end of December.

The budget used has been a comparatively straightforward example, but the system used can be applied to all personal finance planning situations. If you have access to a computer with a spreadsheet programme, then it is possible to look at many alternative solutions to budgeting problems. At the end of this chapter you will find more situations to look at.

RECORDING PERSONAL TRANSACTIONS

Most of us attempt to make some record of our financial transactions, if only marking bills as 'Paid' and filing them, but the bank statement balance is always different to what we expected it to be! To maintain a firm control over personal expenditure and to maximise the benefit obtained from a given level of income, requires a good records system used in conjunction with a realistic budget. The records kept can be numerous, but the following basics should be sufficient for most individuals.

Basic guidelines

1 Pay all but general living expenses by cheque, then you will have two records of your transactions:
(a) cheque book stubs;
(b) bank statements.

The cheque book stubs allow you to keep a check on your current bank balance. This record is simply kept up-to-date; on pay day increase the balance by the amount shown on your payslip, then deduct immediately any regular standing orders or direct debits, thereafter simply reduce the balance each time you write a cheque.
2 Withdraw cash for general living expenses and stick to the amount allowed by your budget. Any over-budget deviation will jeopardise the rest of your financial plans.
3 Compare bills received with the budgeted figure when they are received; this will enable you to take appropriate action if the bill is significantly different from the budget.
(a) Under budget: check to see if a mistake has been

made and rectify if so. If no mistake, then your budget for that category of expense may need recalculating. The difference between budget and actual is therefore available for increased consumption or savings.

(b) Over budget: check for mistakes – if none then the budget needs amending. Overspending in one category will mean first reduced spending in other areas to make up for the shortfall within the total budget period; and/or second the need for additional finance to make good the shortfall in individual budget periods. This usually means an overdraft, although credit cards can be useful at these times.

4 File all bills received and any tariff schedules obtained as these will form the data for the next budget. Take note of any press comment about future price changes and build these into your budget. The more accurate the picture about consumption levels, based on past records and the more up-to-date the prices available, the better. This type of information will allow you to make very accurate estimates of revenue expenditure. The more accurate your estimate of revenue expenditure, the more confident you can be about committing yourself to financing capital expenditure. For example, if a 25-year mortgage cost £10 per month, per £1000 borrowed, to repay then every extra £10 that you have to allow for revenue expenditure to cover up for inaccurate forcasting will reduce the amount you can risk borrowing by £1000. The need for a £50 buffer will cost you a potential borrowing of £5000, possibly the difference between the house you would like and the house you will have to put up with! Under-estimating by a similar amount could lead to over-borrowing with its attendant problems.

5 Keep separate records for any other accounts held, e.g. building society. For an additional level of sophistication, the use of an analysed cashbook can help to establish expenditure patterns and trends. (*See* Chapter 8.) However, a simple cashbook is not much better than cheque book stubs plus statements and probably not worth bothering with.

OPPORTUNITY COST

Financial planning helps with the problem of choosing between the various demands that we wish to meet from our limited resources. This is often referred to as looking at the opportunity cost, i.e. assessing the cost of a choice in terms of the alternatives forgone. In practice the situation we find ourselves presented with is not often a straightforward choice between A or B, it is rather deciding how much of A should be acquired at the expense of less of B and C; in other words assessing priorities. Economists talk in terms of *maximising total utility*. This is obtaining the greatest benefit from the resources available.

We have seen from our previous work on budgeting that it is possible to set out various needs or wants, so that by a combination of direct expenditure from income and finance from other sources, the best use is made of the income available. This is then making opportunity cost decisions in such a way as to maximise the satisfaction obtained from income.

SAVINGS

Saving is simply not spending all of your income, this may be a matter of a few pounds surplus one week which is spent the next or it could be a planned course of action whereby a sum of money is set aside for investment in some way. Savings are often considered to be regular amounts set aside from income, whereas investment is seen as the use of a lump sum, e.g. £100 to buy a national savings deposit bond. We will not draw this distinction and consider all amounts in such places that they gain a return, rather than being spent, as investments.

Considerations before investing:

1 How much is available – some investments require a minimum initial investment or a minimum regular commitment;

2 The level of liquidity required in your investment, i.e. the speed of access to your funds;

3 The type of return required – capital growth, that is the rate at which your investment grows independent of any dividends or interest, or income, the interest or dividends being paid to you;

4 Your tax situation and the tax liability arising on receipt of your interest.

Risk-free investments

The least risky investments are those made in the High Street banks and building societies, along with national savings. In all of these investments you are sure to receive the return of the original sum invested. Unless specifically deposited for a set term, access to these funds is usually very quick, at the possible cost of a loss in interest. There are a large number of investment opportunities available in this category and those on offer should be assessed in the light of your own personal circumstances. Check the personal finance pages of newspapers for advice on the latest offerings and visit a few of these establishments in your local High Street to compare terms and conditions. Non tax payers should remember that the majority of this type of investment pays interest net of tax, which cannot be recovered.

Risk investments

The risk referred to is the chance that the value of your initial investment may fall. The hope is that, unlike risk-free investments, the value of your capital will rise as well as pay interest or dividends. With this type of investment, the level of interest or dividends is often of secondary importance to capital growth.

These investments are usually in shares, although the capital may not be invested directly into shares, but via the medium of a unit trust or similar scheme. (*See* Chapter 1, 'Stock market investment' and the addresses for further information about investing in shares.)

In order to minimise the risk, it is considered necessary to invest in a range of shares. It has been suggested that a minimum of £25 000 needs to be invested by the individual making his or her own decisions – that is £1000 in 25 different shares, to ensure reasonable income from the investment and obtain some overall capital growth, i.e. minimise risks by spreading the investment. If an individual wishes to make their own investment, it is best to seek professional advice before making any decisions.

Advice on investments

Unless one's investment requirements are simple and straightforward, it is best to seek some advice. General advice is available from various publications, daily newspapers, or specialist periodicals and there are a number of books readily available on the subject. Personal advice on your particular situation can be obtained from banks, insurance brokers, solicitors, stockbrokers and accountants, but it should be remembered that these persons all have their own preferences and self-interests, however hard they try to be objective, and their advice will always be biased. In the end, you must make the decision, but if you have made plans and set objectives applying the advice received and the results of your own researches, it should result in a successful investment.

Accountants and personal finance

Chartered and Certified Accountants in public practice are able to provide advice and assist in the planning of personal finances. Their services can be of particular use when your circumstances are more complicated than usual, e.g. when you have a second income.

They can provide advice on:

1 Investments – tax implications, balance of investments to provide income with capital growth, assessment of risk, etc.
2 Borrowing – the most advantageous way of financing capital expenditure, i.e. type of mortgage etc.
3 Pensions – planning of pension providing investments.
4 Taxation – income tax, capital gains tax, inheritance tax, plans can be drawn up to minimise these.

SUMMARY

Revenue expenditure must be met from income. Capital expenditure can be financed from the balance of income after revenue expenditure. Savings also come from this income balance after revenue expenditure. Planning and budgeting allow income to be utilised to provide maximum benefit from that level of income.

TASKS

Tasks 1 to 3

Edward is working in an office in the next town, his net income is £250 per month. He has savings of £300 in a building society which he is planning to spend on a holiday in a year's time. Unfortunately the holiday will cost £600, so can you set out Edward's budget based on transactions through his bank account for the next 12 months to discover if he will be able to afford the holiday.

His salary is paid into his bank current account which today, 31st October, has a zero balance. He would like to save by a regular standing order from his bank to the building society.

Current expenditure:

(a) payment to mother for 'housekeeping', £20 per week;

(b) travelling expenses £40 per month (season ticket);

(c) clothes purchased by revolving credit, payment £10 per month by standing order;

(d) cash withdrawn for general expenses and entertainment £20 per week.

Ignore interest on savings.

Tasks

1 Prepare budget to show if he can afford the holiday.
2 Can he afford driving lessons at £10 per week for an estimated 16 weeks, commencing the first week in November? (The test fee will be part of his birthday

present from his parents). If he cannot afford them can you suggest changes that will enable him to afford them?

3 If you learn that Edward is due a pay increment on 1st May that will increase his net income by 6% per month, does it change your budget for question 2 and can savings be increased?

Tasks 4 to 7

Jennifer will start work on 1st September (note, effectively half-way through the tax year). She will receive a salary of £4500 p.a. for the first year of employment. She will not be in an occupational pension scheme. Jennifer would like to live in a flat near to her work with three friends. She estimates her expenses as:

(a) share of rent £65 per month, paid monthly;
(b) share of gas and electricity bills, £80 per quarter paid in arrears;
(c) clothing £50 per month;
(d) general expenses and entertainment £20 per week;
(e) housekeeping/food expenses £120 per month.

Task 4

Sent out Jennifer's budget for the first 12 months to see if her plans are financially realistic.

Task 5

Suggest ways that the budget may be adjusted to ensure that no overdraft will occur and to have built up savings of £100 by the end of the year to provide funds to meet unexpected expenditure.

Task 6

If one of the persons sharing the flat left at the end of June, so that the flat expenses had to be shared between the remaining friends until the end of the budget period, would Jennifer be overdrawn at the end of the 12 months, and by how much?

Task 7

Estimate the weekly hours required, working weekends in a supermarket for £2.20 per hour, for Jennifer to make up for any shortfall in income during the situation described in Task 6. The ideal level of income will achieve the balance obtained in Task 5.

Tasks 8–10

Task 8

Richard and Elizabeth are to be married and from the following information they provide, prepare a 12-month budget for them after marriage. Savings have been used for house deposit and purchase expenses.

Income (gross):
Richard: £9400 p.a., company pension, contribution 5% of gross salary;
Elizabeth: £8700 p.a., no company pension scheme.

Expenditure:
(a) mortgage £195 per month including household insurances;
(b) life insurance policy £36 per month;
(c) Gas, Electricity, Telephone – total £240 per quarter paid in arrears in months 3, 6, 9 and 12;
(d) Rates £300 per year paid in two equal instalments in months 2 and 8;
(e) travel and car running expenses £50 per month;
(f) car tax and insurance £180 due in month 8;
(g) Elizabeth has been making regular monthly payments of £25 to a savings scheme. They would like to continue with these;
(h) housekeeping £200 per month;
(i) cash for general expenses, etc., £20 each per week;
(j) clothing estimated at £70 per month, using credit cards to spread the cost.

Task 9

Richard is keen to buy a second hand car so that they do not rely on their rather old existing car, except for Elizabeth's comparatively short journey to work. The new car will cost £6300 of which £6000 will be financed by hire purchase at a flat rate of 10% p.a. over 3 years. The car is available in month 1. In addition to the deposit of £300, tax and insurance totalling £360 will have to be paid in the month of purchase. Advise Richard of the feasibility of this purchase and suggest any budget changes required to accommodate it, avoiding any overdraft if possible.

Task 10

What would the effect of Elizabeth becoming pregnant and leaving work in month 8 have on the budgets prepared for Tasks 8 and 9. Assume her income is maintained until half-way through month 9 (maternity pay) and that it is replaced after the baby is born, at the end of month 10, by child benefit of £7.25 per week. A tax rebate of £140 can be expected in month 12.

5

The finance of private sector organisations

INTRODUCTION

The UK economy is divided into *public* and *private* sectors. This distinction is drawn by looking at the ownership and primary source of finance for the organisations within a sector. You must be aware of recent *privatisations*, such as British Gas – this is where the source of finance is being transferred from government, the public sector owner, to the private sector by selling shares in the company to private individuals who then participate in the organisation's ownership.

Private sector organisations are then financed and owned by individuals, or groups of individuals, who act in their own interest. This is in contrast to the public sector where the government, as owner, acts in the 'public interest'.

There are three main categories of private sector organisation.

1 sole trader: a business owned and financed by an individual person:
2 partnership: a business owned by two or more individuals up to a normal maximum of twenty.
3 limited liability company: a business owned by two or more shareholders, the number of owners or shareholders is only limited by the number of shares issued.

It is often possible to tell what type an organisation is from its name. Limited companies must acknowledge their type of ownership in their name (this is to warn potential creditors that the shareholders liability is limited and therefore creditors risk remaining unpaid if the company becomes bankrupt). Private limited companies must have *limited* or its abbreviation *Ltd* as part of their title. Public limited companies tend to use the abbreviation *plc*.

A partnership is the form of business often chosen by professional people (they are not allowed to be limited companies) and the name used often reflects this. Sole trader status may be revealed by the business name or notices stating who the proprietor is. However, care must be taken as businesses are allowed to trade under names that could, with the exception of limited companies, disguise their organisation type.

Examples of business types and names:

Sole trader	D Grant (Painter & Decorator)
Partnership	Appleby Hope & Co. (Solicitors)
Limited liability company	Marks & Spencer plc Fordworths Ltd
Sandlebridge Tyre & Battery	unclear, but not a limited company as Ltd or plc would appear in the name.

SOLE TRADERS

There is no legal distinction between the business and its owner. The business's profits and losses are considered to be those of the owner, and although, for technical reasons, accountants draw a clear distinction between the owner's funds and those invested in the business, the law does not. This means that the owner has responsibility for the business assets and liabilities, this is *unlimited liability*. If the business becomes insolvent the owner is personally responsible for the business liabilities, to the full extent of his or her personal possessions, even if this results in personal bankruptcy.

The main source of finance for this type of business will be the owner's own resources, i.e. savings, profits reinvested rather than taken for personal use, and borrowings for which the owner will have to provide security. This means that the funds available for investment in the business will be limited in comparison with other organisation types. However, with provision of funds comes control of the business and since they are mainly provided by the owner, control remains firmly in his or her hands. Sole traders are not obliged to make public any information about their business's financial situation.

PARTNERSHIPS

If a sole trader is unable to provide sufficient finance for the business as an individual, then he or she has the option of joining with other individuals to form a partnership. Jointly they will have sufficient funds. The individual partners will still have the same sources of finance as a sole trader, but the 'pooled' resources will obviously facilitate a much larger joint investment than can be provided by a sole trader of similar means.

Unlimited liability is still a feature of this business type unless an individual partner elects not to participate in the organisation's management. This situation is provided for by the Partnerships Act 1907. Most trading organisations that expand beyond sole trader status see unlimited liability as a major disadvantage and adopt the form of a limited company. However, the legal obligation for limited companies to disclose certain financial information is not imposed upon partnerships; they retain the same level of confidentiality as a sole trader, and this can be seen as an advantage partnerships have over limited companies.

The majority of partnerships are to be found in the professions, such as accountants, solicitors, etc., whose professional associations will not allow their members to form limited companies. This is to ensure personal liability of these people for their actions in carrying out their duties for clients.

The relationships between the partners are governed by the Partnership Act 1890. The financial aspects covered include the sharing of profits and the provision of capital by the partners. These provisions can be avoided if the partners draw up a Partnership Agreement to cover the regulation of the business; under these circumstances the partnership agreement has precedence over the Partnership Act.

LIMITED COMPANIES

The capital of a limited company is provided by the selling of 'shares' in the company to people who wish to invest in it. The total capital required is divided into a number of shares of a nominal value, e.g. 500 000 shares of £1 each. Investors purchase as many shares as they wish to subscribe for. Any individual or group of individuals who have purchased over 50% of the shares have control of the company. The profits of the company are distributed to the shareholders by means of a *dividend per share,* hence the share of profits received is in proportion to the investor's shareholding.

Shareholders appoint directors, who may be shareholders, to run the company and do not directly participate in the management of the company. From the company's point of view, this has the advantage of allowing it to raise considerable amounts of capital from a large number of investors who can invest large or small amounts as individuals without incurring an obligation to participate in the management of the business.

It was recognised back in the nineteenth century that small investors would not be prepared to risk any money in an enterprise if, on the failure of that business, they could be forced to sell their personal possessions in order to satisfy the company's creditors. In order to protect these persons and make finance available to the large companies being formed, *limited liability* was given to shareholders by the Companies Act of 1856. A shareholder in a limited liability company has only risked the initial investment in the company's shares and liability for the business's debts is limited to the extent of that investment. Therefore, in the event of the company becoming insolvent, the original investment may be lost but no claim can be made on the shareholder's personal assets. It is the ability to sell shares to a wide population of investors that enables limited liability companies to raise far more capital than other forms of business organisation. Private individuals with no personal involvement in the business are prepared to invest because they will enjoy the protection of limited liability.

There are two types of limited company, *public* and *private.* Public companies can be recognised by *plc* in their title and private companies usually adopt the abbreviation *Ltd.* (Note the public and private companies are not be be confused with the public and private sectors of the economy, both types of company are in the *private sector.*)

1 A public company is allowed to offer its shares to the general public by its own rules. However, it is legally required to have a minimum issued share capital of £50 000.
2 A private company is one which restricts the sale of its shares.

Although the main source of finance for companies is the sale of shares, it may use other means to obtain capital. Share capital is permanent and is therefore not issued to obtain shorter-term finance, particularly if the issue of new shares allows control of the company to slip from the existing shareholders. Other means include:

(a) selling loan stock (debentures) for long-term finance at a fixed interest rate for a fixed period;

(b) bank loans and overdrafts are used to meet medium and short-term needs.

Shares, debentures and loans are all sources external to the organisation and so, after the initial investment to commence trading, most businesses will look for internal finance from retained profit as their first source.

OTHER FORMS OF PRIVATE SECTOR ORGANISATION

The majority of businesses have the formats described above. However, there are other types of organisations, some of which we are in regular contact with. Examples include:

1 *Mutual organisations*: companies without shareholders found in the life assurance business. They are owned by the policy holders who receive the profits of the business in the form of bonus added to the value of their policies. Without shareholders to pay dividends to, these organisations are able to apply their income to the mutual benefit of the policy holding owners.
2 *Building societies*: these non-profit making organisations have a similar philosophy to mutual companies. The members of the society are the investors and mortgagors, and they appoint directors to run the organisation on the members' behalf. The basic objective of these societies is to accept members' investments in return for interest and to lend these deposits as mortgages to members who wish to buy houses.
3 *Co-operatives*: there are (a) *retail* co-operatives which are associations of consumers who have joined the society by the purchase of shares. Each member is entitled one vote, irrespective of the size of shareholding, when appointing a committee to manage the business. In this way, the members can exercise democratic control over the organisation. Profits are often distributed to members in proportion to the amount of business the individual member has with the society.

(b) *worker* co-operatives where there is no rigid format, but all function on the basis that the business is entirely owned and controlled by the workforce. In a typical workers' co-operative, members of the co-operative will be able to participate in and vote on major decisions. Day-to-day control will be vested in individual members who will have been appointed by the membership to the various offices of responsibility.

These types of organisations have their roots in the nineteenth century self-help movements and often had socialist as well as business objectives. Their founders were persons who hoped to improve the lot of working class people and to avoid the exploitation of workers by employers.

Not all private sector organisations are businesses, there are a vast number of clubs and societies with social and recreational objectives. All of these have to be financed and this usually comes from members' subscription. Control of these organisations lies with the members who often appoint a committee to look after the running of the society on their behalf. Assessment of these societies' financial management has to be based upon their non-profit making motives.

FINANCING PRIVATE SECTOR ORGANISATIONS

There are four types of finance that a business is likely to need at some time or another. For the purpose of this section, we will be considering companies but the basic principles apply to all business forms.

1 *permanent capital* – the issued share capital and reserves;
2 *long-term finance* – loans for over ten years;
3 *medium-term finance* – loans for a three to ten year period;
4 *short-term finance* – loans for up to three years.

Permanent capital

This is the investment that the owners have made in the business and the funds provided have been used to acquire fixed assets which are needed by the business to perform profitably. It is not only the initial investment in the business, i.e. the issued share capital, but includes profits that have been reinvested in the organisation. In companies these reinvested or retained profits are known as *reserves*. The total of issued share capital and reserves is called the *shareholders' funds* which is a good description of the total amount that the owners have committed to the business. In general all businesses will look to profits as their first source of finance whatever the timescale of the proposed project. If the project is a particularly long-term one then new shares may be issued and sold to raise the finance; thus increasing the permanent capital in the business.

There are institutions who will help companies raise capital by purchasing their shares and through share ownership participate in the control of the organisation, e.g. 3i (Investors in Industry Group plc). Long- and medium-term loan capital may also be part of the package of financial assistance.

Medium- and long-term finance

The clearing banks are the main providers of finance in this and all other areas of business finance. Even the organisations mentioned above as purchasing shares in companies are often owned by the big banks. The loans provided come with various terms and conditions attached but, unlike personal loans, are often tailored to meet individual business requirements. The banks will almost always require security so this means that the loans are often secured on the assets of the company by a mortgage. In effect, in the event of the company's failure, the asset may be sold to repay the loan. The banks often have leaflets on display giving details of this type of loan (*See* Fig. 5.1).

Businesses may also sell 'loan stock', known as *debentures,* in the same way as shares, but usually in £100 blocks. The stock will have a fixed rate of interest payable by the company and a set date on which it will be repaid. Again, security is provided by securing the debenture on a company asset or class of asset.

With types of loan finance, it is important to ensure that the loan term is compatible with the useful life of the asset to be acquired or the project to be financed. Hence medium-term finance is seen as suitable for the purchase of plant and equipment and long-term finance is regarded as being mainly used for the acquisition of land and buildings.

Short-term finance

This usually refers to overdraft facilities on current

Fig. 5.1 Bank leaflet

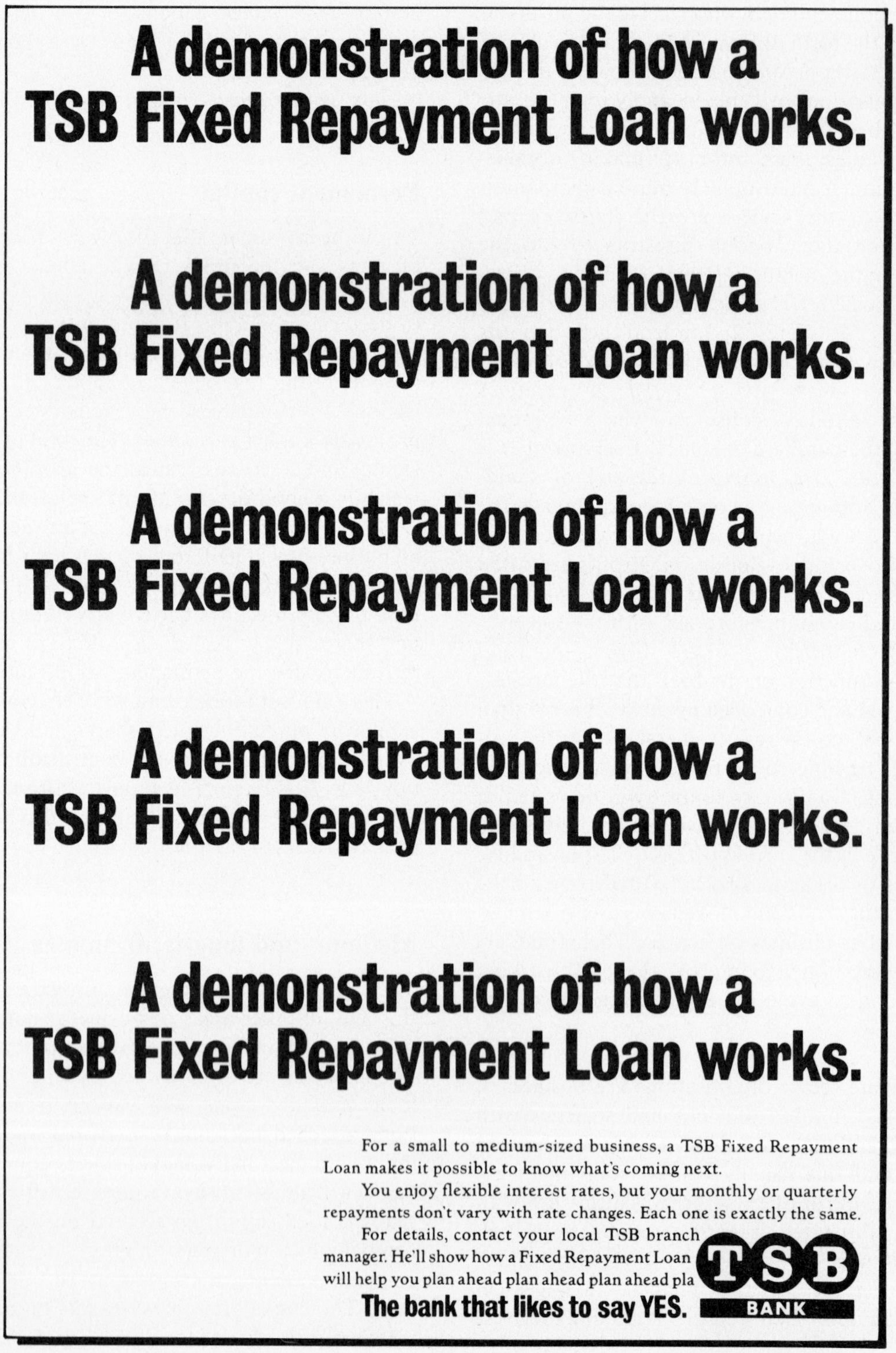

accounts. The bank will need to see cashflow forecasts to show the timing and quantity of the overdraft required before granting facilities. Overdrafts have limits attached which set the maximum amount that can be borrowed and the timescale in which the account is expected to return to a credit balance. Many businesses have a seasonal or cyclical trade with a corresponding need for overdraft facilities and will regularly swing from debit to credit balances and back again. Under these circumstances banks will grant an on-going overdraft facility, subject to regular review. Unlike normal loans which attract interest on the whole loan from the moment the loan is made available, overdraft facilities only incur interest charges when used and then only on the amount used. This makes an overdraft a comparatively cheap form of finance when used appropriately.

Other forms of finance available from bankers and other financial institutions include:

Fig. 5.2 Matching finance and uses

Type of finance	*Normally used for*	*Main sources*
Short-term	1 Financing seasonal/cyclical fluctuations, 2 Financing general working capital requirements; 3 Purchasing minor fixed assets with short working life	Bank overdrafts, short-term loans, hire purchase, leasing, debt factoring, invoice discounting, trade creditors.
Medium-term	1 Financing fixed assets with medium-term life 2 Providing increased working capital requirements.	Medium term loans on a fixed or floating rate basis, hire purchase, leasing.
Long-term	1 Financing major fixed assets with a long life; 2 Providing 'permanent' working capital.	Mortgage loans, redeemable preference shares, debentures.
Permanent	Fixed assets and growth of the business.	Ordinary shares, retained profits.

Hire purchase

This is available to businesses as well as private individuals. It can be an expensive form of finance but an alternative to a bank medium/short-term loan for the small business which may have some difficulty obtaining a loan directly from a bank. A finance company may accept slightly more risky business than the banks, even though a lot of finance companies are owned by banks, because the higher interest charged compensates for the extra risk.

Leasing

This is similar to hire purchase but the item leased remains the property of the finance house. The system is very similar to rental, the business has the use of the leased asset in exchange for regular payments. Maintenance may be included in the cost of the lease. This is a reasonable cost method of obtaining the use of technical goods that the organisation does not wish to accept the responsibilities of ownership for. For example, a leased fleet of cars not only removes the need to raise finance for capital expenditure, it takes from the business all of the troubles associated with car ownership. Lease agreements can be made that provide a substitute car in the event of a breakdown.

Factoring

This is the taking over of trade debts by an organisation known as a *factor*. The factor will provide the value of the invoices sent to customers in cash, less a charge for the service. This type of service can be of use as an alternative to an overdraft. When providing credit to customers a business is depriving itself of the use of the amount owed for the credit period. If the money is needed by the business for other trading opportunies, it can be

(a) borrowed by means of overdraft;
(b) recovered by factoring the debt.

Either way, the business has funds for continued trading. Management must decide upon the most advantageous method.

The government also provides finance to private sector business in the form of loans and grants. They also act as guarantor for some clearing banks lending to businesses where the risk factor is higher than the banks will normally accept. It is in the nature of governments to be continuously changing, introducing and dropping schemes of assistance. It is therefore important to obtain the latest information. The DTI – Department of Trade publish a useful booklet called 'How To Make Your Business Grow', a practical guide to government schemes, and it is obtainable from the Small Firms Service. Other government departments and post offices often have details of these schemes, particularly those aimed at new business start-ups.

GEARING

Gearing is the relationship between issued ordinary share capital, i.e. the finance provided by the owners, and interest bearing finance, provided from external sources. A *high-geared* company is one which has a high proportion of its finance provided by interest-bearing loans. *Low gearing* is the reverse, the majority of finance being provided by the ordinary shareholders.

The importance of gearing to shareholders can be illustrated by the following example.

A business has an issued share capital of 100 000 ordinary shares of £1, it has borrowed £150 000 from a bank to finance the building and equipping of a new extension to the factory making it a high-geared company. Interest is charged on the loan at 15% per annum. The shareholders have been paid a dividend of 12 pence per share for the past few years. Ignoring taxation the annual payments to shareholders and the bank will be:

Dividend payments

100 000 shares × 12p per share =	£12 000
*Interest charges on loan 150 000 × 15% =	£22 500
Total	£34 500

*Loan repayments will include capital, but only interest is a charge against profits.

The business must make at least £34 500 profit after all expenses, except interest, have been met in order to maintain the same level of dividend to shareholders and pay the interest charges.

If profitability falls to, say, £28 500 before payment of interest, it is the shareholders who have their payments reduced. In this situation, they can only receive:

$$\frac{£28\,500 - £22\,500}{100\,000 \text{ shares}} = 6\text{p per share}$$

Note: profits must be maintained at a minimum of £22 500 before interest in order to service the loan.

Persons buying shares in high-geared companies should therefore be aware that the interest charges must be met from trading profits before any dividends can be paid and if profits are low it is the shareholders who receive a reduced income.

However, when high profits are obtained the shareholders can enjoy all of the extra profit because the loan interest remains constant. If profits before interest rose to £46 500, the dividend that could be paid to shareholders is:

$$\frac{£46\,500 - £22\,500}{100\,000 \text{ shares}} = 24\text{p per share}$$

Under these circumstances, high gearing seems a good thing. The project is financed without the issue of new shares and possible changes in the control of the company with a fixed interest rate the shareholders can benefit from higher dividends.

SUMMARY

The quantity of finance needed to set up a particular business dictates the type of organisation that will be used. If a large number of people invest in a business to provide capital, then they gain a measure of control which reduces the freedom to control enjoyed by the sole trader.

It is important to match the finance source and type with the need. Shareholders may be exposed to a potential loss of income if a business is too dependent on external finance because of the effect of gearing.

TASKS

Task 1

The following is a list of typical business names that could be found in Yellow Pages or any other business directory. Can you work out from their names what type of business organisation they are?

(a) Bernard Hebden (Motors) Ltd
(b) Downlands Coach Hire (prop. J Orwell)
(c) Grant and Cooper (Certified Accountants)
(d) Falcon and Bird Ltd
(e) James Porter (Solicitor)
(f) Frank Brown (decorators)
(g) TTR plc
(h) Davis, Smith and McLean Ltd
(i) Brownstone Bros, plc
(j) Office Supplies

Task 2

In order to illustrate a talk you have to give to a group of people who are interested in starting their own businesses, you need to make up a handout. A friend suggests a table showing the main features of the different types of business and sets down the outline shown below. All you have to do is fill in the columns to complete the table.

	Sole trader	*Partnership*	*Limited company*
Who owns the business?			
Who has overall control?			
Who has day-to-day control?			
Who provides the major finance?			
Who receives the profits?			
What limit to liability?			

Tasks 3 to 5

Investigate the options available for the following businesses which require some finance in addition to that already invested or available for investment by the owner or owners. Write a short letter to each enclosing some literature on *one* scheme you think is appropriate.

Task 3

Jean has not worked for some time, she has savings of just over £1000 and wishes to start her own business offering a word processing service. She proposes to work from home initially, preferring to invest all of her funds into the best computing facilities she can obtain with that amount. She will also use some of her savings for a series of adverts in the local press and a display entry in a local trade directory. Jean will need some finance to help her with day-to-day expenses while the business becomes established.

Task 4

David runs a local delivery and courier service, which he started 18 months ago and business has grown steadily. The van he started with was old then, it is now in need of replacement because unreliable transport and late deliveries would do considerable damage to the business's reputation. A new vehicle would cost £6000 and could be expected to need replacement in 3 years' time.

Task 5

Allman Engineering Developments believe that they have developed a revolutionary new central heating control system that will enable home owners to be far more economical in the running of their heating systems. The directors have invested heavily in research and development for the product and are confident that it is a technically sound product. They believe the market for the system is vast but they do not have the facilities to make the product in the volume that will enable demand to be met at a competitive price. Unfortunately the high street banks are not prepared to provide the finance for equipping the required production line, they see the product as too 'high tech' and risky.

Task 6

ABC Ltd has reported the following profit (taxation is ignored):

Extract from ABC Ltd's Accounts

	£
Operating profit	90 000
less Interest charges	30 000
Net profit	60 000
less Dividends	20 000
Retained profit	40 000

It is company policy to reinvest, i.e. retain profit, of £40 000 per year as part of a long-term investment programme. The interest charges are for external finance on the same project. All profit is paid as dividend subject to the retention of £40 000 and the interest charges of £30 000. The issued share capital is 100 000 £1 ordinary shares and the dividend paid this year was 20p per share. Chandra has been invited to purchase shares in ABC Ltd. Can you explain to him the effect on his dividend income of *plus* or *minus* 10% fluctuation in the operating profit shown above.

6

The finance of public sector organisations

INTRODUCTION

The public sector of the economy is more than the *nationalised industries* – it contains government departments, local authorities and organisations like the water boards. Control of these organisations is in the hands of Government, local and central, who are responsible for their activities to the public through the election system. In reality, the public have little influence on the actions of these bodies, they can only vote for the general principles put forward at election time.

The three main types of organisation in the public sector (*see* Fig. 6.1) that we are aware of on a day to day basis are:

(a) public corporations; the nationalised industries;
(b) local authorities; county and district councils;
(c) central government departments; e.g. defence, transport, health.

Fig. 6.1 Public sector organisations

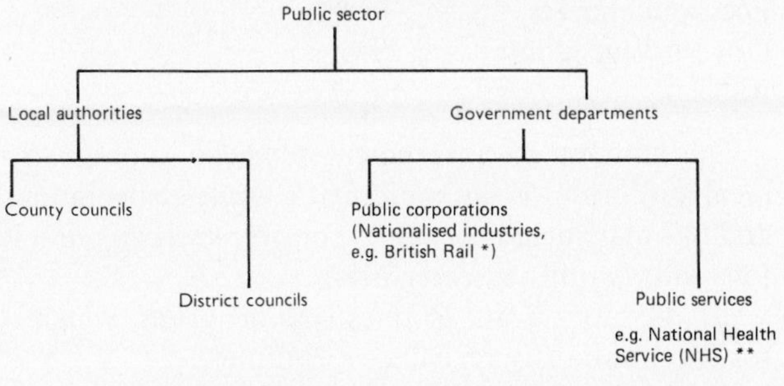

* British Rail is the responsibility of the Department of Transport.
** The National Health Service is administered by the Department of Health and Social Security.

Note: The Government is steadily transferring ownership of corporations to the private sector by restoring them as public limited companies and then selling their shares to the public and financial institutions. This removes control of the organisation from the 'sponsoring' government department. For example, the Department of Energy was responsible for British Gas, which is now under the control of its board of directors acting for the shareholders.

PUBLIC CORPORATIONS

Each public corporation must operate in accordance with the provisions of the act that created it. The government sets the general policy of the organisation and the policy is overseen by the minister responsible. The minister has the power to appoint a board of governors to implement the policy and be responsible for the management of the organisation. They have day-to-day control of the corporation in the same way as directors of a limited company. However, the board of governors will not have the same freedom of action as a board of directors, because their decision-making powers will be limited by political constraints imposed by government through the minister. These constraints must be acknowledged by the board of governors because their finance has been provided by government and government will be required to approve further finance. Shareholders do not exist for public corporations, the government is the sole shareholder with the controlling interest. Other finance may be available from sources such as the EEC regional fund grants and borrowing is permitted in appropriate circumstances on home and overseas capital markets, subject to the government set constraint of the External Financing Limit. Internally generated funds are available to profitable organisations.

The financial objectives of these corporations may differ from companies in the private sector where profitability is the major consideration – the position as part of the government's overall activities can make them play a social and economic role in the government's overall objectives which may clash with purely commercial activities.

Financial objectives fall into three broad categories:

1 *Return on capital*: this is the profit expressed as a percentage of the total investment in the industry or particular project. It is often set as a target to be achieved and can be used as a reasonable basis for comparing the efficiency of a public corporation with the private sector.

Failure to achieve the required return will result in
(a) cost cutting measures;
(b) increased prices to customers;
(c) a combination of (a) and (b).

Exceeding the target for return on capital can, because maximising profit is not an overriding objective, result in prices being cut or at least maintained at the same level for long periods.

2 *Meeting budget for the period*: ensuring that the planned income and expenditure meet the targets for the period. Some public corporations are not profitable and to make them profitable would reduce the level of service provided to unacceptably low levels, i.e. there would be a high social cost. Government provide the corporation with a subsidy on the services it does not want withdrawn so that the corporation can meet its financial budget. British Railways has good examples of this type of government action.

(a) Withdrawal of some loss-making rural services could deprive large numbers of people of their links with urban areas. This may be considered to be socially unacceptable even though closure would make economic sense for the system as a whole. So a subsidy is provided to maintain the service.

(b) Commuter services may show unacceptably low levels of return on capital, but the traffic chaos that would result from withdrawal of these services could not be tolerated. So again a subsidy is provided. When looking at British Railways results for a financial year it may appear that they have made a vast loss and needed a subsidy. However, if the subsidy provided was the budget figure then technically there has not been a loss. It is perfectly reasonable to receive considerable income from subsidies and claim a profit, if income exceeds budgeted costs.

3 *Value for money*: public organisations should be seen to be providing a service that is good value for the public money spent. There is considerable effort expended by the management of public sector organisations to ensure that they operate efficiently with the scarce resources available. The recent introduction of budgeting systems designed to ensure that all expenditure is justified and methods developed to measure the effectiveness of the services provided have enabled managers to move towards a situation where the use of resources is maximised.

LOCAL AUTHORITIES

Certain services are provided and controlled by local authorities. These are elected bodies who are responsible for specific local services, e.g. education and fire service. They work through committees of elected councillors which formulate policy on services and, after council approval, oversee the implementation of the policy. Day-to-day management of the service is in the hands of council employees who report to their appropriate committee.

There are three tiers of local authority, at the bottom level are *parish councils* with minor responsibilities. They can play an effective role as channels through which local opinion is expressed on planning matters and other issues of local interest. Above parish councils are *borough* or *district councils* whose services include houses, parks, car parks and refuse collection. The highest tier of local authority is the *county council* whose responsibilities are headed by education, police and social services. It is the county councils which provide the most expensive services such as education and therefore need to raise the most revenue. In the year 1987–88, Hampshire education budget was 62% of the total revenue expenditure.

At county level, local authorities obtain finance in four main ways:

(a) from charging rates on domestic and business premises;

(b) from central government, the rate support grant and other specific grants;

(c) charging for services, hire of halls, recreation facility entrance fees, etc.

(d) raising loans for capital expenditure.

Hampshire accounts for 1987–8 reveal that revenue expenditure is financed by:

Fees and charges	16.5%
Government grants	29%
Rates	54.5%

The amount of government financial support for local authorities is the subject of complex calculations and this may include penalties for over spending, but it falls into two broad categories:

(a) the block grant or rates support grant, which is for local authority revenue expenditue;

(b) specific grants, these are often assistance with capital expenditure programmes.

Central government has been increasing the restrictions on local authority spending in order to reduce public spending as a whole. In addition, the proportion of local revenue expenditure financed by government has been steadily falling, particularly in the 'shire counties', e.g. Hampshire, where government grants have fallen from 51% of income in 1974–5 to 29% of income in 1987–8.

The main source of income for meeting revenue expenditure needs are the rates and the charges made for services, and of these two, rates are the major source of income. Indeed, rates often provide more income to meet revenue expenditure than the others combined.

Rates calculations – the householders' bill

Householders will receive in March of each year a *general rates bill.* This is sent by the district council who collect rates on the behalf of the county council and parish council; the district council is known as the

Fig. 6.2 Rates bill

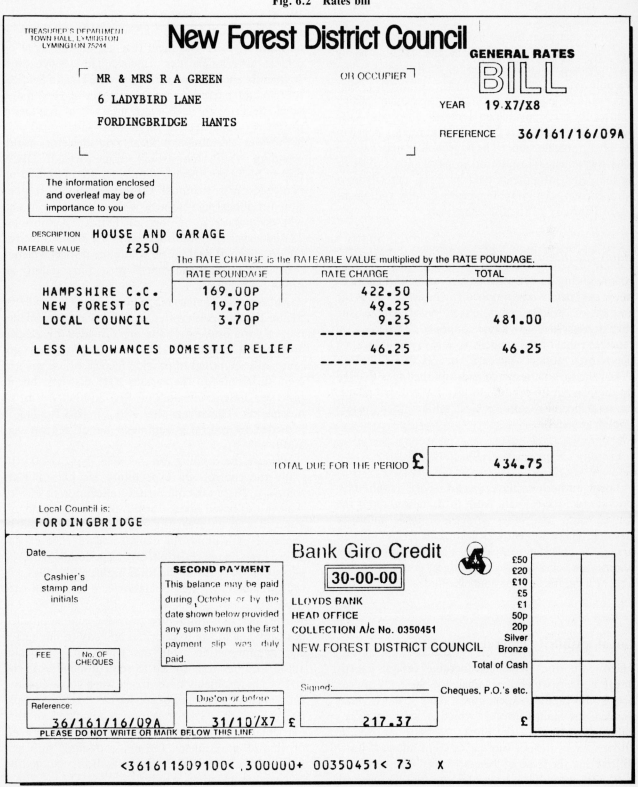

TREASURER'S DEPARTMENT
TOWN HALL, LYMINGTON
LYMINGTON 75244

New Forest District Council

GENERAL RATES BILL

MR & MRS R A GREEN
6 LADYBIRD LANE
FORDINGBRIDGE HANTS

OR OCCUPIER

YEAR 19 X7/X8

REFERENCE 36/161/16/09A

The information enclosed and overleaf may be of importance to you

DESCRIPTION HOUSE AND GARAGE

RATEABLE VALUE £250

The RATE CHARGE is the RATEABLE VALUE multiplied by the RATE POUNDAGE.

	RATE POUNDAGE	RATE CHARGE	TOTAL
HAMPSHIRE C.C.	169.00P	422.50	
NEW FOREST DC	19.70P	49.25	
LOCAL COUNCIL	3.70P	9.25	481.00
LESS ALLOWANCES DOMESTIC RELIEF		46.25	46.25

TOTAL DUE FOR THE PERIOD £ 434.75

Local Council is:
FORDINGBRIDGE

Date____________

Cashier's stamp and initials

SECOND PAYMENT
This balance may be paid during October or by the date shown below provided any sum shown on the first payment slip was duly paid.

Bank Giro Credit

30-00-00

LLOYDS BANK
HEAD OFFICE
COLLECTION A/c No. 0350451
NEW FOREST DISTRICT COUNCIL

£50	
£20	
£10	
£5	
£1	
50p	
20p	
Silver	
Bronze	
Total of Cash	
Cheques, P.O.'s etc.	
£	

FEE

No. OF CHEQUES

Signed:____________

Reference: 36/161/16/09A

Due on or before 31/10/X7

£ 217.37

PLEASE DO NOT WRITE OR MARK BELOW THIS LINE

<361611609100< 300000+ 00350451< 73 X

rating authority. The bill will demand payment of rates calculated on the basis of a property's *rateable value* which is a notional value placed on the property taking into consideration its location, size, facilities and use. The amount is set by the Inland Revenue when a property is built and at periodic intervals thereafter. The rates charge is set at 'x' pence in the pound of rateable value. This is the *rate poundage* and the householder must pay 'x' pence times the rateable value. (*See* Fig. 6.2.)

Notice that each tier of local authority has its own rate poundage. You can check the calculation by multiplying the rate poundage for each council by the rateable value of the property. Domestic relief represents a grant from central government which reduces the rates payable on domestic property. In the period of this bill it was the equivalent of 18.5 pence in the £1 of rateable value. The householder may pay the rates by two equal instalments in April and October or by ten equal instalments paid by direct debit from a bank current account, commencing in May and finishing in February of the following year.

Rates calculations – setting the rate poundage

Before setting the rate poundage, a council will need to know the '*penny rate product*' for its area. This is the amount of revenue that would be raised by charging each householder with a rate poundage of 1p, i.e. total rateable value of the councils area is £17 million, then penny rate product will be £17m × £0.01 = £170 000. When the income required is established it is divided by the penny rate product to give the rate poundage, i.e. total income required is £25.5 million, then the rate poundage will be

$$\frac{£25\,500\,000}{£170\,000} = 150\text{p in the £1}$$

Local authorities have recently been required to provide rate payers with more information about the use of rates and other sources of local authority revenue. These are sent with each general rates bill and are quite informative. More detailed information about your local authority's budgets is usually available at local libraries or council offices.

Local authority capital expenditure

Local authorities have considerable capital expenditure budgets which are financed in methods appropriate to capital expenditure. This means, loan finance, the main source of which is central government in the form of the Public Works Loan Board. Other sources include mortgages from financial institutions and the issue of loan stock and bonds.

Capital expenditure by local authorities has been on the decline since the mid 1970s as part of a reduction in general public sector expenditure. Expenditure on housing has been notably reduced.

GOVERNMENT DEPARTMENTS

While the majority of services provided by public sector organisations are under the control of local authorities, there are some that are administered by central government departments. The service most frequently encountered is the National Health Service; this is administered by the Department of Health and Social Security, through which most of the funding is provided. The NHS is organised with local area authorities deciding on local priorities for health spending within the overall framework of DHSS policy. Local area health authorities are organised on two levels: first, Regional Authorities who are responsible for allocating resources within the region, which will encompass a number of District Authorities; second, District Authorities which are responsible for the provision of health care within the district which is often the natural catchment area surrounding an urban conurbation.

Although small amounts of income may be available to the District Authorities, e.g. from charges made, the vast majority of funds are provided by central government. National Insurance contributions are notionally supposed to provide finance which government distributes to the various NHS districts, but in practice these contributions are another form of income tax. This means that 97% of NHS funding is provided by central government out of general taxation.

Because the funding for the NHS is provided centrally the controls on expenditure are naturally set centrally. These take the form of allocation to Health Authorities based upon a health profile of the population in a given area; the allocation is expressed in terms of cash limits for capital and revenue expenditure for a financial period. Over a period of years the allocation of funds to the local health authorities will reflect changes in the population and its health care needs.

The fact that funds are provided and controlled centrally but spending priorities and day-to-day financial administration is in the hands of the health authorities has recently led to some difficulties in the NHS. The problems have arisen when local demand for a particular element of service has exceeded supply because of the lack of resources allocated to that particular branch of the NHS. Is the problem the fault of central government for not providing sufficient funds? Or, the fault of the health authority for getting its spending priorities wrong?

Central Government income and expenditure

No consideration of public sector finance is complete without showing details of Central Government finance. Each year in the Budget the government sets out its monetary and fiscal policy for the next year. These policies resolve themselves into a balance between planned expenditure and income required to finance that expenditure. The actual details are determined by economic and political factors.

Figure 6.3 shows the Central Government income and expenditure for 1986.

Fig. 6.3

Central Government Income (1986)

Direct Taxation	£1000m
Income tax	37.6
Petroleum revenue tax	2.7
Corporation tax	12.0
Other	0.1
Total taxes on income	52.4
Indirect taxation	
Customs and Excise revenue	
Alcohol and tobacco	8.9
VAT	22.7
Customs levies	1.2
Petrol and oils	7.1
Other	2.1
Motor vehicle duties	2.5
Other taxes and levies	2.7
Total taxes on expenditure	47.2
Social security contributions	26.0
Total taxes and contributions	125.6
Rent, dividends and interest etc.	9.3
Miscellaneous items	1.1
Total current receipts	136.0
Central Goverment borrowing requirement	8.5
Total income	144.5
Current expenditure on goods and services	
Health	18.2
Defence	18.2
Public order and safety	1.9
Education	1.1
Other	9.3
	48.7
Subsidies	5.4
Social security, benefits and other grants (not local authority	46.3
Grants to local authorities	21.8
Grants paid abroad, including net receipts from the EEC	2.2
Debt interest	16.0
Net Capital Account expenditure	4.1
Total expenditure	144.5

Source: HMSO Annual Accounts

SUMMARY

Because public sector industries have Government as their 'shareholder' and controller, they may have different objectives to private sector companies, even though commercial criteria may be used to assess their performance. Central Government also exercises control over local authorities through its grants system and spending restrictions. All householders provide local authorities with income through the rates system. *Note*: It is proposed to replace rates with a 'community charge' which will be a charge for local authority services levied on all adults living in the authority's area.

TASKS

Task 1

The householder whose rates demand was shown in Fig. 6.1 is considering an extension to his existing property or a move to another house within the district. If he extends his house it is expected that his rateable value will increase to £325.

He has seen other properties and is actively considering to buy:

(a) a house at Whitsbury with a rateable value of £350. Local council rates for Whitsbury are 0.2p in the £1.

(b) a house at Hyde with a rateable value of £290. Local council rates for Hyde are 1.8p in the £1.

Provide the householder with a statement showing the potential rates bill for the extension and the two houses he is considering.

Task 2

Wessex county council has a total rateable value in its area of £25 million. It estimates that it needs a £45 million contribution from rates in the next year to meet its revenue expenditure plans.

(a) Act as an officer in the finance department and calculate the general rate poundage for the coming year.

(b) The treasurer is preparing an information leaflet to be sent with the rates bill. You are asked to complete the following table to the nearest whole number.

	Income £000	*Percentage of total* %
Rates	45 000	
Government	23 000	
Users of services	12 000	
Total	80 000	

Task 3

After a further year Wessex county council have to set the general rate poundage again. You are still the officer responsible for the calculation. The following changes have taken place.

(a) the total rateable value has risen to £26 million;

(b) the total income required by the council has risen by $7\frac{1}{2}$% from last year's level;

(c) charges for services are to rise by an average of 5% in line with inflation;

(d) government grants have been announced and are to total £24 000 000 in the year.

Calculate the general rate poundage and set out the table of income as before.

Task 4

The government is to replace the rating system with a 'community charge' also known as a *poll tax*. This has been the subject of much publicity and will continue to be so because the change-over is to be phased in over a period of years for the majority of the UK.

Research the subject, and write a short leaflet for your local authority to circulate to households in its area explaining the difference between the two systems of raising finance for the council. Your leaflet should be factual and not give your opinion on the subject.

Information sources:

(a) the library for government information papers and journals with articles on the subject, including back numbers;

(b) the local council may have published information on the subject;

(c) organisations that may have an opinion on the subject, e.g. rate payers' associations, chambers of commerce, political parties. Remember not to bias your leaflet with opinions.

7
The accounting profession

THE PURPOSE OF ACCOUNTING

Accounting has four main purposes:

(a) To collect, classify and record transactions in monetary terms;

(b) To prepare financial statements, using the recorded transactions in such a way as to report to the members of the organisation on its financial performance and state of affairs;

(c) To use the financial statements in assessment of past performance and from this and other information, make forecasts of future performance;

(d) To provide the financial information to parties external to the organisation; first, information that is required by law, e.g. Company Reports and VAT returns, and second, information that the organisation wishes to provide in order to facilitate its good relationships with these external parties, e.g. public relations, creditors, providers of finance.

HISTORY

Book-keeping is as old as trade – archaeologists have discovered that records in the form of tally stick and tablets were in use over 5000 years ago in organised societies. Modern book-keeping has its origins in the fifteenth century Italian business world – during that period a scholar, Lucia Pacioli, published a paper on mathematics in which he describes the theoretical background to the *double-entry book-keeping* system used today.

Even as early as the sixteenth century the concepts and conventions of accounting were developing as a separate function from book-keeping. A notable early contribution was from Don Pietra who put forward the *separate entity concept*, i.e. the separating of the business from the owner (*see* Chapter 5 on sole traders).

Accounting as a profession developed in the Industrial Revolution when businesses became much larger and more sophisticated in their financial transactions.

Stewardship accounting was the way of reporting to the owners of a business how their investment had been used and the profit or loss for the financial period. This form of accounting has developed into modern *financial accounting*. At the end of the nineteenth century the Institutes of Chartered Accountants were set up by practising accountants in order to establish a professional association which could regulate the activities of its members. This move was in response to some scandals concerning accountants' work in the field of company insolvency. Public and business confidence in accountants had to be restored by the setting of the highest standards for professional conduct and competence.

The increasing complexity of the manufacturing processes developing in the early twentieth century meant that accountants were increasingly looking at the detailed costs of production and estimating future costs, rather than simply reporting on the past. From this has developed *cost accounting* which is a branch of accountancy now found under the overall title of *management accounting*.

In general terms, we have two types of accounting function today:

(a) *financial accounting* which is concerned with the recording of transactions and the reporting of the effect of these transactions on the business over a period of time;

(b) *management accounting* concerns itself with providing management with the financial information required to effectively employ the resources at its disposal and to make sound decisions on future activities.

TYPES OF ACCOUNTANT AND AREAS OF WORK

Accountants work in three broad areas: public practice, industry and commerce, and the public sector.

There are five main professional bodies to which the accountants working in these areas belong. The table in Fig. 7.1 shows the main work areas and professional bodies.

Note that this is the general pattern, but it is possible to find all types of accountant working in all sectors, e.g. a firm of chartered accountants may employ public sector accountants for their specialised knowledge.

Public practice

Accountants working in public practice are independent accountants acting for clients. These businesses can range from a sole trader working on his own to large partnerships with branches in every major city employing a large number of accountants and other financial specialists. The proprietor or partners in these businesses must be holders of public practice certificates from either the Institutes of Chartered Accountants or the Chartered Association of Certified Accountants. The services they offer to clients include:

1 *Accounting and audit:*
General book-keeping services;
Monthly and quarterly accounts/reports;
Preparation of annual accounts;
Annual audit under Company Law;
Audits under other regulations.

2 *Taxation:*
VAT returns;
Operation of payroll – PAYE/NIC;
Agreeing tax assessments;
Minimising business tax;
Personal tax planning – capital gains tax/capital transfer tax

3 *Business planning and management:*
Business start-up advice and assistance;
Assistance with raising finance;
Annual budgets and cashflow forecasts;
Three or five year plans/financial appraisals;
Acquisitions and disposals;
General management advice.

4 *Personal finance:*
Investment advice;
Mortgages;
Pensions.

Industry and commerce

These accountants perform many financial functions for the businesses in which they are employed. Figure 7.2 shows the relationship between the accountants and other functions within the organisation and lists the activities of those accountants.

Public sector

This refers to the public sector of the economy. Accountants working in this area perform similar tasks to their colleagues in industry and commerce. Because of the different nature of these organisations' objectives, and the financial systems employed, the accountants who work in them have developed their own professional body and methods of working in this specialist field.

Fig. 7.1 Work areas and accounting professional bodies

*Accounting body**	*Place of work*		
	Public practice	*Industry and commerce*	*Public sector*
Chartered Accountants	main area of work	large numbers	—
Certified Accountants	some members	the majority of members	—
Cost and Management Accountants	—	the majority of members	some members
Chartered Institute of Public Finance and Accounting	—	—	all but a few members
Association of Accounting Technicians	Members are found in all areas of accountancy, they specialise in a particular area at final examination level.		

*The full names and addresses are given at the end of the chapter.

THE ACCOUNTING ENVIRONMENT

Irrespective of the influence on accountants' work from their employing organisations, there are three major constraints on the work on an accountant.

The law

The law, in particular the Companies Act 1985 and taxation legislation. The Companies Act 1985 lays down the format for presenting company accounts and states what detail must be made public about the state of the company's affairs. Taxation is constantly changing, if only in its administrative details and accountants must be up to date with these changes in order to discharge their responsibilities effectively.

Statements of Standard Accounting Practice (SSAPs)

The Accounting Standards Committee is a body formed by the major professional associations to set down the accountants' 'own rules' for the practice of their profession. This committee responds to changes in the business, legal, economic and accounting environment by drawing up:

(a) SSAPs which are mandatory for accountants and their set down procedures must be followed.

(b) Recommendations on how to deal with specific accounting situations. These are not mandatory but it is usual for them to be followed unless good reason can be given.

Accounting conventions

As accounting developed, so a number of conventions grew with it. The purpose of these is to ensure that accounts are prepared on the same basis by all accountants for whatever type of organisation. During the eighteenth and nineteenth centuries businesses became more complex with a number of owners, and the preparation of accounts became a statutory requirement for companies, so financial reports were being seen and used by a wider readership. This meant that accounts needed to be prepared using a universally accepted and understood set of basic assumptions. These are what we know today as *accounting conventions* or accounting concepts, they are not necessarily legal rules, although some are incorporated into the Companies Act 1985, but a framework of professional practice used by all accountants.

Fig. 7.2 Accounting functions within the organisation

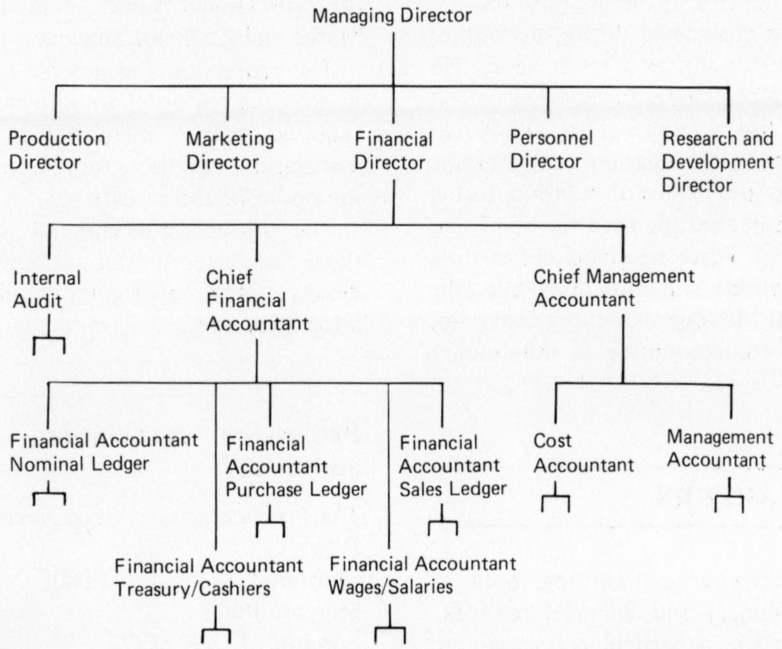

The main accounting conventions may be summarised as follows:

1 *Going-concern convention*: the accounts are prepared on the assumption that the organisation is going to continue to exist in the foreseeable future.
2 *Accrual convention*: profits and losses are calculated on the basis of revenue earnt and expenses incurred for a period rather than cash received and cash paid.
3 *Prudence convention*: profits are not anticipated and losses are reported in full as soon as they become apparent.
4 *Consistency convention*: the same accounting policies are used in every financial report for every financial period. If there is a change in policy it is declared and the effect of the change made clear.

The above four conventions are incorporated into the Companies Act 1985.

5 *Business entity convention*: the business has a separate identity to its owner or owners and the accounts prepared are those of the business.
6 *Materiality convention*: small items of capital may be written off revenue expenditure in the period incurred.
7 *Money measurement convention*: all transactions are recorded in monetary terms; if a transaction cannot have a money value placed upon it, it cannot be recorded.
8 *Realisation convention*: when the organisation enters into a contractual obligation to receive a payment in exchange for goods or services, the revenue generated by that contract is recognised for the purpose of calculating profits.
9 *Historical cost convention*: transactions are recorded at their cash value and assets and liabilities are recorded at their original cost to the organisation.

This convention was challenged during periods of high inflation in the 1970s and as a result SSAP No 16 was issued requiring companies to report the effect of inflation upon their final accounts. This is known as *current cost accountancy* or *inflation accountancy*. However, the return to lower rates of inflation during the mid 1980s largely removed the need for SSAP No 16 and it was withdrawn. There are guidelines existing for reporting the effects of inflation but the accountancy bodies, at the time of writing, have not established new rules for accounting in inflationary condition.

ACCOUNTING CAREERS

A career in accountancy can be rewarding, both in terms of personal fulfilment and financial rewards. The work can be varied or a particular area can be specialised in (*see* the section on types of accountant and areas of work). It should be remembered that accountants control the information system of business and their ability to extract, interpret and use this information places them in a powerful position in any organisation. The image of accountants has, in the past, been unfortunately one of boring people doing boring work in a boring environment. This is far from the truth and a short spell of work placement in an accountants' office could be a worthwhile experience for any student considering this career.

The examination structure of the various bodies all differ in detail but entry requirements and progressions will be general as set out in Fig. 7.3. For those who do not wish to progress to full professional qualifications, the major accounting bodies have sponsored a lower tier association whose examinations can be used to gain a qualification in its own right, or as a step in the progression to full accounting qualifications at a later stage, this is the Association of Accounting Technicians.

Fig. 7.3 Accounting examinations structure

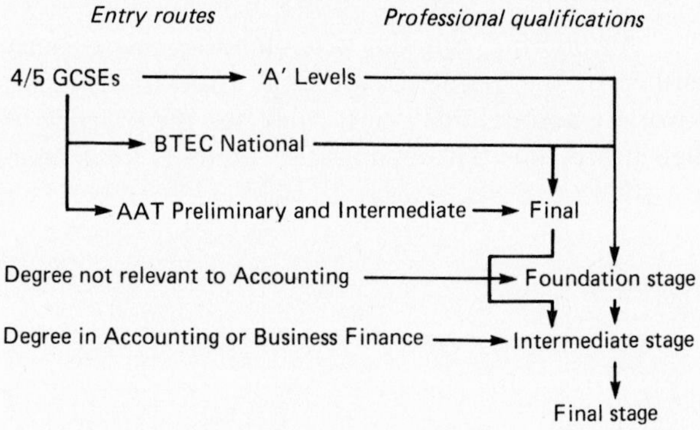

Irrespective of other qualifications, you can expect the professional bodies to insist on 'O' level/GCSE Maths and English Language.

The professional exams are taken at the same time as working, in order to gain the practical experience required before membership of the professional association can be granted, and this is usually a minimum of three years.

The profession bodies all produce literature for those interested in an accounting career and give details of their own entry requirements and examination structure.

Profession associations (full titles and addresses)

The Institute of Chartered Accountants in England & Wales
Chartered Accountants Hall
Margate Place
London EC2R 6EQ

The Institute of Chartered Accountants of Scotland
27 Queen Street
Edinburgh EH2 1LA

The Chartered Association of Certified Accountants
29 Lincolns' Inn Fields
London WC2A 3EE

The Chartered Institute of Management Accountants
53 Portland Place
London W1N 4AB

The Chartered Institute of Public Finance & Accounting
1 Buckingham Place
London SW1E 6HE

The Association of Accounting Technicians
21 Jockey's Fields
London WC1R 4BN

8

The Books of Account, cash records

INTRODUCTION

We have seen in Chapters 3 and 4 that the maintaining of records enables the individual to plan his or her financial affairs and to keep effective control over them. Businesses should also maintain records of their financial affairs, these records are known as the *Books of Account*, for exactly the same reasons. A properly kept book-keeping system can provide the proprietor with a lot of information for use in the effective management of the business.

In addition to the management's obvious need for reliable financial information, other parties will require information and some will insist on records being maintained.
For example:

1 VAT registered businesses are required to maintain detailed records by HM Customs and Excise.
2 The Inland Revenue will expect a financial statement at the end of the businesses' financial year with documentation to support the transactions listed.
3 External sources of finance will require evidence of the businesses' profitability and cashflow.

A book-keeping system should be kept simple, it need be no more complicated than the business whose transactions it is recording. If the business grows and the transactions increase in volume and complexity, then the book-keeping system can be expanded or changed to accommodate the changed circumstances.

CASH TRANSACTIONS

The basic system

In accounting, the use of the term *cash* refers to payments and receipts that take place at the time of the transaction. Hence a cheque received at the time goods were sold is a *cash transaction*. The opposite to a cash transaction is a *credit transaction*. Here time is given to pay after the goods have changed hands.

Recording the flow of cash is the most important record; the type of record will depend upon the trading activities but the following are required for a business that mainly engages in cash transactions:

1 a *Cash Book* to record the transactions that pass through the bank account;
2 a *Petty Cash Book* to record small cash payments;
3 a record of the *daily sales turnover*: this may be obtained from the till and it is of more use if it can be analysed into categories of goods sold;
4 all invoices, receipts, credit notes, bank statements, and correspondence must be filed in an accessible way. These documents are required to support the profit/loss figures sent to the Inland Revenue at the end of each year, they should be kept for at least six years.

In addition the following records may be required:

(a) If employing staff, wages records must be maintained in order to account for PAYE and National Insurance contributions deducted.

(b) VAT registered businesses must maintain the records demanded by HM Customs and Excise.

THE CASH BOOK

The Cash Book records:

(a) all transactions that pass through the bank account, cheques received and issued, standing orders, credit transfers, etc.

(b) all transactions that are in actual cash, with the exception of small cash payments, which are recorded in the petty cash book.

Note As a general rule, it is best to bank all cash on receipt and make all payments, other than petty cash ones, by cheque. This is for security and record-keeping reasons. Retail establishments which take cash are also advised to regularly bank the cash received, recording this transaction in the Cash Book. It is not good practice to take money from the till to make payments.

Cash books are often 'analysed', that is extra

Fig. 8.1 Analysed Cash Book (see also p. 56)

Receipts

	Date (1)	Details, (2)	Ref (3)	Bank £ p (4)	Goods £ p (5)	VAT £ p (6)	Sundry £ p (7)	Notes (8)
	1988							
(a)	May 7	Brought forward		750 –	400 –	60 –	290 –	
(b)	May 8	R Stone	430	92 –	80 –	12 –		
(c)	May 8	Sales (till)		115 –	100 –	15 –		
(d)	May 9	Office Surplus Ltd	431	25 –			25 –	sale of old typewriter
	Other transactions until							
	May 12	Sales (till)		138 –	120 –	18 –		
(e)		Carried forward		1465 –	1000 –	150 –	315 –	

Note This layout assumes that the business does not maintain any cash balance except petty cash and a till float.

Key to columns

1 Date of each transaction recorded.
2 Brief detail given, sufficient only for identification of transaction type. The receipt will show further details.
3 A reference number for transaction documentation, e.g. receipt no.
4 Headed by the total banked by the end of the previous sheet. Then the amount banked for each transaction. Closed by the accumulated total banked by the end of this sheet.
5 That part of the total, and each transaction, that represents the sales value of the goods sold. It could be sub-divided into classes of goods sold to provide information of product sales performance.
6 The VAT within the amounts banked.
7 This column is for recording receipts that arise other than by way of normal trading activities.
8 An explanation of the transactions entered in column 7.
Columns 5, 6 and 7 are known as analysis columns.

Key to rows

(a) The accumulated totals brought forward from the end of the last sheet. Note that column 4 is the total of 5, 6 and 7 added together.
(b) Receipt of £92 from R Stone. The payment for goods that were chargeable with VAT as shown by the split of £92 in the analysis column, £80 goods, £12 VAT.
(c) Retail sales banked, total £115, this splits to goods £100, VAT £15.
(d) A self-explanatory transaction, but note that it is not a sale and so it must be analysed as Sundry.
(e) The accumulated total at the end of the sheet, note that column 4 is the total of columns 5, 6 and 7 added together. These totals are carried forward to start the next sheet.

columns are added to the basic receipts and payments columns and are used for example to analyse payments into the type of expense or split the VAT element in the price paid (*see* Fig. 8.1).

As can be seen from Fig. 8.1, the use of the Cash Book is quite simple even in its analysed form. Receipts are simply entered when banked and the sum banked is analysed into its constituent parts. Similarly each time a cheque is written, it is recorded on the payments sheet and the sum paid analysed appropriately. If a running balance at the bank is not kept on the cheque book stubs, then the balance at bank can be obtained by subtracting the accumulated total payments from the accumulated total receipts at any time. This is known as *balancing the account* (*see* Fig. 8.2).

The Cash Book entries for October are shown in Fig. 8.2. However, you must remember that these entries could extend over several sheets for both receipts and payments and are only shown on single sheets as they have been summarised. Entry (a) shows the balance at bank on 1 October: as it is recorded on the receipts side we can tell that the business is in credit

Fig. 8.2 Balancing the account

Receipts Date	Detail	Bank £ p
(a) Oct 1	Balance b/d	100 00
	Receipts for the month	750 00
		850 00

Payments Date	Detail	Bank £ p
	Payments for the month	650 00
(b) Oct 31	Balance c/d	200 00
		850 00

Note b/d means *brought down* and is used to indicate that a balance has been 'brought down' from a previous acounting period. c/d means *carried down* and is used to indicate that a balance is to be 'carried down' to the next accounting period.

Fig. 8.1 Analysed Cash Book (*cont'd*)

Payments

	Date (1)	*Details* (2)	*Cheque* (3)	*Bank* £ p (4)	*Purchases* £ p (5)	*Expenses A to Z* £ p (6)	£ p (6)	*VAT* £ p (7)	*Petty Cash* £ p (8)	*Sundry* £ p (9)	*Notes* (10)
	1988										
(a)	May 7	Brought forward		620 –	315 –	100 –	85 –	60 –	45 –	15 –	
(b)	May 8	Bright & Co	247100	230 –	200 –			30 –			
(c)	May 10	Central garages	101	69 –		60 –		9 –			
(d)		Cash	102	20 –					20 –		
		Other transactions until									
(e)	May 12	Stationers Ltd	108	23 –			20 –	3 –			
(f)		Carried forward		1361 –	615 –	260 –	176 –	230 –	65 –	15 –	

Key to columns

1 Date of each transaction recorded.
2 Brief detail of transaction which should include any document references.
3 Number of cheques used to make the payment.
4 Headed by the total of payments to date from the end of the previous sheet, followed by the value of the cheque used for each transaction. The column is closed by the total of transactions to be carried forward to the next sheet.
5 The value of goods bought for resale ex-VAT. *Note, purchases* is a term used in accounting that specifically refers to goods bought for resale. It should not be used in any other context.
6 These columns represent expenses analysis columns. The number depends upon the various categories of expense the business incurs and the degree of analysis required. Typical headings would include Rent and Rates, Heat and Light, Stationery, Postage, Telephone, Motoring expenses, Wages and PAYE and NIC.
7 The VAT within the payments made.
8 Petty cash is for recording the amount withdrawn from the bank and placed in the petty cash box. Petty cash expenditure is recorded on a different sheet.
9 Used for payments that cannot be analysed into any other column.
10 An explanation of the transactions recorded in 9.

Key to rows

(a) The accumulated totals brought forward from the end of the previous sheet. Note that column 4 is the total of columns 5 to 9 inclusive.
(b) A payment for purchases from Bright and Co. Paid by a cheque for £230 which was made up of goods value £200 and VAT £30.
(c) Paid garage bill of £69 which includes VAT of £9.
(d) Cash withdrawn for petty cash.
(e) Paid for stationary £23 including VAT of £3.
(f) The accumulated totals of the columns to be carried forward to the next sheet. Note that column 4 is the sum of columns 5 to 9 inclusive.

with the bank. (An opening entry of balance b/d on the payments side would indicate an overdraft.) Entry (b) is the balance at bank at the end of October and it is calculated by adding together all the entries on the receipts side: £100 + £750 = £850, and deducting all of the entries on the payments side (prior to entering (b) the balance): £850 receipts less £650 payments = £200 balance at bank. The balance at the end of the month, £200, is recorded on the payments sheet. Then both the receipts and payments sheets are totalled: £850 on both sheets. The balance of £200 reappears at the start of November on the receipts sheet.

Receipts *Date*	*Details*	*Bank* £ p
Nov 1	Balance b/d	200 00

We have balanced the Cash Book at the end of a month but this can be done at any interval that suits the business. The bank columns of the Cash Book are the businesses' own record of the transactions passing through the bank account, and should be periodically compared with a bank statement. The *bank statement* is of course a copy of the bank's own records of the same transactions. Any discrepancies should be investigated.

Reconciling the Cash Book and the bank statement

This procedure is known as *bank reconciliation* and is a necessary step to be taken on receipt of a bank statement, because the balance shown on the bank statement is unlikely to be that revealed by the Cash Book on any given date (*see* Fig. 8.3). The difference between the balances must be shown to arise for reasons other than error.

Receipts Date	Details	**Sheet 25** Bank £ p
May 1	Balance b/d	110 00
5	Sales	470 00
16	J Brown	136 00
19	Sales	512 00
24	V James	242 00
27	L Mallard	66 00
28	Sales	154 00
	Carried forward	1690 00

Payments Date	Details	**Sheet 25** Bank £ p
May 3	B. Jones	60 00
5	Rent	190 00
13	R. Dean	120 00
18	R. Cooper	40 00
26	Supplies Ltd	80 00
26	Bryant Bros	210 00
27	P. Payne	440 00
28	ABC Co	500 00
	Carried forward	1640 00

Bank Statement

Date	*Details*	*Debits*	*Credit*	*Balance* £ p
May 1	Balance brought forward			110 00
5	Sundry credit		470	580 00
6	Cheque	60		520 00
10	Cheque	190		330 00
11	Sundry credit		136	466 00
15	Cheque	120		346 00
16	Insurance standing order	300		46 00
	Sundry credit		512	558 00
21	Cheque	40		518 00
24	Sundry credit		242	760 00
26	Cheque	80		680 00
	Investment account interest		50	730 00

Fig. 8.3 Cash Book (bank columns only shown)

Procedure

The balance at bank as shown by the statement is the figure in the balance column after the last transaction has been recorded; i.e. £730.

The Cash Book balance can be found by deducting total payments from receipts:
£1690 total receipts less £1640 total payments = £50 balance at bank. Note that the statement shows £730 and the cash book £50.

Compare the Cash Book and the statement to reveal any differences in transactions recorded. These will fall into two categories:

(a) receipts and payments that do not appear in *the Cash Book*, possibly standing orders paid and credit transfers received directly into the bank account. If these are agreed they should be entered into the Cash Book and the Cash Book balanced. This procedure is shown in Fig. 8.4.

Fig. 8.4 Cash Book (bank column only)

Receipts Date	Details	**Sheet 26** Bank £ p
May 28	Brought forward	1690 00
(a)	Investment interest	50 00

Payments Date	Details	**Sheet 26** Bank £ p
May 28	Brought forward	1640 00
(b)	Insurance	300 00

Inspection of the Cash Book and statement in Fig. 8.3 reveal that:

(i) investment interest received has not been recorded in the Cash Book £50;

(ii) a standing order for insurance has been omitted from the Cash Book £300;

These have been recorded in the Cash Book which must now be balanced.

Total receipts £1740 less total payments £1940 = £(200) (overdrawn because payments exceed receipts). Note that negative amounts, like overdraft, are denoted by accountants with brackets. The final balance is shown in the Cash Book on p. 58.

Notice how, in the case of an overdraft, the balance c/d appears on the receipts side. On the next sheet, at the start of a new month, the balance b/d will have to appear on the payments side.

(b) receipts and payments not appearing *on the statement*. These probably arise because receipts have been paid in after the statement was prepared, and payments made may not have been debited to the account if the cheque has not been presented to your bank for payment. Make a list of these receipts and payments not shown on the statement. Look for these items in Fig. 8.3.

Now prepare a reconciliation statement as shown in Fig. 8.5.

Cash book (bank columns only)

Receipts Date	Details	Sheet 26 Bank £ p
May 28	Brought forward	1690 00
	Investment interest	50 00
	Balance c/d	200 00
		1940 00

Payments Date	Details	Sheet 26 Bank £ p
May 28	Brought forward	1640 00
	Insurance	300 00
		1940 00

If after adding the receipts and subtracting the payments to the statement balance as shown, and the bottom figure is not as in the Cash Book after stage one then a mistake has been made. The figures should be checked to find the difference, assuming that the number and type of transaction are agreed when comparing the Cash Book and statement the error will lie in a quantity recorded or a difference not identified.

Fig. 8.5 Bank reconciliation

Bank Reconciliation Statement as at 26 Sept 1988		
Balance at bank as shown on statement		730.00
Add receipts banked after statement date	154.00	
	66.00	220.00
		950.00
less Payments not yet debited by the bank		
(*see* Fig 8.3)	210.00	
	440.00	
	500.00	1150.00
from Fig 8.4 balance shown in Cash Book		
(overdrawn)		(200.00)

THE PETTY CASH BOOK

Small items of expenditure, that are paid for in cash, are recorded in a Petty Cash Book. The petty cash system requires:

1 The Petty Cash Book for recording transactions (Fig. 8.6);

Fig. 8.6 Petty Cash Book

	Receipts £ p (1)	Date 1988 (2)	Details (3)	PCV (4)	Payments Total £ p (5)	VAT £ p (6)	Postage & stationary £ p (6)	Travel expenses £ p (6)	Sundry expenses £ p (6)
(a)	50 –	May 4	Balance b/d						
(b)		5	Post	82	2.16		2.16		
(b)		5	Petrol	83	9.89	1.29		8.60	
(b)		8	Red pens	84	3.45	0.45	3.00		
(b)		9	Newspapers	85	4.50				4.50
(c)					20.00	1.74	5.16	8.60	4.50
(d)	20 –	10	Cash book						
(e)		10	Balance c/d		50.00				
(e)	70.00				70.00				
(e)	70.00	10	Balance b/d						

Key to columns

1 Receipts recorded, these are obtained by cashing a cheque drawn specifically for petty cash. This cheque will also appear in the Cash Book.
2 Date of transaction.
3 Details of all receipts and payments are shown in this column. Only a short explanation is required, the full details will appear on the documentation.
4 A record of the *petty cash vouchers* (PCVs). Each one is numbered for reference and has full details of the transaction and a signature authorising the expenditure. Any receipts for the expenditure are usually clipped to the PCV.
5 The total of expenditure recorded on each PCV and the total of expenditure for that sheet. The column will also show the balance c/d if the accounting period end occurs.
6 The analysis columns are used in a similar manner to those in the Cash Book – the total of each transaction is analysed into its constituent parts, usually VAT and the actual expense. The sundry expenses column often has a space for notes alongside so that a further explanation can be given.

Key to rows

(a) A £50 balance b/d from the previous period. This is available in the cash box to meet expenditure as it is incurred.
(b) Various transactions involving payment for expenses. Note that each has an individual PCV number and that the total is analysed into its constituent parts.
(c) In this row the payments are totalled to give totals for each class of expense and a grand total for one period. Note that the analysis column totals should sum to the same amount as the grand total:

$$£1.74 + £5.16 + £8.60 + £4.50 = £20$$

(d) The expenditure is reimbursed by means of a cheque cashed for the purpose. This cheque will have been recorded in the Cash Book, payments side. (*See* Fig. 8.1.)
(e) The balance is found by totalling receipts and deducting payments (£50 + £20) less £20 = £50 balance. The balance c/d, balance b/d and totals are recorded in the columns and on the rows shown.

2 A petty cash box, for the security of the cash and to hold any documents relating to the transaction;
3 Petty cash vouchers detailing the expenditure (Fig. 8.7).

To be valid a petty cash voucher requires the following:

(a) Voucher number, needed for cross reference with Petty Cash Book;
(b) Details and amount of expenditure;
(c) Signature of person receiving the cash in order to make the payment or receiving reimbursement for payment made;
(d) Signature of person authorising the expenditure;

Operation of a petty cash system is quite simple. A float is provided, known as the *imprest*, in Fig. 8.6 it is £50; from this float petty cash payments are made. When the float is low the amount spent is reimbursed, in exchange for PCV to the same value, thus the imprest is restored. It is not necessary to balance the Petty Cash Book each time the imprest is restored. Balancing only takes place at the end of the accounting period for petty cash. There is some security built into the system as the person responsible for petty cash must always be able to produce the imprest or cash and PCVs to the value of the imprest.

SUMMARY

The use of a Cash Book and a Petty Cash Book have been shown to provide:

1 A record of every transaction and a reference to the supporting documents;
2 The ability to check the balance at bank when required;
3 The ability to easily check the bank statement for accuracy;
4 Extraction of VAT from receipts and payments to form the basis of acceptable VAT records;
5 Analysis of receipts and payments to show:
(a) receipts: by class of goods sold, sale of goods or other source;
(b) payments: by category of expense, cost of goods bought for resale.

All of this is useful information for the day-to-day management of the business and will be of considerable help to the accountant who prepares the end of year accounts, thus possibly minimising the fee charged for this service by auditors.

In addition, their use encourages security of cash held on the premises by regular bankings, making all but minor payments by cheque, and maintaining a petty cash system.

Fig. 8.7 Petty cash voucher

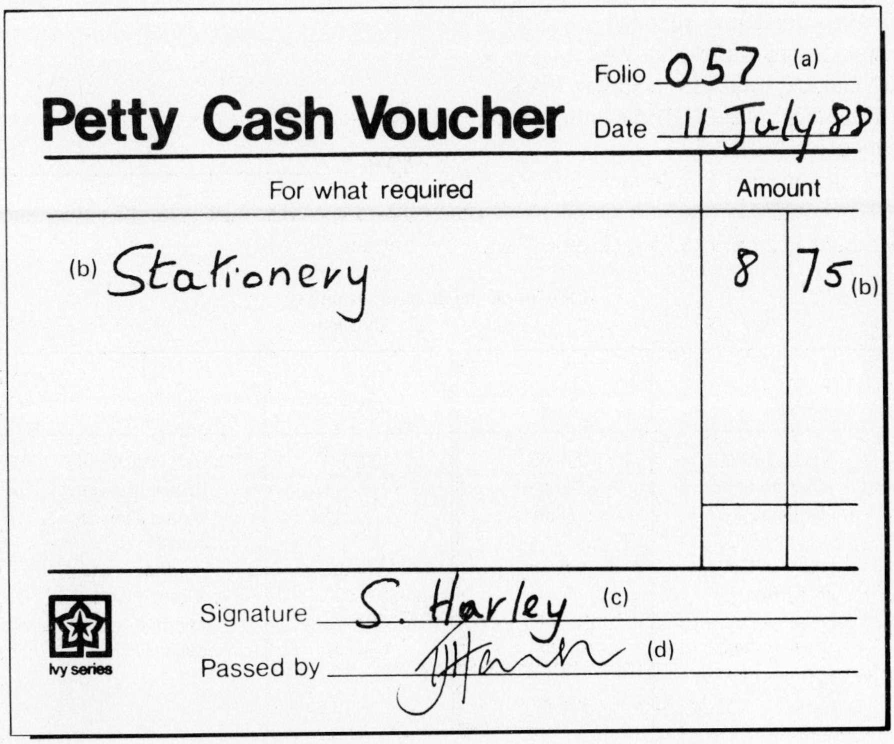

Petty Cash Voucher

Folio 057 (a)
Date 11 July 88

For what required	Amount	
(b) Stationery	8	75 (b)

Ivy series

Signature S. Harley (c)
Passed by [signature] (d)

TASKS

Note VAT is at a rate of 15% in all the following tasks.

Task 1

Acting as cashier for Hardy Bros, write up their cash book with the transactions for the last week of June. Balance the book and total the analysis columns set out below. It is suggested that this is set out on cash analysis paper.

Receipts

Date 1988	*Details*	*Ref*	*Bank £ p*	*Goods £ p*	*VAT £ p*	*Sundry £ p*
Jun 22	Brought forward		450.00	300.00	45.00	100.00

Payments

Date 1988	*Details*	*Ref*	*Bank £ p*	*Purchases £ p*	*Rent and Rates £ p*	*Gas and Elec £ p*	*VAT £ p*	*Sundry £ p*
Jun 22	Brought forward		280.00	140.00	100.00		21.00	19.00

Transactions

Jun 22 Sales cash banked, total £23 including VAT.
23 Paid JJ Wholesalers £60 plus VAT.
23 Sales cash banked, total £34.50 including VAT.
24 Received a cheque from R Bright for £46 including VAT for goods supplied.
24 Paid Grange Supplies £20 plus VAT.
24 Sales cash banked total £23 including VAT.
25 Sales cash banked total £11.50 including VAT.
26 Paid electricity bill £45.
26 Sales cash banked total £17.25 including VAT.
27 Paid week's rent £25.
27 Sales cash banked total £28.75 including VAT.

Task 2

It is 1 July at Hardy Bros. Having established that the balance at bank is £192 which is, of course, the closing balance c/d for June, you are able to start July with this as the balance b/d. The same analysis columns will be in use but as this is the start of a new period, there will not be any total brought forward in them. Enter the transactions for the first week of July and then total the book.

July 1 Bought various stationery items £23 including VAT.
1 Sales cash banked £34.50 including VAT.
2 Paid insurance premium £25.
2 Received a cheque from D White, £115 including VAT, for goods supplied.
2 Sales cash banked £40.25 including VAT.
3 Paid Wessex Wholesale, by cheque for £40 plus VAT.
3 Sales cash banked £28.75 including VAT.
4 Paid JB Supplies Ltd £60 plus VAT.
4 Paid week's rent £25.
4 Sales cash banked £46 including VAT.
5 Cashed a cheque for petty cash £50.
5 Sales cash banked £23 including VAT.
6 Sales cash banked £11.50 including VAT.

Task 3

The Cash Book of your business shows the following entries for May:

Cash Book (bank columns only)

Receipts / **Payments**

Date 1988	*Details*	*£ p*	*Date 1988*	*Details*	*£ p*
May 1	Balance b/d	210.00	May 3	JKL Wholesale	121.00
2	Cash to bank	170.00	11	British Telecom	145.00
10	R. Shipley	58.00	15	James Downer and Co	84.00
14	Cash to bank	235.00	26	Multiport Ltd	60.00
23	P. Mellor	72.00	27	Grant Properties (rent)	200.00
28	Cash to bank	220.00	31	Balance c/d	355.00
		965.00			965.00

The following bank statement has arrived, covering the same period. Your task is to reconcile the two documents.

Bank Statement

27 May 1988 — o/d indicates an overdrawn balance

Date	*Details*	*Payments* £ p	*Receipts* £ p	*Balance* £ p
Apr 30	Balance b/f			210.00
May 2	Sundry credit		170.00	380.00
8	Cheque no	121.00		259.00
10	Sundry credit		58.00	317.00
14	Sundry credit		235.00	552.00
	Cheque no	145.00		407.00
20	Cheque no	84.00		323.00
23	Sundry credit		72.00	395.00
27	Insurance Services standing order	100.00		295.00
	Account charges	10.00		285.00

Task 4

You have written up the Cash Book of the firm you are employed at and have only the balancing to do when a bank statement arrives. The owner would like the Cash Book and bank statement reconciled before you go home at the end of the day.
The Cash Book and statement are shown below.

Cash Book (bank columns only)

Receipts / **Payments**

Date 1988	*Details*	£ p	*Date 1988*	*Details*	£ p
Sep 1	Balance b/d	50.00	Sep 2	Building supplies	147.00
6	Cash to bank	310.00	5	Apex Garage	38.00
13	Davis Bros	125.00	9	Hire specialists Ltd	25.00
17	Cash to bank	284.00	16	Dean & Co	160.00
25	Fordware Ltd	91.00	26	Office Wages	320.00
28	Cash to bank	340.00	29	Inland Revenue (Tax)	600.00

Bank Statement

27 Sept 1988 — o/d indicates an overdrawn balance

Date	*Details*	*Payments* £ p	*Receipts* £ p	*Balance* £ p
Aug 30	Balance b/f			50.00
	Account charges	25.00		25.00
Sep 1	Equipment financing Direct debit	200.00		225.00 o/d
6	Sundry credit		310.00	85.00
8	Cheque no	147.00		62.00 o/d
9	Cheque no	38.00		100.00 o/d
13	Sundry credit		125.00	25.00
	Cheque no	25.00		00.00
17	Sundry credit		284.00	284.00
20	Cheque no	160.00		124.00
25	Sundry credit		91.00	215.00
26	Cheque no	320.00		105.00 o/d

Task 5

It is your first day as petty cashier. The previous cashier has balanced the book and obtained a reimbursement of the imprest. You have therefore received £50 with which to start the week. It is a small organisation with only a few transactions; your duties are to record the transactions, balance the book at the end of the week and establish the value of cheques required to reimburse the imprest.

The following is a list of transactions for your first week. Analyse them under the headings of VAT, Postage, Stationery, Travel and Sundry expenses..

August 4 Started with an imprest of £50
5 PCV no 327
Postage on parcel £3.20
6 PCV no 328
Envelopes, paper and pens inc VAT £5.75
plus Bus fares £0.65
Total £6.40
7 PCV no 329
Newspaper bill £7.00
8 PCV no 330
Train fare £15.10
Taxi fare £ 4.00
Meals on train £13.80 inc VAT

Task 6

The organisation, for which you are petty cashier, has quite a number of petty cash transactions, which means that the imprest may have to be reimbursed twice during the week. The Petty Cash Book is balanced at the end of each week and a cheque drawn on each Monday to provide the imprest at the start of the week. Small cash receipts are also paid into petty cash. The analysis columns in use are VAT, Postage, Stationery, Travel, Office sundries, General expenses.

Transactions for the week February 19/23 inclusive were as set out below. These should be recorded, reimbursing the imprest when necessary and balancing the Book on 23 February. Take care not to spend more than the cash available!

Feb 19 Balance b/d £7.20
Cheque drawn to restore the imprest to £50.00
PCV no 1732
Correcting fluid £1.15 inc VAT
20 PCV no 1733
Printing £36.80 inc VAT
Bus fare £0.52
Total £37.32
Received from staff member 50p for private telephone call
21 PCV no 1734
200 13p stamps
200 white envelopes £10.35 inc VAT
22 PCV no 1735
Travelling expenses £9.20
PCV no 1736
30 miles at 35 pence per mile
PCV no 1737
Window cleaner £8.00
23 PCV no 1738
Parcel post £6.70
PCV no 1739
Pack of floppy disks for word processor £6.90 inc VAT, Bus fare 52p

Task 7

Mr Jacobs started in business on 1 March 1988, he has found keeping records difficult and has employed you to be his part-time book-keeper/administrator.

All transactions have been documented but not formally recorded. You sort all of his paperwork into transaction types and list them as set out below. Your next task is to recommend to Mr Jacobs a suitable records system then write up the first month's entries, balance the books and reconcile them with a bank statement that arrived today, 31 March 1988, *Note* Mr Jacobs is not registered for VAT.

Bank account
Receipts and Payments

March 1 Deposited £2400 in the account.
2 Paid Property (Holdings) Ltd for rental of shop unit £300.00.
Paid Retail Surplus Ltd £210.00 for various items of second-hand shop and office equipment.
Paid WH Wholesale for various items of stock £710.00
Paid Cash and Carry (Southern) plc for various items of stock £240.00.
5 Banked cash takings of £170.00.
6 Withdrew £25 for use as office cash (petty cash).
10 Banked cash takings of £280.00.
13 Paid various insurance premiums to Brokers & Co £320.00.
15 Banked cash takings of £340.00.
18 Withdrew from bank £200.00 for Mr Jacobs' personal use.
19 Banked a cheque from Z Crier for goods sold value £75.
20 Withdrew a further £25 for office use.
22 Purchased further stock from Cash & Carry (Southern) plc £180.
24 Banked cash takings £470.00.
25 Central Garages £87.00 for vehicle repairs.
28 Sold goods to J Kirkup received a cheque for £64.00.
31 Mr Jacobs withdrew a further £200 for his own use.

Office cash (petty cash)
Receipts and Payments

March 6 Received £25.
7 Paid for postage stamps 10 @ 18p each.
11 Paid for various stationery items £10.60.
14 Petrol for car £10.00.
19 Pens and pencils £2.60.
22 Petrol for car £10.00.
28 Window cleaners £4.00.

Bank Statement

27 March 1988 — o/d indicates an overdrawn balance

Date	*Details*	*Payments* £ p	*Receipts* £ p	*Balance* £ p
Mar 1	Opening deposit		2400.00	2400.00
5	Sundry credit		170.00	2570.00
	Cheque no	240.00		2330.00
6	Cheque no	710.00		1620.00
	Cheque no	25.00		1595.00
7	Cheque no	210.00		1385.00
	Cheque no	300.00		1085.00
10	Sundry credit		280.00	1365.00
15	Sundry credit		340.00	1705.00
17	Cheque no	320.00		1385.00
18	Cheque no	200.00		1185.00
19	Sundry credit		75.00	1260.00
20	Cheque no	25.00		1235.00
24	Sundry credit		470.00	1705.00
26	Cheque no	180.00		1525.00
27	Trade Association Direct Debit	50.00		1475.00

9

Credit transactions

INTRODUCTION

The giving and receiving of credit is common in business, in some trades there are standard periods of credit, e.g. the furniture industry gives its retailers 90 days (three months) credit. It is only when goods are retailed that it is expected that the purchaser will pay for them when taking delivery. (There are, of course, retail credit schemes – *see* Chapter 3 – but in most cases the retailer receives payment from a finance company and it is the finance company that allows time to pay.)

When time to pay is given then the transaction is known as a *credit transaction*. Once established, a business will expect to receive most of its supplies of goods and services on credit and, unless it is a retail business, its customers will also expect to be allowed credit, indeed an organisation that does not extend credit to its customers may find difficulties in obtaining business.

DISCOUNTS

Having allowed customers a period of credit businesses often offer a discount to those who are prepared to give up all or most of the credit period. This is because it costs the business providing the credit a lot to make what are effectively interest-free loans to its customers. The cost can be viewed in two ways:

1 If the business has an overdraft and it must wait for payment, then the overdraft cannot be reduced until the payment is received. For example, one month's credit given when paying 18% p.a. for an overdraft will cost the supplier of the goods 18%/12 months = $1\frac{1}{2}$% per month, or £1.50 for every £100 of credit given per month.
2 The organisation has lost the opportunity to use the money within the business while waiting for payment. This could mean lost profits if the funds to take advantage of profitable situations are not available. For example, if £10 profit is made every time goods were sold then if the company allowed one month's credit they would make £10 profit from that type of transaction each month. If however the customers could be encouraged to pay within one week, the money would be available for buying more goods for sale after one week. Assuming the goods purchased could be resold immediately, making a further £10 profit, the potential for four profitable deals per month can be seen. Using the same funds but circulating them through the business more quickly yields 4 × £10 profit = £40 profit per month.

In order to reduce the amount of credit taken by customers a system of discounts is used. There are two types of discount that should not be confused.

(a) *Trade discount* – given to persons or organisations in the same trade or business. This is a reduction from list or retail price given to trade customers in recognition of the volume of business they will provide to the seller. Trade discount is not given to encourage prompt settlement it is part of the calculation of price to charge.

(b) *Cash discount* – this is given to credit customers in order to encourage prompt settlement. Not to be confused with a discount given for cash in a retail situation; this is simply negotiating the price.

DOCUMENTS

Credit transactions require more careful documentation than cash transactions. There are three main documents to consider, i.e. invoices, credit notes and statements of account.

Invoices

Sales invoices are sent to customers; purchase invoices are received from suppliers. They are used to give details of goods supplied, the price calculation and the payment terms. There may be a host of other details but it is the financial ones that we are concerned with.

In Fig. 9.1 the invoice shows the total payable made up from the value of goods supplied + VAT; the calculation of this total requires some explanation:

(a) trade discount is deducted on the invoice prior to calculating the invoice total. It should be noted that the pre-discount price is not being charged, it only appears as part of the calculation.

(b) VAT is charged on the invoiced amount. In this case it might be expected to be £40.00 × 15% = £6 VAT but VAT is charged on the lowest amount that can be paid for the goods invoiced and a cash discount is offered which would reduce the invoiced amount to below £40.00 if taken. VAT due is found by

$$\begin{aligned}(\text{£}40 \text{ less } 5\% \text{ cash discount}) \times 15\% &= (\text{£}40 - \text{£}2) \times 15\% \\ &= \text{£}38 \times 15\% \\ &= \text{£}5.70\end{aligned}$$

Note that this amount of VAT is paid whether the discount is taken or not.

(c) The amount of cash discount is not calculated and shown on the invoice, it is up to the customer to calculate and deduct it if payment is made within the specified time. You should also notice that the discount is calculated on the value of the goods supplied after deduction of any trade discount. It is not a further discount from list or retail price.

Fig. 9.1 Invoice (basic outline)

INVOICE

B. TEC and Co Ltd, 2 High Street, Forest Ville, Hants.

Customer address	Despatch to
Invoice number	Your order number

Quantity	*Details*	*Total* £ p
10	Part number 372158 at £5.00 each	50.00
	less trade discount of 20%	10.00
		40.00
	VAT at 15%	5.70
	Total payable	45.70

Terms:
Net monthly account or 5% cash discount for settlement within 7 days

Credit notes

These are similar in most details to invoices but are used to acknowledge an allowance given for goods returned by a customer. Because of the common details and layout between credit notes and invoices, credit notes are often printed in red to distinguish them from invoices. (*See* Fig. 9.2.)

Notice that the basis of the price calculation is shown and that VAT must also be refunded. The VAT is again charged on the price that would be paid for the goods after cash discount is deducted.

Fig. 9.2 Credit note

CREDIT NOTE

B. TEC and Co Ltd, 2 High Street, Forest Ville, Hants.

Customer address

Credit note number

Quantity	*Details*	*Total*
2	Part no 372158 at £5 each	10.00
	less trade discount at 20%	2.00
		8.00
	VAT at 15%	1.20
	CREDIT GIVEN	9.20
	Terms 5% 7 days	

Credit note issued because : ....

....

Fig. 9.3 Statement

STATEMENT

B. TEC and Co Ltd, 2 High Street, Forest Ville, Hants.

Customer address

Date	*Invoice*	*Details*	*Debit*	*Credit*	*Balance*
1988			£ p	£ p	£ p
Feb 1		Balance b/f			109.25
4		Payment received Thankyou		109.25	00.00
	2144	Goods	45.70		45.70
	C172	Credit Note		9.20	36.50

Statement of account

Unless an invoice is for a one-off transaction with a customer, it will not be a request for payment, but simply financial details of a specific transaction. Requests for payment come in the form of a *statement of account*. This shows details of all transactions since the last statement and indicates the balance owing (*see* Fig. 9.3).

The last figure in the balance column is the amount now due.

RECORDING CREDIT TRANSACTIONS

There are four books required to record credit transactions:

1 Sales Day Book (Fig. 9.4);
2 Sales Returns Book (Fig. 9.5);
3 Purchases Day Book (Fig. 9.6);
4 Purchases Returns Book (Fig. 9.7).

Each book has analysis columns enabling identification of the type of goods sold, VAT, category of expense paid, etc. If a business needs these books to record credit transactions, it may be possible to reduce the amount of analysis that takes place in the Cash Book, thus avoiding duplication of records.

Fig. 9.5 Sales Returns Book

Date	*Customer*	*Credit note*	*Total*	*VAT*	*Notes and Reference*
Jun 14	Castle plc	CN0472	22.85	2.85	Faulty goods supplied on invoice 3724
	Continued with other entries until end of period				
			114.25	14.25	

The headings and entry in Fig. 9.5 illustrate the information recorded in the Sales Returns Book. It is made up from credit notes issued, which need to be cross referenced with:

(a) the Sales Day Book in order to explain why a lesser amount than expected has been received or

(b) the Cash Book to show the cheque sent to the customer by way of refund for goods returned.

Totals are shown at the end of the same accounting period as used by the Sales Day Book.

Note The VAT refunded has been calculated on the basis of a 5% cash discount being offered on the original invoice for the goods being returned.

Fig. 9.4 Sales Day Book

Sales Day Book

Date (1)	*Customer* (2)	*Invoice* (3)	*Total* (4) £ p	*VAT* (5) £ p	*Goods* A (6) £ p	*Goods* B (7) £ p	*Amount Rec'd* (8) £ p	*Discount allowed* (9) £ p	*Rec'd* (10)	*Ref* (11)
19X8										
Jun 1	R Bryant	AT3714	137.10	18.10	120.00		137.10		28 Jun	CB24
	XYZ Co	AT3715	91.40	11.40	80.00					
2	Able Bros	AT3716	109.68	13.68	96.00		104.88	4.80	27 Jun	CB24
	Hall Ltd	AT3717	182.80	22.80		160.00	174.80	8.00	28 Jun	CB24
		Continued with other transactions until								
30	Manor & Co	AT3791	159.95	19.95		140.00				
			4734.52	590.52	1494.0	2650.0				

Key to columns

1 Date of issue of invoice.
2 Customer's name.
3 Invoice number.
4 Invoice total including VAT
5 VAT charged on invoice, these amounts have been calculated on the basis of a 5% cash discount being offered.
6 and 7 Analysis columns allowing classification of the sale into class of goods.
Only two columns are shown but these can be increased to any suitable amount.
8 Amount received from customer.
9 Any discount taken by customer. Note this should be checked against the column 6 or 7 amount times the discount rate.
10 Date payment received from customer.
11 Reference column allowing cross referencing. In this case a cross reference to the Cash Book has been indicated to show the entry recording the deposit of the customer's cheque in the bank account – CB 24 means Cash Book sheet 24, which is where the deposit record will be found.

Fig. 9.6 Purchases Day Book

(1) Date	(2) Supplier	(3) Invoice	(4) Total £ p	(5) VAT £ p	(6) Goods A–Z £ p	(7) Expenses A–Z £ p	(8) Amount paid £ p	(9) Discount taken £ p	(10) Date paid	(11) Ref
Jun 1	Wholesale Ltd	R43721	205.65	25.65	180.00		196.65	9	Jun 5	
4	P & L Smith	006171	275.10	35.10	240.00					
6	British Gas	D327145	165.00			165.00	165.00		Jun 10	
	Continued with other transactions until									
30	British Telecom	54718	241.50	31.50		210.00				
			2451.70	262.35	1670.0	519.35				

Key to use of columns

1 Date of receipt of invoice from supplier.
2 Name of supplier.
3 Suppliers invoice number.
4 Total of suppliers invoice.
5 VAT charged on invoice.
6 Example of analysis column for goods; there may be any number required.
7 Example of analysis column for expenses; there may be any number required.
8 Amount paid to supplier.
9 Any discount allowed by supplier and taken.
10 Date payment made to supplier.
11 Cross reference to Cash Book showing where payment is recorded.

Fig. 9.7 Purchases Returns Book

Date	Customer	Credit note	Total £ p	VAT £ p	Notes and Reference
Jun 19	P & L Smith	000943C	22.94	2.94	Goods supplied on invoice 006171 returned damaged in transit
		Continued with other entries until end of period			
			53.75	5.75	

Similar headings to the Sales Returns Book are used. The originating documents for these entries are the credit notes sent by suppliers. The same accounting period as used in the Purchase Day Book will be applied and cross referencing to that book will be necessary.

CREDIT CONTROL

It is very important to ensure that those persons and organisations to whom the business has given credit, i.e. the *debtors*, abide by the trading terms. This is in order to keep the cost of providing credit to the minimum. Of equal importance is ensuring that those to whom money is owed by the business, i.e. the *creditors*, are paid on time. Continuity of supply may be affected by late payment.

Debtor control is comparatively easy using the Sales Day Book because any empty spaces in the columns used to record receipts from customers indicate an amount owing. If payment has not been received shortly after the end of the credit period then the payment should be requested from the debtor. Control of payments to creditors can use a similar system but because of the variation in credit period allowed by suppliers it is probably best to use a separate diary in which the date on which payment must be made is recorded. If creditors offer a cash discount for prompt settlement a decision between taking the discount or the full credit period must be made.

THE EXPANDED RECORD SYSTEM

The books of accounts and other records maintained we have considered are now:

1 Cash Book;
2 Petty Cash Book;
3 Sales Day Book;

Fig. 9.8 Expanded record system

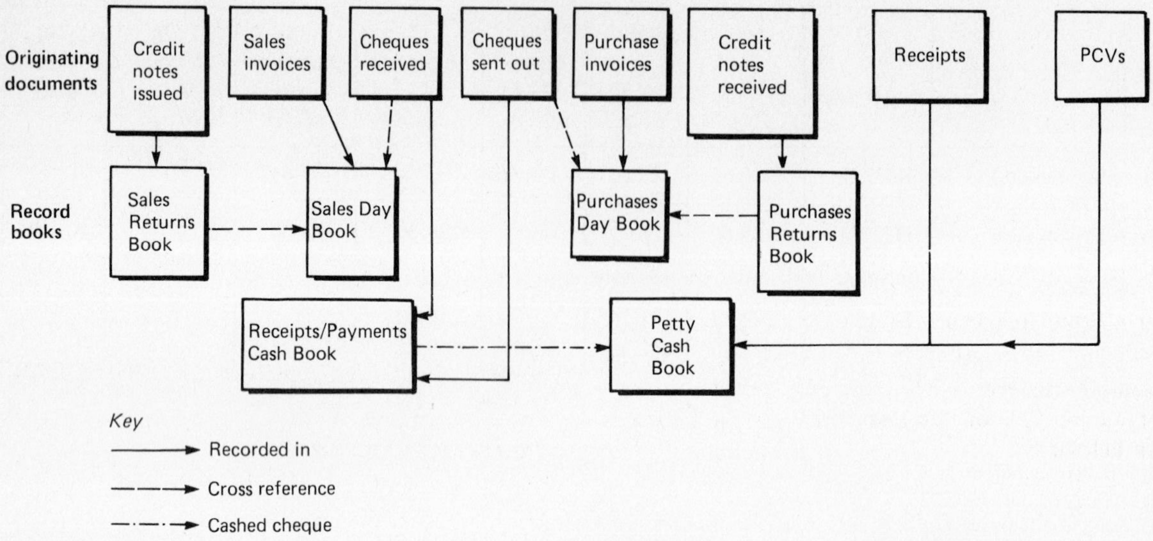

4 Sales Returns Book;
5 Purchases Day Book;
6 Purchases Returns Book.

The diagram in Fig. 9.8 explains how they all are used together.
Note that
(a) each transaction has an originating document;
(b) each transaction is recorded;
(c) cross referencing is made between records where necessary.

SUMMARY

1 Credit transactions are transactions where time to pay is given.
2 Cash discounts may be offered to encourage prompt settlement of bills.
3 Credit transactions in any quantity require their own record books: Sales and Purchase Day Books, Sales and Purchase Returns Books.
4 Control of credit is important to ensure that payments received and made are on time.
5 The continued use of analysis columns enables business information to be extracted from the records system. But duplication of this information is unnecessary and as the record system is expanded, analysis in a new book may take over from a previous record.

TASKS

Tasks 1–6

As the clerk in a small business it is your job to make out invoices for goods supplied.

Tasks 1–6: in each case calculate the total amount to charge, including VAT at 15%, for the following goods supplied.

Task 1
200 kg of SUPERPLAS 3 at £0.50 per kg.

Task 2
1000 kg of PLASTIFULL Z at £30 per 25 kg bag.

Task 3
800 kg of MAKROPLAS at £0.65 per kg less 20% trade discount.

Task 4
1500 kg or MIRAPLAS TT at £0.45 per kg less 15% trade discount.

Task 5
900 kg of SUPERPLAS 3 at £0.50 per kg less 20% trade discount. A 5% cash discount for prompt settlement is offered on the invoice terms.

Task 6
1200 kg of PLASTIFULL Z at £30 per 25 kg bag less 15% trade discount. A 5% cash discount for prompt settlement is offered.

Task 7

An invoice received by your business showed the following details

Goods	£520
VAT at 15%	75
	595

Terms Net monthly account or 4% cash discount 7 days.

Your clerk checked the invoice details and discovered the VAT calculation was wrong – it should be £78. On checking, you cannot find an error.

(a) Write a brief note for your clerk to refer to, explaining how VAT was calculated on the invoice.

(b) Advise the clerk how much should be paid

- if settled within 7 days
- at the end of the month.

Tasks 8–9

You have been taken on as a trainee clerk with a firm whose business involves a lot of credit transactions. Your first training task (Task 8) is to enter up sales invoices and credit notes issued to customers into the Sales Day Book and Sales Returns Book.

For the purpose of this task, use only the headings shown below:

Sales Day Book
Date Customer Invoice Total VAT Goods

Sales Returns Book
Date Customer Credit Note Total VAT Goods

Transactions

Date	*Credit note or Invoice*	*Invoice/Credit note value including VAT*	*Customer*
Oct 1	I 007143	£230.00	R Style Ltd
	I 007144	£69.00	J. Jourdans
2	I 007145	£172.50	M Howel
	CN 000621	£11.50	P Deacon
	I 007146	£138.00	Davis Bros
3	I 007147	£241.50	R Style Ltd
	CN 000622	£28.75	Adams & Co Ltd
	I 007148	£92.00	Dee Van Ltd
4	I 007149	£182.80 a 5% cash discount was offered	Mitchel & Co
	I 007150	£80.50	M Howell
	I 007151	£207.00	Grantly DC
	CN 000623	£46.00	J. Jourdan
5	CN 000624	£57.50	P Woodhams
	I 007152	£230.00	R Style Ltd
	I 007153	£137.10 a 5% cash discount was offered	D O'Leary
	I 007154	£228.50 a 5% cash discount was offered	S Best

After completing a week working with sales invoices and credit notes, you are transferred to learn how to deal with the Purchases Day Book and Purchases Returns Book, (task 9). The transactions to be recorded are set out below. Use only the headings shown.

Purchases Day Book
Date Supplier Invoice Total VAT Goods Expenses

Purchases Returns Book
Date Supplier Credit note Total VAT Goods Expenses

Transactions

Date	*Invoice/ Credit note*	*Invoice/Credit note value including VAT 15%*	*Supplier*
Oct 8	V 0832	£126.50 Invoice for goods supplied	Victor Ltd
	4001	£143.75 Invoice for goods supplied	Bath & Co
9	R 773210	£13.80 refund on service over charge	Gas Services Ltd
	XX 321	£114.25 for goods supplied, 5% cash discount offered	Bean Bros
	A 4447	£92.00 van service	Apex Garage
10	TM 07449	£200.00 rent no VAT charge	Property Ltd
11	67742	£276.00 Invoice for goods supplied	Wholesalers Ltd
	CN 241	£45.70 credit for damaged goods supplied on invoice offering 5% cash discount	Carrymuch Ltd
12	BW 1289	£207.00 Invoice for goods supplied	Retail Suppliers

10

Double-entry book-keeping – an outline of the system

INTRODUCTION

A consideration of accounting record systems cannot pass without mention of double-entry book-keeping. This system is the standard system of book-keeping for organisations which have outgrown the systems described in the previous two chapters. It moves beyond the systems described so far, which were only *single*-entry methods, and increases the range of records that can be kept. The end result is the facilitating of profit calculations and preparation of the *Balance Sheet*.

The accounting records are held in the *ledger* which is split for convenience into three separate ledgers:

1 Sales Ledger holds the accounts of debtors;
2 Purchase Ledger holds the accounts of creditors;
3 Nominal Ledger holds accounts that record assets, liabilities, revenues and expenses.

These ledgers are in addition to the Cash Book, Petty Cash Book, Sales and Purchase Day Books, Sales and Purchase Return Books. So the basic system operates as previously described.

The originating documents include: sales invoices, purchase invoices, credit notes received and issued, cheques received and issued, receipts, etc. All of these remain as the source documents for the record system. They are recorded in *the Books of Prime Entry*.

BOOKS OF PRIME ENTRY

Sales Day Book, Sales Returns Book, Purchases Day Book, Purchase Returns Book are the true Books of Prime Entry. They are used to collect data before recording in the ledgers.

Included with them, for practical reasons, but really part of the ledger are the Cash Book, now without the need for analysis beyond VAT and discounts, and the Petty Cash Book.

Entries into the ledgers are said to be *posted to the ledger*. This posting takes the form of two entries in the ledger accounts, hence the term 'double' entry.

TWO ENTRIES

Each transaction can be said to have two aspects to it:
(a) the giving of value;
(b) the receiving of value.

Let us take an example: the purchase of a newspaper for 25 pence. The value given, is money worth 25 pence; the value received, a newspaper worth 25 pence. All transactions have this dual aspect: value is always exchanged.

As each transaction has a value *given* and a value *received* then *two* accounts are required to record them.

For example goods purchased by cheque £20.

This requires:

(a) a Purchases Account to record the value of goods received and;

(b) a Bank Account to record the value of the payment.

An account in a modern system will look like this:

Date	*Particulars*	*Debit,*	*Credit*	*Balance*
		£ p	*£ p*	*£ p*

To record the entries requires a decision on which column to use, i.e. debit or credit (The balance column shows the net effect of all debit and credit entries in an account.) Debit is used to record value *received*. Credit is used to record value *given*.

So from the example above we can see that the entry in the Purchases Account must be in the debit column to record the value of goods received. The Bank Account entry is in the credit column to record the value of the payment.

Note Do not confuse the banking terminology, debit and credit, with the debit and credit entries to be made in the Books of Account. *In the business's records of bank account transactions debit is for receipts and credit for payments.*

Fig. 10.1 Basic double-entry system

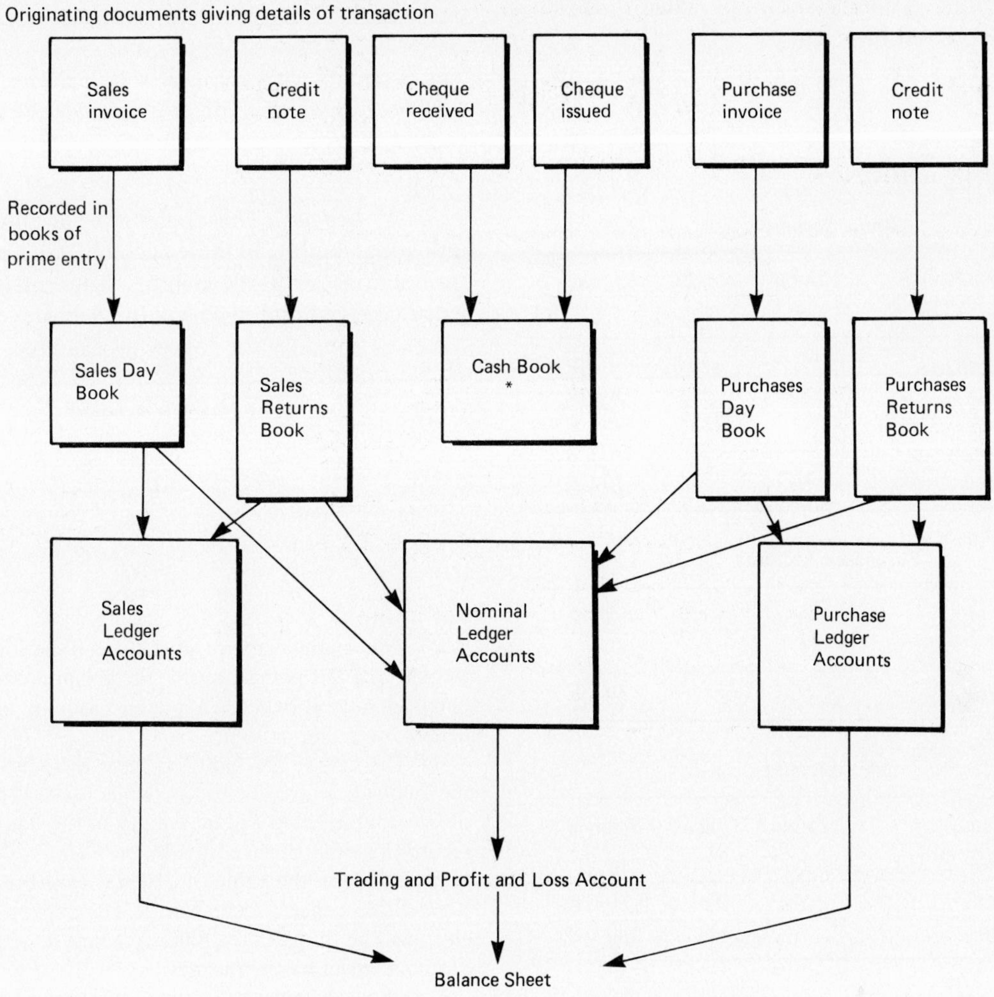

* The Cash Book is part of the 'ledger' and therefore has entries connecting it with the individual ledgers. These are omitted as it is only intended to show how the data in the Books of Prime Entry is posted to the ledgers.

A SIMPLE WORKED EXAMPLE

Note Ignore VAT. A/c means account.

Transactions

	Account to record: *Value received* Debit	*Value given* Credit
1 Bought goods for resale, paid £50 by cheque	Purchases a/c	Bank a/c
2 Sold goods, received payment by cheque £80	Bank a/c	Sales a/c
3 Paid rent by cheque £120	Rent a/c	Bank a/c
4 Paid for petrol by cheque £20	Motoring expenses a/c	Bank a/c
5 Sold goods, received payment by cheque £60	Bank a/c	Sales a/c

Reasons for debit and credit entries

Note The numbers refer to the ones in the transactions record.

1 Value received, debit purchases a/c to record the value of goods received.

Value given, credit bank a/c to record the value of the payment made.

2 Value received, debit bank a/c to record receipt of a cheque for £80.

Value given, credit sales a/c to show value of goods supplied to customer.

3 Value received, debit rent a/c to show the value attached to receiving the use of premises.

Value given, credit bank a/c to show the value of the payment made.

4 Value received, debit motor expenses a/c to show the value of petrol received.

Value given, credit bank a/c to show the value of the payment made.

5 Value given, credit sales a/c to show the value of goods given in exchange for the cheque for £60.

Note Only the bank a/c shows the movements of money, the other accounts show the value of goods and services received or given.

Book-keeping entries

Bank Account

Date	*Details*	*Debit* £	*Credit* £	*Balance* £
Sept	Purchases		50	50 CR
	Sales	80		30 DR
	Rent		120	90 CR
	Motor expenses		20	110 CR
	Sales	60		50 CR

Purchases Account

Date	*Details*	*Debit* £	*Credit* £	*Balance* £
Sept	Bank	50		50 DR

Sales Account

Date	*Details*	*Debit* £	*Credit* £	*Balance* £
Sept	Bank		80	80 CR
	Bank		60	140 CR

Rent Account

Date	*Details*	*Debit* £	*Credit* £	*Balance* £
Sept	Bank	120		120 DR

Motor Expenses Account

Date	*Details*	*Debit* £	*Credit* £	*Balance* £
Sept	Bank	80		80 DR

Notice how the Details column is used to record the name of the other account that forms the double entry. This applies to all transactions.

Accounting records can only show monetary values for transactions (the money measurement concept), it is not possible to indicate any worth or value in a transaction if it cannot be stated in monetary terms. Hence the employment of scientists in a research department can only be recorded in terms of the cost of employing them, their value to the company as reflected in the products they are developing cannot be quantified and therefore not shown in an accounting record.

CREDIT TRANSACTIONS

The accounts we have used were held in the *Nominal Ledger*, but when credit transactions are recorded the other two ledgers are required:

1 *Sales Ledger*. This holds an account for each individual debtor, in these accounts are a record of the transactions with the debtor. The entries show the value received and given by the debtor.

Let us consider the following example.

R Smitherson Account

	Date	*Details*	*Debit* £	*Credit* £	*Balance* £
(a)	Mar 1	Balance b/f			100.00 DR
(b)	2	Bank		85.00	15.00 DR
(c)	10	Sales	125.00		140.00 DR

Key to entries

(a) This is the balance owing by R Smitherson on 1st March. The DR note alongside the balance indicates a *Debit* balance. A debit balance in a debtor account means that the debtor owes that amount.

(b) The debtor has paid £85. It is a credit entry because the debtor has given value, a cheque for £85, the other half of the double entry will be a debit in the Bank Account to record the value received by the business.

(c) Goods to the value of £125.00 have been received by the debtor, hence a debit entry. The corresponding credit entry will be found in the Sales Account recording the value of goods given by the business.

Note how the balance column changes with each transaction reflecting the amount owed by the debtor after each transaction.

2 *Purchase Ledger*. This holds accounts of individuals, i.e. creditors. The entries indicate the value given and received by the creditors, and any sums owed by the business to its creditors.

Southern Wholesalers Ltd Account

	Date	*Details*	*Debit*	*Credit*	*Balance*
(a)	Mar 1	Balance b/f			50.00 CR
(b)	4	Purchases		240.00	290.00 CR
(c)	16	Bank	50.00		240.00 CR

Key to entries

(a) The opening balance shows how much the business owes to Southern Wholesalers on 1st March. CR indicates a credit balance; a credit balance in a purchase ledger account is an amount owing by the business to the creditor.

(b) Goods bought from Southern Wholesalers valued at £240. This is a credit entry showing value given by the creditor, note that the balance changes to show a total of £290 owing after this transaction.

(c) The business pays the £50 owing from the beginning of the month. The entry is a debit, showing value received by the creditor. The balance is reduced by the payment to £240.

A SIMPLE WORKED EXAMPLE INCLUDING CREDIT TRANSACTIONS

Transactions

Note Ignore VAT. All transactions take place in March.

	Account to record	
	Value rec'd *Debit*	*Value given* *Credit*
1 Sold goods value £260, received a cheque	Bank a/c	Sales a/c
2 Bought goods on credit from Traders Ltd value £200	Purchases a/c	Traders a/c
3 Paid rent by cheque £150	Rent a/c	Bank a/c
4 Sold goods on credit to R Biggs £50	R Biggs a/c	Sales a/c
5 Paid wages by cheque £60	Wages a/c	Bank a/c
6 R Biggs sent a cheque for £45	Bank a/c	R Biggs a/c
7 Paid Traders Ltd £100 by cheque	Traders a/c	Bank a/c

R Biggs Account will be in the Sales Ledger. Traders Ltd Account will be in the Purchase Ledger. Bank Account is found in the Cash Book. All of the other accounts such as Purchases Account, Sales Account, Rent Account, Wages Account are found in the Nominal Ledger.

Book-keeping entries

Sales Ledger
R Biggs Account

Date	*Details*	*Debit* £	*Credit* £	*Balance* £
March	Sales (transaction 4)	50.00		50.00 DR
	Bank (transaction 6)		45.00	5.00 DR

Purchase Ledger
Traders Ltd Account

Date	*Details*	*Debit* £	*Credit* £	*Balance* £
March	Purchases (transaction 2)		200.00	200.00 CR
	Bank (transaction 7)	100.00		10.00 CR

Cash Book
Bank Account

Date	*Details*	*Debit* £	*Credit* £	*Balance* £
March	Sales (trans. 1)	260.00		260.00 DR
	Rent (trans. 3)		150.00	110.00 DR
	Wages (trans. 5)		60.00	50.00 DR
	R Biggs (trans. 6)	45.00		95.00 DR
	Traders Ltd (trans. 7)		100.00	5.00 CR

Nominal Ledger
Purchases Account

Date	*Details*	*Debit* £	*Credit* £	*Balance* £
March	Traders Ltd (trans. 2)	200.00		200.00 DR

Sales Account

Date	*Details*	*Debit* £	*Credit* £	*Balance* £
March	Bank (trans. 1)		260.00	260.00 CR
	R Biggs (trans. 4)		50.00	310.00 CR

Rent Account

Date	*Details*	*Debit* £	*Credit* £	*Balance* £
March	Bank (trans. 3)	150.00		150.00 DR

Wages Account

Date	*Details*	*Debit* £	*Credit* £	*Balance* £
March	Bank (trans. 5)	60.00		60.00 DR

Trace the transactions through and check that each transaction has
(a) been recorded in two accounts;
(b) one entry was a debit and the other was a credit.

SUMMARY

This has been a very brief introduction to the principles of double-entry book-keeping which increases the range of records that can be kept and as a result facilitates profit calculations and preparation of the Balance Sheet.

Those students who study the option unit Accounting in the second year of the BTEC National Course will study the system in greater depth.

TASKS

Tasks 1 and 2

Before entering transactions into the ledger note the two accounts needed to complete the entries. Below are a list of transactions; complete the table to show the accounts in which entries will be made.

Task 1

Transaction	*Account to receive a debit entry (value rec'd)*	*Account to receive a credit entry (value given)*
1 Bought goods for resale, paid by cheque		
2 Sold goods to customer who paid by cheque		
3 Paid telephone bill by cheque		
4 Paid gas bill by cheque		
6 Paid wages by cheque		

Task 2

Note: credit transactions are included

Transaction	*Account to receive a debit entry (value rec'd)*	*Account to receive a credit entry (value given)*
1 Sold goods, received a cheque in payment		
2 Sold goods on credit to F Davies		
3 Paid rent by cheque		
4 Paid electricity bill by cheque		
5 Bought goods, paid by cheque		
6 Bought goods on credit from Zill Ltd		
7 Paid wages by cheque		
8 F Davies sent a cheque to pay for goods supplied		
9 Sent a cheque to Zill Ltd in settlement of their bill		
10 Bought goods, paid by cheque		

Tasks 3 to 7

Your junior accounts clerk is unsure of the meaning of the entries in various accounts. Write a short note explaining what is being recorded by the entries in these accounts as shown below:

Task 3

Park District Council Rates Account

Date	*Details*	*Debit* £	*Credit* £	*Balance* £
April	Bank	400.00		400.00 DR
Oct	*Bank	400.00		800.00 DR

Task 4

Cash Book – Bank Account

Date	*Details*	*Debit* £	*Credit* £	*Balance* £
April	Balance b/f			1000.00 DR
	Rates		400.00	400.00 DR
	Sales	120.00		520.00 DR
	*Purchases		80.00	440.00 DR
	Cantor Supplies Ltd		100.00	340.00 DR
	*Rent	130.00		210.00 DR

Task 5

Sales Accounts

Date	*Details*	*Debit* £	*Credit* £	*Balance* £
April	Bank		120.00	120.00 CR
	J Baker		200.00	320.00 CR

Task 6

Sales Ledger
J Baker Account

Date	*Details*	*Debit* £	*Credit* £	*Balance* £
April	Balance b/f			140.00 DR
	Sales	200.00		340.00 DR

Task 7

Purchase Ledger
Cantor Supplies Account

Date	*Details*	*Debit* £	*Credit* £	*Balance* £
April	Balance b/f			100.00 CR
	Bank	100.00		00.00

Task 8

In Tasks 3 to 7 you could see the double entries for some transactions. However, apart from 'Balance b/f' the other entries marked * do not have their double entry shown. For the benefit of your junior, make a list of these entries and note against each where the double entry can be found.

Task 9

As a book-keeper it is your job to enter transactions into the ledger accounts. From the following list of transactions:

1 Draw up a list of accounts required.
2 Record the transactions in the accounts.
(a) Goods sold, cheque received for £120;
(b) Stall rent paid £25 by cheque;
(c) Paid for purchases by cheque £80;
(d) Sold goods, payment received by cheque £100;
(e) Business owner took £50 for personal use (use a drawings a/c).

Task 10

The following transactions, including credit transactions need to be recorded.

1 Draw up a list of accounts and the ledgers in which they appear.
2 Record the transactions in the accounts.
(a) Bought goods on credit from Middleton & Co Ltd value £400;
(b) Sold goods, received payment by cheque £150;
(c) Sold goods on credit to M Small value £180;
(d) Sold goods on credit to D Large value £210;
(e) Paid rent on premises £50 by cheque;
(f) Paid part-time employee £40 by cheque;
(g) Received a cheque for £160 from M Small;
(h) Paid Middleton & Co Ltd £200 by cheque;
(i) D Large sent a cheque for £210.

11

Book-keeping and information technology

INTRODUCTION

In the recent past, the cost of computer hardware has fallen dramatically making a basic computing system easily affordable by all but the smallest businesses. The software for these cheap systems has also fallen in price and some applications software is often given away with the hardware, e.g. word processing software.

Because of the routine nature of book-keeping, it can be easily computerised and this has become one of the most widespread applications of information technology in business today. Standard book-keeping packages are available in high street stores at reasonable cost and these will handle the financial record keeping of the majority of small businesses. Large organisations may have tailor-made software for their specific requirements.

ACCOUNTING PACKAGES

The majority of these book-keeping software packages are 'integrated', which means that:

1 it has the full range of books of prime entry, ledgers and accounts that are normally encountered in business;
2 the accounts are linked together (integrated) so that a single entry into the system will update all the records appropriate to that transaction.

For example, when an invoice is made out to a customer, a basic software system will:

1 record the transaction in the Sales Day Book;
2 record the transaction in the Nominal Ledger, Sales Account;
3 record the transaction in the Sales Ledger, Customers Account.

Although integrated, these packages are often sold in a modular form allowing the customer to build up a system to suit the specific needs of their business. If, in addition to the usual Sales, Purchase and Nominal Ledger modules, Stock Control were included, the list of records update by a single entry could be extended to include:

4 stock level reduced by the quantity sold to the customer. Other add-on modules may include:
(a) payroll;
(b) costing;
(c) budgeting.

The ability to accurately update the accounting records by a single entry for each transaction has removed the time-consuming element from record-keeping, thus reducing the cost of keeping records and reducing errors to those caused by operator input. Other organisations which previously had not bothered with record-keeping beyond that forced upon them by outside agencies now have access to systems that will enable far greater control to be maintained over the finances of the business.

Error reduction is achieved by a number of features built into book-keeping software.

1 *Security codes* are used to ensure that only authorised personnel are able to have access to the system. Several layers of security may be available, allowing almost open access at the level of making enquiries of the system, through to very tight control over those who can enter non-routine transactions.
2 *Computer prompted response*, i.e. the operator enters transactions into the system through a familiar format displayed on the screen, e.g. a sales invoice. The computer works through the format requesting information from the operator. This reduces the chances of entries being omitted as the computer forces the operator to consider each stage of the data entry sequence.
3 *Verification procedures*, when data is entered the computer checks to see if the data it has been given is reasonable in that situation. Any unsuitable or illogical data is rejected and the operator is invited to try again.

4 *Automatic processes*, the operator is not required to make routine calculations like VAT calculation, totalling and sub-totalling, discount deductions, etc.
5 *Automatic sequencing of documents* removes the chances of duplication or omission of documents.

Apart from the specific features of book-keeping software, the introduction of a computerised system that operates in a logical and systematic way will often force a haphazardly administered organisation to introduce more routine into its operation, thus reducing the opportunities for errors.

OPERATING A TYPICAL SYSTEM

Most systems are 'menu driven', that is on starting up and loading the system into the computer the operator is presented with a list of options, the menu, from which a choice of activity is made, which in turn will lead to another menu offering further choices. Fig. 11.1 shows a typical book-keeping menu.

After working through the menus until an entry format is displayed, the operator enters details as prompted by the computer. When the form is complete the operator will be asked to confirm that it is correct:

(a) if *yes* the format is displayed again for entering the next transaction;

(b) if *no* the format is represented for the correct information to be entered.

When all of the transactions have been completed, the operator will work back through the menus, while the computer updates the records and prints any documents required. At the end, the operator chooses 'Exit' from the main menu and the computer returns to its operating system.

Fig. 11.1 A typical book-keeping menu

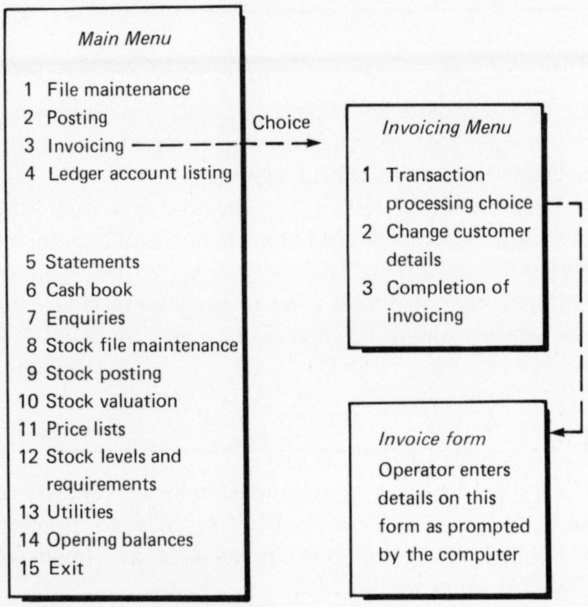

Practice

Computerised systems, while using the same basic mode of operation, all have their own individual features that mean data provided for practice on one system may not be suitable for another. Furthermore, these systems are capable of processing vast numbers of transactions in a few minutes, making the provision of exercises impractical. You should therefore make yourself familiar with the system available to you at your college where there will be sets of data available for practice.

OTHER FINANCIAL SOFTWARE

Financial planning and record keeping can be enhanced by the use of two other types of software.

Spreadsheets

These can be considered as electronic sheets of paper, divided up into rows and columns, on which figures can be set out. 'Multiplan' has 63 columns and 255 rows. The intersections of the rows and columns form '*cells*' (*see* Fig. 11.2) and it is into these cells that the figures are entered.

Fig. 11.2

	Columns			
Rows	1	2	3	4
1				
2				
3		Cell		
4				
5				
6				

The cell shown in Fig. 11.2 is described by its co-ordinates, i.e. Column 2, Row 3 or C2R3. The spreadsheet programme allows the figures in the cells to have calculations performed upon them and the answer placed in another cell (*see* Fig. 11.3).

Fig. 11.3

	1	2	3	4
1	Price	Quantity	Sales	
2	2.00	50	100.00	
3				
4				
5				

The sales figure in C3R2 is calculated by telling the spreadsheet programme to multiply price and quantity together, i.e. C1R2 * C2R2, and put the answer in C3R2.

The method of giving instructions to carry out the task shown in Fig. 11.3 will be different for each spreadsheet programme but they will all perform this type of calculation.

After setting the formula for the calculation any change to the figures in C1R2 and C2R2 will automatically result in an amended result in C3R2. In this automatic recalculation of the answer to calculations lies the value of a spreadsheet, this is known as the '*what if*' *function*.

Management can set up a complex set of relationships on a spreadsheet, e.g. a cashflow forecast and investigate alternative courses of action. Thus the most advantageous combination of variables can be established.

Databases

Databases are simply filing systems that are set up in such a way as to enable the user to extract information in a form that is useable by the person interrogating the database. The information filed is broken down into *records* and then sub-divided into *fields*.

Example

Fields

Stock reference	Description	Price	
732	Bolts	0.35	Record

The record is all of the details about the stock item but the individual details are separate fields.

Information is retrieved from the database by specifying information stored in the fields, the program will show all records that have fields corresponding to the field description given. For example, if 'bolts' was specified then the database would provide details of the item shown above and any other bolts listed.

The interrogation of the database can be very specific and the parameters of the information required can be tightly set (*see* Fig. 11.4).

Fig. 11.4 Database interrogation

Stock Reference	Description	Price
732	Bolts	0.35
733	Washers	0.10
734	Flanges	2.00
735	Bolts	0.50

A simple interrogation of this database for stock reference 734 will produce the required details of this stock item. A more complex request, say, for stock items valued at less than 75p, would produce details of stock items 732, 733 and 735. A request for details of bolts held worth more than 40p would provide details of stock item 735 only.

The number of records and fields within the record, the complexity of the interrogation possible and the style of output will depend upon the database software but the above should be considered simple examples.

SUMMARY

Computer based book-keeping systems are quick to process records and accurate. They offer the opportunity to obtain reports on various aspects of the firm's finances instantly. Standard systems are available that are suitable for most small businesses and, as they replicate the familiar manual book-keeping systems, the terminology and method of operating is well-known to users.

TASKS

Task 1

Using a standard set of data, e.g. sales invoices, enter the transactions into two or more different accounting packages and compare the systems.

Write a short report on the systems used and highlight any problems from an operator's point of view.

If you cannot obtain a set of invoices to enter, use the transactions in Chapter 9, Task 8.

Task 2

Use a spreadsheet program and its 'what if' capacity to look at Chapter 4, Tasks 8–10. You will need to set up a Cash Budget on your spreadsheet as shown in Chapter 4 Figs 4.1 and 4.2.

Task 3

Survey the banks, building societies and other financial institutions in your area and find out their rates to savers/investors and borrowers. You should also gather information about special conditions etc. Then set up a database with this information; you will then be able to look for the best rates for investors and the most advantageous terms for borrowers.

Note This type of information dates quickly and if the database is to be of continuing use it should be updated regularly.

12 The financial statements of business organisations

INTRODUCTION

Whatever the organisation structure, it is usual for statements to be drawn up at the end of each financial period to show:

1 the profit or loss for the period; this is done by comparing revenue and expenditure for the period in a statement known as the *Trading and Profit and Loss Account*, or *Income Statement*;
2 the assets, liabilities and financing of the organisation in a document known as a *Balance Sheet*. This lists the assets of the organisation, its external liabilities and the funds provided by the owner or owners.

CAPITAL AND REVENUE EXPENDITURE

These ends of period statements reveal some aspects of expenditure for the period. Expenditure is classified as:

1 *revenue expenditure*, the day-to-day running expenses of a business and the cost of goods sold, e.g. rent, rates, heat, light, wages, vehicle running costs.
2 *capital expenditure*, expenditure of the permanent assets of the organisation, e.g. purchase of land, building, machines, motor vehicles. These are known as *fixed assets*.

The distinction is important because profit is calculated by deducting all revenue expenditure for a period from the income for that period; capital expenditure is not a charge against income. Let's take an example.

	£
Sales income	90 000
Cost of goods sold and running expenses	70 000
Profit	20 000

This is the *correct* way to calculate profit.

	£	£
Sales income		90 000
Cost of goods sold and running expenses	70 000	
Purchase of new car	10 000	80 000
Profit		10 000

This is the *wrong* way to calculate profit, the purchase of a new car is capital expenditure and should *not* be included in the profit calculation.

DEPRECIATION

Having said that capital expenditure is not to be included in the profit calculation, it is obvious that capital expenditure is a cost to the business and therefore has an effect on profitability. The transfer of capital expenditure to the profit calculation as a revenue expense is achieved using *depreciation*.

Depreciation is normally considered to be the loss in value of a piece of equipment over time, and this is true, but the accountant is more concerned with using depreciation as a way of charging the cost of that equipment to the profits earned during its useful life. The most common method of calculating the depreciation on fixed assets is the straight line or *equal instalment method*, the calculation is shown below.

$$\text{Annual depreciation charge} = \frac{\text{Cost of asset} - \text{Residual value}}{\text{Number of years' life}}$$

Cost of asset is the purchase cost plus any installation expenses. *Residual value* is an estimate of any second-hand or scrap value the fixed asset is likely to have at the end of its useful life to the purchasing organisation. *Number of years' life* refers to the number of years the purchasing organisation intends to keep the fixed asset.

The annual depreciation charge is then a revenue expense that is charged each year, along with all of the other expenses, in the profit calculation, the *Trading and Profit and Loss Account*. For example, a machine is installed for a cost of £10 000. The business expects to use it for four years, after which they anticipate selling it for £2000 on the second-hand market.

$$\text{Annual depreciation charge} = \frac{£10\,000 - £2000}{4 \text{ years}}$$

$$= \frac{£8000}{4 \text{ years}}$$

$$= £2000 \text{ p.a.}$$

The annual depreciation charge can be expressed as a percentage of cost if the straight line method is employed. Using the information in the above example:

Annual depreciation charge as a percentage of cost

$$= \frac{£2000}{£10\,000} \times \frac{100}{1}$$

$$= 20\% \text{ p.a.}$$

Note: Although depreciation is shown as an expense in the profit calculation, it is not a 'cash' expense. That is, the expense may be an annual charge, but the asset was paid for on acquisition, therefore no further cash payments leave the business because of the ownership of the fixed asset.

Consider your car standing outside your house, it is losing value, depreciating, month by month, but you are not paying month by month for that depreciation. You paid for the car when purchased, that was when the cash left your hands.

THE TRADING AND PROFIT AND LOSS ACCOUNT

The heading of this account suggests one single account and although the presentation also gives this appearance, there are in reality two separate accounts.

The Trading Account

This records the sales income or turnover and deducts from it the cost of the goods sold to give a *gross profit*. *Note*: All stock values are shown as 'at cost'. This is in accordance with the rules set out in Statement of Standard Accounting Practice (SSAP) 9, which in summary requires that stocks are valued at the lower of cost or net realisable value. *Realisable value* means the amount for which the goods may be sold, which is, in the majority of cases, greater than cost hence cost is the valuation used as it is usually the lower valuation. The Trading Account is only used for organisations that purchase goods to resell in one form or another.

Fig. 12.1

J Keen
Trading Account
for year ending 31 December 19X1

		£	£
(a)	Sales		80 000
	Cost of sales		
(b)	Stock 1st January 19X1	4000	
(c)	add Purchases	46 000	
(d)		50 000	
(e)	*less* Stock 31 December 19X1	5000	
(f)			45 000
(g)	Gross profit		35 000

Key to entries

(a) The income from sales, this can be called the *turnover*.
(b) The cost value of stock at the start of the period.
(c) The cost value of total purchases for the period.
(d) The total of (b) and (c), it is the total cost value of goods that were offered for sale during the year.
(e) The cost value of stocks held at the end of the period, i.e. the unsold part of (d).
(f) The cost of sales figure found by deducting stock at the end of the period (e), from the total cost value of goods offered for sale (d).
(g) The *gross profit* is the difference between the cost value of the goods sold (f) and the sales value of the same goods (a).

The Profit and Loss Account

Within this account the revenue expenses for the period are deducted from gross profit to reveal if there is anything left. If income exceeds total revenue expenses then a *net profit* is obtained, when revenue expenses exceed income the business has sustained a *loss*. (*See* Fig. 12.2, page 82.)

As indicated earlier, these two accounts are presented as one under the title of *Trading and Profit and Loss Account* or alternatively the use of the title *Income Statement* is becoming more popular. The two are shown combined in Fig. 12.3, page 82.

Key to entries for Fig. 12.2 (page 82)

(a) Gross profit from the Trading Account.
(b) The expenses, revenue expenditure, for the period are listed. The expenses' shown are examples of the types of expense incurred. It is not an exhaustive list.
(c) The total of expenses listed at (b).
(d) The net profit, found by taking the total expenses (c) away from the gross profit (a). Net profit is the profit after all expenses and the cost of goods sold have been met out of income for the period.

Fig. 12.2

J Keen
Profit and Loss Account
for year ended 31 December 19X1

		£	£
(a)	Gross profit		35 000
(b)	*less* Expenses		
	Wages and salaries	12 000	
	Rent and rates	2000	
	Heat and light	1000	
	General expenses	2000	
	Depreciation of equipment	2000	
(c)			19 000
(d)	Net profit		16 000

Fig. 12.3

J Keen
Trading and Profit and Loss Account
for year ended 31 December 19X1

	£	£
Sales		80 000
Cost of sales		
Stock 1st January 19X1	4000	
Purchases	46 000	
	50 000	
Stock 31 December 19X1	5000	
		45 000
Gross profit		35 000
less Expenses		
Wages and salaries	12 000	
Rent and rates	2000	
Heat and light	1000	
General expenses	2000	
Depreciation of equipment	2000	
Net profit		19 000
		£16 000

ACCRUAL CONCEPT

This is a fundamental concept. It refers to the process of matching costs and revenue for the same time period. There are two factors to consider:

1 Any cost directly incurred in obtaining the revenue for the period must be deducted from the revenue. This is usually the *cost of sales* which we have seen deducted from income/revenue in the Trading Account.
2 Any revenue expenses incurred for the period during which the income was obtained must be deducted from that revenue. This process takes place in Profit and Loss Account.

The problem arises when you ask yourself what to do with items like insurance when payments are made in advance, and electricity where payments are made in arrears? The solution is to calculate that proportion of an expense that applies to the period under consideration and include only this amount. This is known as dealing with *prepayments and accruals*.

Prepayments occur when payment is made in advance for an expense, the benefit of which will be obtained in more than one period. Accruals, or expenses owing, are a problem which occurs when an expense has been incurred but payment has not been made. The payment will be made in the next financial period but the benefit from the expense was enjoyed during the current financial period.

Example 1 Prepayment

If a business takes out insurance cover on a new machine purchased on 1st October 19X1, the premium will be for one year's cover and paid in advance, say £120. Assuming a financial year of 1st January to 31st December, you can see that only 3 months' insurance cover is used during the year ending 31 December 19X1 although a full year's cover was paid for during that year.

Under these circumstances, the appropriate amount of £120 × 3/12 of a year = £30 will be charged as an expense in the Profit and Loss Account for year ended 31 December 19X1. The balance of the payments, £90, is known as a *prepayment* and will be included in the expenses for year ended 31st December 19X2. If the premium for the next year, payable on 1 October 19X2, rises to £148 p.a. then the amount charged to the Profit and Loss Account for year ended 31 December 19X2 will consist of:

Prepaid last year	90
plus 3/12 of this year's payment (£148 × 3/12)	37
Expense shown in the Profit and Loss Account	£127

Example 2 Accrual

Payments for certain services are made after the service has been used and the cost of the service provided assessed by the supplier, e.g. telephone services. If a business has a financial year from 1st January to 31 December and the telephone bill may be presented in the following pattern:

Charging period 19X1	*Date bill presented*	*Amount*
1 January–31 March	12 April	£240.00
1 April–30 June	14 July	£255.00
1 July–30 September	8 October	£225.00
1 October–31 December	not yet received	?

From this information it is impossible to show the total charge for telephone services in the Profit and Loss Account for year ended 31 December 19X1. It would be an error to show only (£240 + £255 + £225) £720 as this is obviously not the correct total for the cost of this service during the year. The missing amount is known as an *accrual*, and its magnitude must be estimated in order to calculate the profit for the year.

In practice, the bill will often have arrived before it becomes necessary to prepare the Profit and Loss Account and therefore estimates are not always necessary. However, the sum is an amount owing at the end of the year and will appear in the accounts as such.

THE BALANCE SHEET

The *Balance Sheet* (Fig. 12.4) is a statement of an organisation's assets, external liabilities and sources of finance on a given date, usually the date on which the financial year ends. It is drawn up in two parts:

1 Net assets employed section, this lists the assets of the organisation, divided into *fixed assets* (the

Fig. 12.4

D Starkey
Balance Sheet as at 31 December 19X1

	£	£	£
Net assets employed			
Fixed assets			
(a) Premises at cost			40 000
(b) Equipment at cost		10 000	
(c) *less* Accumulated depreciation		6000	4000
			44 000
Current assets			
(d) Stock		1700	
(e) Trade debtors		1100	
(f) Cash at bank		2700	
(g) Cash in hand		100	
(h) Prepayments		200	
		5800	
Current liabilities			
(i) Trade creditors	1200		
(j) Accruals	300	1500	
(k) Net current assets			4300
(l) *Total* assets *less* current liabilities			48 300
Long term liabilities			
(m) Mortgage on premises			20 000
			28 300
Financed by:			
(n) Capital Account 1 Jan 19X1			25 800
(o) Net profit			11 500
			37 300
(p) *less* Drawings			9000
(q)			28 300

Key to entries

(a) The purchase cost of premises is shown, if the current value of premises is considerably different to the price paid then the accounts will probably be changed to reflect this.

(b) and (c) The cost of equipment is shown, but as this capital expenditure is being charged to the Profit and Loss Account over a number of years via depreciation, it is necessary to show the accumulated depreciation and the *book value* of equipment. Book value is the undepreciated element of the original cost of equipment. Note that it is the book value that is used to give a total value for fixed assets.

(d) Stock is the cost value of stock held on the Balance Sheet date, in this case 31 December 19X1. This is found by 'stocktaking'.

(e) Trade debtors is the total amount owed by trade debtors on the Balance Sheet date. To establish this figure, all of the balances on the sales ledger accounts are added.

(f) and (g) Simply the balances of cash held in the bank and on the premises at the Balance Sheet date. Note that it may be necessary to prepare a bank reconciliation statement to establish the bank balance accurately.

(h) The total amount of any expenses prepaid for the next period.

(i) Any sum owed to suppliers of goods at the Balance Sheet date. This can be found from the balances on Purchase Ledger Accounts.

(j) Accruals are the total of amounts owing for expenses incurred to date but as yet unpaid.

(k) Net current assets is found by deducting current liabilities from current assets. This figure is also known as *working capital* and, as the name implies, it shows the funds available to finance the trading operations of the business.

(l) Total assets less current liabilities is a sub-total required if long-term liabilities exist. The figure is exactly what its description states.

(m) An example of a long-term liability. These are deducted from the sub-total (l) above to give the final total for this part of the Balance Sheet, i.e. the total for net assets employed.

The second part of the balance sheet explains how the net assets employed are financed. This section deals with the owner's permanent investment in the business.

(n) The capital invested by the proprietor at the start of the period just ending. Any new capital invested would be shown as an addition at this stage.

(o) The net profit for the year, it is added to the opening capital balance as it represents the return on the capital invested.

(p) Drawings are the funds taken from the business by the owner for his/her personal use. They are that part of the profits the owner wishes to withdraw from the business. Any profits not taken as drawings are said to be *retained profits*, that is they are retained in the business as a further investment.

(q) The new capital balance, showing how much is invested in the business at the end of the period. In this case, the investment is increased by the amount of the retained profits, i.e. net profit £11 500 less drawings £9000 = retained profit £2500. Opening capital £25 800 add retained profits £2500 = new capital £28 300.

permanent assets of the business) and *current assets* (the assets generated in the trading activities of the business). From the assets are deducted the business liabilities, current liabilities – amounts due within one year, and long-term liabilities – amounts due after one year.
2 Financed by section, this gives details of the permanent finance for the business provided by the owner or owners.

Together the Trading and Profit and Loss Account and the Balance Sheet make up what is known as the *Final Accounts* of a business.

LIMITED COMPANIES

Limited companies construct their final accounts in the same way as sole trader organisations, they follow the same basic rules and use similar terminology. However, because they are not reporting to a single individual the format has to be changed slightly to take these circumstances into consideration.

Trading and Profit and Loss Account

This is expanded to show shareholders how much Corporation Tax has been paid on companies' profits and how the remaining profits have been allocated between dividends to shareholders and retained profit for reinvestment in the business. This is recorded in an *Appropriation Account*, which follows directly after the calculation of profit for the period. (*See* Fig. 12.5.)

Balance sheet

The general format of the 'Net assets employed' section remains the same although items specific to limited companies appear in some sections:

1 Current liabilities will show the taxation of profits as

Fig. 12.5

Grant and Sons Ltd
Trading and Profit and Loss Account
for year ended 31 October 19X2

		£	£
	(a) Turnover		40 000
	(b) *Cost of sales*		
	Stock 1 November 19X1	30 000	
	Purchases	210 000	
		240 000	
	Stock 31 October 19X2	35 000	
			205 000
	(c) Gross profit		195 000
	(d) *less* Expenses		
	Rent and rates	14 000	
	Heat and light	6000	
	Wages and salaries	75 000	
	Debenture interest	3750	
	General expenses	6250	
	Depreciation of equipment	6000	
			111 000
	(e) Profit before taxation		84 000
Appropriation Account	(f) Taxation on profits		28 000
	(g) Profit after taxation		56 000
	(h) Dividends:		
	interim dividend on ordinary shares	15 000	
	proposed final dividend on ordinary shares	22 500	37 500
	(i) Retained profit for the year		18 500
	(j) Profit and Loss Account balance brought forward		41 500
	(k) Profit and Loss Account balance carried forward		60 000

Key to entries
(a) Turnover, this means revenue from sales; the term is often used in company accounts.
(b) and (c) The usual calculation of cost of sales and its deduction from turnover to give gross profit.
(d) The expenses we have seen before, remember the figures shown will have been calculated taking any prepayments and accruals into consideration. Debenture interest is an extra item; this is loan interest, *see* Fig. 12.6 entry (d).
(e) Profit before taxation corresponds with net profit in the previous examples.
(f) Limited companies have to pay Corporation Tax on their profits. The rate of taxation is 35% of profits, but various writing down allowances can reduce taxable profit to below the figure for profit before taxation.
(g) The profit remaining after deduction of taxation.
(h) A company distributes its profits to its owners, the shareholders, by making a dividend payment. This is expressed as so many pence per share or as a percentage of nominal value. The distribution often takes place twice during the year, at the half-year point an interim dividend is paid, then at the end of the year a final dividend is declared. Both are shown as a deduction from profits in the Appropriation Account.
(i) After making allowances for taxation and the payment of dividends there remains the profit that has been reinvested in the business, i.e. the retained profit.
(j) and (k) The retained profit for each year is accumulated with that of previous years. The accumulated total is known as the *Profit and Loss Account balance*. In the example the accumulated total from previous years (j) is shown being added to the current year's retained profits to give a new balance to carry forward (k). This new balance will appear in the Balance Sheet.

an amount owing, and the final dividend will not have been paid on the Balance Sheet date and is therefore a liability.

2 Long-term liabilities may have *debentures* as an item. This is loan stock usually with a fixed rate of interest, which will be a revenue expense charged to the Profit and Loss Account, and bearing a repayment date, e.g. 6% debenture 19X8.

Because of the nature of ownership and financing of limited companies the 'Financed by' section changes to 'Capital and Reserves'. It is usual to state both the *authorised* and *issued share capital* in this section and then to list the company reserves. Reserves are established for a number of reasons, but we will confine ourselves to *revenue reserves*, these are created from retained profits and are shown as the profit and loss account balance.

Published final accounts of limited companies

The accounts shown so far have been for internal use by the organisation for which they were prepared. Limited companies are required to publish their final accounts so that all who have dealings with, or an interest in, the company are made aware of the company's financial state.

The detailed method of preparation of these accounts is set out in the Statements of Standard Accounting Practice (SSAPs), so that all who read them can compare company with company, and look at the year by year trends in an individual company, knowing that the basis of preparation for all the accounts is the same and that any material difference in accounting method or policy will be disclosed.

The rules about the method of presentation and the deals that must be disclosed are contained in the Companies Act 1985. The layout for published final accounts is given in the Act and all of the final accounts in this chapter have, in general terms and where possible, followed Format 1 of the Companies Act 1985 for both Trading and Profit and Loss Accounts and Balance Sheets. From Fig. 12.7, the Trading and Profit and Loss Account, you will see that the information shown in the account itself is minimised, all required and relevant disclosures are made in notes to the accounts. Fig. 12.8 shows a Balance Sheet in published form, again the information shown on the face of the statement is abbreviated, but notes following it explain the legally required disclosures in detail.

The preparation of published accounts with all their detailed notes in such a way that they conform to the Companies Act 1985 and comply with all the requirements of the SSAPs is not a subject for a BTEC National course. However, it is worthwhile obtaining a

Fig. 12.6

Grant and Sons Ltd
Balance Sheet as at 31 October 19X2

		£	£	£
	Net Assets employed			
(a)	*Fixed Assets*			
	Premises			340 000
	Equipment at cost		50 000	
	less Depreciation		18 000	32 000
				372 000
(b)	*Current assets*			
	Stock		30 500	
	Trade debtors		40 000	
	Cash at bank		30 000	
	Cash in hand		500	
	Prepayments		1000	
			102 000	
(c)	*Current liabilities*			
	Trade creditors	13 000		
	Accruals	500		
	Corporation Tax	28 000		
	Proposed dividend	22 500	64 000	
	Net current assets			38 000
	Total assets *less* current liabilities			410 000
	Long-term liabilities			
(d)	7½% Debenture 19X9			50 000
				360 000
	Capital and reserves			
(e)	Authorised share capital			
	500 000 Ordinary shares of £1 each			500 000
(f)	Issued share capital			
	300 000 Ordinary shares of £1 each, fully paid			300 000
(g)	Reserves			
	Profit and Loss Account balance			60 000
				360 000

Key to entries

(a) The fixed assets of the organisation are shown with book values as the figures totalled as in a Sole Trader's Balance Sheet.

(b) Current assets: no change from a Sole Trader's Final Accounts.

(c) The additional items of Corporation Tax and proposed final dividends appear. They are linked to Fig. 12.5.

(d) An example of debentures is shown. It should be clear from the layout given that debentures are *not* part of share capital. They are only loan stock and they are treated in a similar manner to any other long-term loan.

(e) The statement of authorised share capital; this is an information item only and is not included in the total of capital and reserves.

(f) The issued share capital is shown at nominal value, that is face value. The market value of shares does not appear on the Balance Sheet.

(g) The accumulated retained profits, this item links with Fig. 12.5.

set of company accounts and reading through them now that you have had an introduction to the topic. Write to the Company Secretary of a public limited company you have an interest in or you think may have an interesting set of accounts, and request a copy of their *Annual Report* and *Accounts*. Alternatively, companies often advertise in the financial pages of newspapers, offering copies of their reports to the public so write for one of these.

SUMMARY

The Final Accounts of a business organisation comprise a Trading and Profit and Loss Account and a Balance Sheet. These are modified to suit the circumstances and type of organisation. All are prepared according to the requirements of the SSAPs and

Fig. 12.7

Grant and Sons Ltd
Trading and Profit and Loss Account
for year ended 31 October 19X2

	£	£
(a) Turnover		400 000
(b) Cost of sales		205 00
Gross profit		195 00
(c) Administration expenses	35 750	
(c) Distribution costs	71 500	107 250
		87 750
(d) Interest payable		3750
(e) Taxation on profit on ordinary activities taxation		84 000
(e) Profit on ordinary activities		28 000
(e) Profit on ordinary activities after taxation		56 000
(f) Dividends		37 500
(g) Retained profit for the year		18 500
(g) Profit and loss account balance brought forward		41 500
(g) Profit and loss account balance carried forward		60 000

This is the Trading and Profit and Loss Account of Grant and Sons Ltd as shown in Fig. 12.5 re-presented in published format. The notes to the account are not shown.

Key to entries
(a) Turnover is shown as before.
(b) The cost of sales total is shown, it is not necessary to disclose the detailed calculation, some detail may be described in the notes.
(c) All of the expenses have been allocated as *administration expenses* or *distribution costs* after the extraction of debenture interest which is shown separately at entry (d). The allocation of expenses to the two categories was for the sake of this example an arbitrary 1/3 Administration 2/3 Distribution.
(d) Interest payable on loans to the company.
(e) These sections, although reworded, remain as before.
(f) Total dividend for the year shown, the notes disclose its make up.
(g) These sections remain as before.

Fig. 12.8

Grant and Sons Ltd
Balance Sheet as at 31 October 19X2

	£	£
Net assets employed		
(a) *Tangible fixed assets*		372 000
(b) *Current assets*		
Stock	30 500	
Debtors	40 000	
Cash at bank and in hand	30 500	
Prepayments	1000	
	102 000	
(c) *Creditors*: amounts falling due within one year	64 000	
Net current assets		38 000
Total assets *less* current liabilities		410 000
(d) *Creditors*: amounts falling due after one year 7½% Debenture 19X9		50 000
		360 000
(e) *Capital and reserves*		
Issued share capital		300 000
Profit and loss account balance		60 000
		360 000

This is the Balance Sheet of Grant and Sons Ltd as shown in Fig. 12.6, re-presented in published format. The notes to the balance sheet are not shown.

Key to entries
(a) Fixed assets, only the book value of the fixed assets is shown, the notes to the Balance Sheet give details about depreciation.
(b) Current assets remain as before.
(c) Creditors, amounts falling due within one year, replaces the use of the term *current liabilities* at this point in the Balance Sheet. Details of individual items in this section are shown in the notes.
(d) Creditors, amounts falling due after one year, replaces the use of the term *long-term liabilities* in the published Balance Sheet.
(e) The 'Capital and reserves' section has authorised capital removed to the notes, where details of the types of share issued are also found.

published company accounts are further constrained and prescribed by the Companies Act 1985.

Two major considerations in the preparation of Final Accounts are

1 distinguishing between *capital* and *revenue* expenditure, and the use of depreciation to charge revenue with the appropriate proportion of capital expenditure.
2 the *accrual concept*, expenses paid must be adjusted to take into consideration prepayments and accruals.

TASKS

Task 1

You have been given a pile of invoices and asked to classify them as Capital Expenditure or Revenue Expenditure. The invoices are listed below:

(a) D Winterslow & Co, Invoice 3921, £325 for property maintenance.

(b) Midlands Electricity, bill for £850, the last quarter's supply.

(c) Park Garages, Invoice 24401, £7521 for a new delivery van.

(d) Deacon and Deacon, Invoice 283, £52 legal fees in connection with debt collection.

(e) Stationery Supplies Ltd, Invoice LT1302, £275 business stationery.

(f) Metro Hire Ltd, Invoice 7319, £68 hire of electrical generator.

(g) Park Garages, Invoice 24523, £120, hire of car for one week.

(h) Downer Bros Ltd, Invoice 1778, £4270, for new computers and ancillary equipment.

(i) Dell Electrical Services, Invoice 2992, £320, electrical installation work for computing facilities.

(j) Holt and Co Ltd, Invoice 899271, £1347, furniture re installation of computers.

Task 2

The company for which you work has just purchased a new production machine, the cost of installing the equipment was £8000. It is planned to keep this machine for six years after which it will be sold and replaced with the latest technology. In the past, this type of equipment has been sold after six years for about 10% of its original cost. Calculate for the business the annual depreciation cost that will be charged in the Profit and Loss Account for the next six years in respect of this machine. Company policy is the use of the straight line method of calculating depreciation.

Task 3

After two years' use of the machine referred to in Task 2 the company decides to purchase another. The new machine will cost £8500 to install and is also expected to last six years before being sold for approximately 10% of its original cost. Calculate for your manager:

(a) The book value of the original machine after two years.

(b) The annual depreciation charge for the new machine.

(c) The book value of machines as shown in the balance sheet after a further year's use and depreciation (original machine three years old and the new machine one year old).

(d) The total charge for depreciation to show in that year's Profit and Loss Account, in respect of both machines.

As a trainee accountant you visit various clients and assist them with the preparation of Final Accounts. In the following tasks take the information provided by clients and produce the required financial statements. Ignore VAT.

Task 4

Andrew Bayliss has been engaged in an end-of-year stock check at his business premises. The cost valuation of his stock is £3275. The Purchase Day Book reveals from its analysis columns that during the year goods to the value of £27 325 were purchased for resale. A copy of last year's Balance Sheet on file at your office showed that at the end of Andrew Bayliss's last financial year he had stock valued at £3100 at cost price. Calculate Bayliss's cost of goods sold.

Task 5

The Sales Day Book of Andrew Bayliss shows that goods with a sales value of £52 300 were despatched to customers. Of these, the Sales Returns Book shows £450 worth were returned making the Net Sales figure £51 850. With this information you can now prepare a Trading Account for the business at the end of the year to 31 October 19X2.

Task 6

Further checking of Bayliss's Purchases Day Book reveals that the grand totals for the expenses analysis columns are:

Stationery £230
Gas and electricity £1320
Rent and rates £4700
Part-time staff wages £3200
Insurance and other general expenses £2570

In addition the Petty Cash Book showed the following totals for the year:

Postage £98.00
Stationery £56.00
Travel expenses £276.00
General expenses £190

The Profit and Loss Account can now be prepared to establish Andrew Bayliss's Net Profit for the year.

Task 7

After preparing the Trading Account and Profit and Loss Account for Andrew Bayliss you return to your office to have them checked by your supervisor who immediately spots your mistake! 'What about depreciation?' you are asked.

After searching through Bayliss's files and yet another check through the books, you discover that the fittings and equipment at Bayliss's business premises originally cost £7500 two years ago, and that they are being depreciated using the straight line method at the rate of 20% per annum on cost. They must now be depreciated for the third year using this rule. There were no sales or new acquisitions of fittings and equipment during the year.

Your supervisor would like Andrew Bayliss's accounts rewritten to include depreciation and as a single account under the heading of Trading and Profit and Loss Account.

Task 8

After solving all of the problems associated with preparing the Trading and Profit and Loss Account you set about drawing up a Balance Sheet as at 31 October 19X2.

In addition to the information already obtained the following is extracted from the books and file.

(a) Last year's Balance Sheet showed that Andrew Bayliss's capital invested in the business was £7640 at 31 October 19X1.

(b) The Petty Cash Book had a balance of £30 cash in hand on 31 October 19X2.

(c) The business bank account had £1980 to its credit on 31 October 19X2 taking all receipts and payments into consideration.

(d) The amounts outstanding from customers total £2815 on 31 October 19X2.

(e) Unpaid bills at 31 October 19X2 amounted to £1900.

(f) Andrew Bayliss paid himself £9000 out of business funds during the year to 31 October 19X2.

Task 9

A fellow trainee has been working at a business owned by David Johnson, and he has obtained all of the figures required to prepare the Final Accounts of this business. Unfortunately, he is off work ill and you have been asked to finish his work by preparing the Trading and Profit and Loss Account for the year ended 31 October 19X2 and Balance Sheet as at that date. Figures from David Johnson's books and files:

	£
Sales for the year	102 400
Purchases during the year	70 100
Stock valued at cost 31.10.X1	4200
Stock valued at cost 31.10.X2	3700
Expenses paid:	
Rates	3200
Heat and light	2000
Insurance	700
Vehicle running expenses	1500
Wages	5200
Other balances:	
Premises valued at	45 000
Equipment at cost	12 000
Motor vehicle at cost	8000
Amounts owed by customers	5500
Amounts owed to suppliers	3100
Cash in hand	60
Cash in bank	1240
Capital invested at 31.10.X1	59 200

Other items to take into consideration:

1 Included in the amount for insurance is a premium prepaid at 31.10.X2 by £100.
2 Heat and light section does not include electricity bill for £300, two-thirds of which is for electricity consumed in the period to 31.10.X1.
3 Depreciation: (a) the equipment is depreciated at 10% per year on cost, 31.10.X2 will be the end of the fourth year of ownership of this equipment.
(b) Motor vehicles are depreciated at 25% per year on cost. The motor vehicle was new at the beginning of this year.
4 David Johnson has paid himself £1000 per month during the year 31.10.X2.

Task 10

Your next job is to deal with a section of the accounts of JB, Cramley Ltd. The Net Profit has been established but the Appropriation needs drafting. The following details are available.

(a) Net Profit for the year £210 000.

(b) Corporation Tax on profits estimated at £50 000.

(c) The directors of the company have paid an interim dividend to shareholders of 10p for every 375 000 ordinary shares issued – they propose payment of a final dividend of 12p per share.

(d) The Profit and Loss Account Balance (undistributed profits) stands at £417 000 prior to preparation of the Appropriation Account.

Task 11

The Final Accounts of Dinlass Ltd need preparing. You are given the following information as at 30.11.X2 and requested to produce a Trading and Profit and Loss Account (including Appropriation Account) for the year ended 30 November 19X2 and a Balance Sheet at that date. In the first instance the accounts will be for internal use so include as much detail as possible.

		£
Turnover for the year		743 000
Purchases during the year		437 000
Stocks: 30 November 19X1		12 000
30 November 19X2		16 000
Trade debtors		62 000
Trade creditors		45 000
Administration, wages and salaries		60 000
Sales, salaries and commission		120 000
Vehicle running expenses		25 000
Heat and light of premises	Admin. costs	3000
Rates	Admin. costs	5000
Insurance	Admin. costs	2000
Premises at cost		180 000
Motor vehicles at cost		120 000
Equipment at cost		75 000
Depreciation on motor vehicles to 30.11.X1		41 000
Depreciation on equipment to 30.11.X1		25 000
General expenses (1/3 used by administration)		12 000
Interest on long term bank loan		8000
Cash in hand and at bank		15 000
Corporation Tax on profits		14 000
Long-term bank loan		50 000
Profit and Loss Account Balance as at 30.11.X1		32 000

Other items to take into consideration:

1 Depreciation: (a) the equipment is to be further depreciated by £8000 for year ended 30.11.X1.

(b) the motor vehicles are to be further depreciated by £20 000 for year ended 30.11.X2.

2 The directors have not paid an interim dividend but propose to pay a final dividend amounting to 7½% on the nominal value of issued share capital. Issued share capital is 200 000 ordinary shares of £1, fully paid. The authorised share capital is 500 000 ordinary shares of £1.

3 Vehicle running expenses include insurance premiums amounting to £1000 that are prepaid as at 30.11.X2.

4 Sales, salaries and commission does not include £2000 of commission owing, but unpaid to sales staff as at 30.11.X2.

Task 12

After the Final Accounts you have prepared for Dinlass Ltd have been checked, you are requested to rewrite them in a format suitable for publication, disclosing only what is necessary. Your supervisor will prepare any notes to the accounts that are required, so you only have to condense the accounts you have already prepared into a Trading and Profit and Loss Account and Balance Sheet in published format, then pass them to your supervisor for completion.

13

The financial statements of organisations – non-trading organisations

INTRODUCTION

The Final Accounts of business organisations as seen in Chapter 12 are designed to highlight those figures of particular concern to the owners of these organisations. Hence the Trading and Profit and Loss Account emphasises profits and the Balance Sheet shows the investment in the business and the assets that investment has acquired.

However, there are many organisations for whom profit is not a major consideration, if it is a consideration at all. Although there are some major non-profit making organisations in the business world, the two areas in which individuals generally have dealings with non-profit making or non-trading organisations is in the social organisation to which they belong and the local authority whose services they receive.

Fig. 13.1

Residents' Club
Receipts and Payments Account

19X1	*£ p*	*19X1*	*£ p*
Jan 1			
Balance at bank	320.00	Rent of community centre	600.00
Cash in hand	10.00	Committee expenses	25.00
Subscriptions received	480.00	New equipment	170.00
Donation received	100.00	Speakers' expenses	75.00
Sale of old equipment	25.00	Dance expenses	120.00
Receipts from dances	155.00	Cost of refreshment	60.00
Refreshment sales	140.00	Dec 31	
		Balance at bank	160.00
		Cash in hand	20.00
	1230.00		1230.00

Note This is not an account prepared under the accrual concept and therefore the balance on the account is not the profit or loss for the period.

SOCIETIES AND CLUBS

The financial objectives of most clubs and societies are to provide the activities required by the members at reasonable cost and to ensure that at the end of each financial period the club's income at least meets it expenditure. They will usually expect to maintain a credit balance in their bank account on a day-to-day basis.

The club official responsible for the finances is the Treasurer, who will probably maintain a record of each transaction in a Cash Book. From the Cash Book it is possible for the Treasurer to present to the club members, at its Annual General Meeting, a summary of the transaction passing through the Cash Book in the form of a *Receipts and Payments Account* (Fig. 13.1).

You can see that this account uses the totals of various analysis columns as the basis for a summary of the club's transactions for the year.

The Receipts and Payments Account is adequate for small organisations with uncomplicated affairs but the preparation of an *Income and Expenditure Account*, the Profit and Loss of non-trading organisations, under accrual concept principles along with a Balance Sheet is the preferred way of presenting members with a financial report. With an Income and Expenditure Account any surplus (profit) or deficit (loss) for the period is revealed and the Balance Sheet will give members details of the assets and liabilities of the club. Although profit is not the overriding objective of these organisations, many of their activities are motivated by profit in order to raise funds and the format adopted should make the profit or loss on individual activities clear to members. Some social organisations have permanent profit making activities such as a bar, and under these circumstances a Trading Account for this particular activity would be appropriate.

Figure 13.2 shows a full set of final accounts for a club.

Fig. 13.2 Final Accounts of a Club, to include Bar Trading Account, Income and Expenditure Account and Balance Sheet

Dean Court Association
Bar Trading Account
for year ended 30 September 19X2

		£	£
	Bar takings		5300.00
	Cost of sales		
	Bar stocks 1 October 19X1	522.00	
	add Purchases of bar supplies	3075.00	
		3597.00	
	less Bar stocks 30 September 19X2	477.00	
(a)	Cost of bar stock sold	3120.00	
(b)	Depreciation of bar equipment	180.00	
(c)	Part-time bar staff wages	1480.00	
(d)			4700.00
(e)	Surplus to Income and Expenditure Account		600.00

Dean Court Association
Income and Expenditure Account
for year ended 30 September 1987

		£	£
	Income		
(a)	Members' subscriptions		700.00
(b)	Bar Trading Account Surplus		600.00
(c)	Receipts from dances and socials	280.00	
	less Expenses	190.00	90.00
(d)	Donations		75.00
(d)	Prize money		15.00
(d)	Sponsorship		100.00
			1580.00
(e)	*Expenditure*		
	Annual rent for club premises	750.00	
	Caretaker's wages	300.00	
	Heat and light	250.00	
	Treasurer and Committee expenses	20.00	
	Depreciation of furniture and fittings	40.00	
	Quiz league fee and fixture expenses	40.00	
	Town carnival entry fee and expenses	50.00	
			1450.00
(f)	Surplus of Income over Expenditure		130.00

Dean Court Association
Balance Sheet
as at 30 September 19X2

		£	£	£
(a)	*Fixed Assets*			
	Furniture and fittings at cost		400.00	
	less Accumulated depreciation		240.00	
				160.00
	Bar equipment at cost		1800.00	
	less Accumulated depreciation		540.00	
				1260.00
				1420.00
(b)	*Current Assets*			
	Bar stocks		470.00	
	Subscriptions owing		10.00	
	Cash in hand and at bank		373.00	
			860.00	
(c)	*Current Liabilities*			
	Creditor for bar supplies	200.00		
	Electricity charges accrued	40.00		
	Subscriptions in advance	20.00	260.00	
	Net current assets			600.00
				2020.00
(d)	Accumulated funds as at 30 September 19X1			1890.00
(e)	Surplus for the year			130.00
(f)	Accumulated funds as at 30 September 19X2			2020.00

Bar Trading Account

The account is prepared as described in Chapter 12; there is more detail in the descriptions because the account is prepared for a non-financial readership. Extra items are included in order to obtain the full cost of providing the bar service.

Key to entries

(a) This is simply the cost price of the bar sales
(b) and (c) Costs specifically related to the bar service are included in the cost of sales figure, in this case it is clear that depreciation of bar equipment and bar staff wages must be included in bar costs in order to calculate the true profit.
(d) Total cost of bar sales (a), (b) and (c).
(e) The profit from the bar service. This is often described as a *surplus* by non-trading organisations. It is transferred to the Income and Expenditure Account as part of Income.

Income and Expenditure Account

Income from various sources is listed, where there are specific expenses associated with generating certain income it is quite in order to net the expenses from the income and show the surplus for that activity, see item (c). The expenses are listed giving as detailed description as practical.

Key to entries

(a) Subscriptions may not be the largest source of income, but it is often the basic form and the cost of membership subscription is an important matter to members, so this item is often given first place in the income list.
(b) Transferred from the Bar Trading Account.
(c) The net income from the dances and socials is shown so that members can clearly see if a profit or loss was made.
(d) Sundry sources of income.
(e) The expenditure items are self-explanatory and this is as it should be in the accounts of this type of organisation.
(f) Note the use of the term surplus instead of profit; this is often employed.

Balance Sheet

The usual categories appear but with some entries peculiar to the individual organisations. The term 'Accumulated Fund' is often employed instead of Capital, this is because it is more likely to have grown from Accumulated Income and Expenditure Account surpluses than have been created by a specific investment.

Key to entries

(a) Fixed assets, normally nothing exceptional, although some organisations may have special fixed assets, e.g. sports equipment. Fixed assets are likely to be depreciated, but the method may be unusual and the rate of depreciation may be low.

(b) Current assets will contain the usual items although the descriptions may be fuller and in some cases different. In this case 'Debtors' is dropped in favour of a more specific description – 'Subscriptions owing'. Members who owe their subscriptions to the club are its debtors in the same way that external parties who owe money are its debtors.

(c) Current liabilities has a new item, 'Subscriptions in advance', in addition to the normal entries. If members have paid their subscriptions prior to the date on which they fall due then these members are the creditors of the organisation until the date on which subscriptions become payable.

(d)(e)(f) In the example, the association's capital is described as accumulated fund and its profit as a surplus. The new labels do not alter the normal treatment of these items. The surplus is added to the opening Accumulated Fund Balance to give a new balance at the end of the financial year.

Note that there are no drawings by a proprietor or dividends paid to shareholders, so the surplus from the Income and Expenditure Account is accumulated without any deductions.

While there are no legal constraints on format and content of the accounts of clubs and societies, they would be advised to follow accepted accounting conventions in the preparation of their accounts to avoid confusion over the information presented. Organisations with charitable status are obliged to submit annual accounts to the Charity Commissioners.

LOCAL AUTHORITIES

Like the clubs and societies just considered, local authorities are concerned with generating sufficient income to meet their planned expenditure on services. Some activities may be profitable but the earning of profits is not the overriding consideration of these organisations. This is reflected in the financial information they produce for ratepayers. The financial statement sent to ratepayers with the rates demand is not so much a report on the past financial performance, rather it is a forecast of the income and expenditure on services for the coming year; this is to explain to ratepayers the services that will be provided, partly financed by their payments. Last year's figures are given, but the emphasis is on the coming year and as a consequence the statement is described as a 'Budget', i.e. a financial plan for the coming year.

Local authorities provide more information about their finances than that shown in Fig. 13.3, not only in the information for ratepayers sent with each demand, but by the publication of an *Annual Report*. However, it is the link between planned spending and the rates which is the important information for the majority of ratepayers.

Local authority expenditure has in recent years become the subject of increasing Central Government scrutiny and control. The objectives of this diminuation of local automony are mainly to be found in the economic and political spheres but in part it is a striving to achieve value for money.

Councils can no longer raise and spend money as they like, they are obliged by the financial constraints placed upon them, to manage their affairs efficiently and to be effective in the delivery of the services they provide, i.e. give value for money. In the light of this, the information provided to ratepayers attempts to demonstrate that the highest level of services is being provided at minimum cost and that any rate rises are kept to the lowest level possible.

SUMMARY

Not all organisations are profit-centred, therefore the financial reports these non-profit making organisations produce will reflect the financial objectives, e.g. break-even, charitable giving, and value for money.

Fig. 13.3 Extract from New Forest District Council Budget

New Forest District Council 1987/88

The Council's Budget

Rates to be collected	1987/88	
	Rate in £	*Amount raised*
	p	£
For New Forest District Council	20.9	5202010
For Hampshire County Council	184.1	45804080
	205.0	51006090

New Forest District Council items of expenditure	1987/88 *Gross expenditure*	*Deduct income*	*Net expenditure*
	£000	£000	£000
Car parks	250	117	133
Cemeteries	103	26	77
Coast protection	282	–	282
Concessionary bus fares	164	–	164
Council housing	10,961	10,776	185
Other housing	3,738	3,140	598
Environmental health	705	98	607
Grant aid schemes	130	–	130
Land charges	141	170	CR 29
Planning & building control	1,688	500	1,188
Public conveniences	201	–	201
Recreation centres and golf course	1,443	961	482
Refuse collection	1,526	97	1,429
Registration of electors	109	3	106
Other services including agency services	2,876	1,993	883
Total expenditure on services	24,317	17,881	6,436
Plus rate rebates	3,014	2,794	220
Cost of collecting rate income	547	16	531
Revenue contribution to capital outlay	560	–	560
Contingencies	270	–	270
Interest on balances	–	850	CR 850
Use of reserves		60	CR 60
	28,708	21,601	7,107
Transfer to balances		113	CR 113
	28,708	21,714	6,994
Less Government block grant	–	1,792	CR1,792
NFDC rate borne expenditure	28,708	23,506	5,202
	(a)	(b)	(c)

Key to entries

(a) The planned expenditure by NFDC.

(b) Income generated from some services plus government grant and the use of funds already held by the Council.

(c) The difference between (a) and (b) which is the expenditure that must be met from the rates. The rates to be collected and this net expenditure figure are linked in the illustration to highlight the source of these funds.

TASKS

Task 1

As the Treasurer of the Northlea Amateur Dramatics Society (NADS), you produce a Receipts and Payments Account for each production. The latest production has just finished and the account can now be drawn up from the following details:

Production of *The Importance of Being Earnest*:
Treasurer's expenses £20.00
Ticket sales £240.00
Refreshment sales £50.00
Hire of hall £15.00 per night for three nights
Hire of costumes £110.00
Purchase of refreshments £17.00
Sales of programmes £23.00
Printing of programmes £45.00
Sale of advertising space in programmes £50.00
Sundry production expenses £40.00
Preparation of scenery and props £95.00
Sponsorship from Blandfords Ltd £50.00
Advertising £15.00
Balance to Bank Account £26.00

Task 2

During a year NADS put on four productions, for each of which the Treasurer produces a Receipts and Payments Account. The membership have requested that a statement be drawn up covering the whole year to show if the society is making a profit or loss on its activities. This you have agreed to do and the following details are extracted from your books and records for the year ended 31.12.X1.

Income received	
Ticket sales	
Pantomime	£360.00
The Importance of Being Earnest	£240.00
West Side Story	£210.00
Major Barbara	£70.00
Sponsorship	
Blandfords Ltd	£50.00
Deacon Financial Services	£100.00
Refreshment sales in total	£160.00
Sale of programmes in total	£80.00
Sale of advertising space in progs	£200.00
Membership subscriptions	£500.00
Expenses paid	
Hire of hall for all performances and rehearsals	£195.00
Hire of costumes, props, etc.	£530.00
Purchase of refreshments	£75.00
Expenses associated with production	£260.00
Treasurer and society officer's expenses	£110.00
Printing of programmes	£180.00
Advertising	£60.00
Materials for scenery and prop preparation	£360.00
Hire of sound equipment	£120.00

At the end of the year the Treasurer reported that one ticket seller had not yet paid to the society £30.00 in respect of tickets sold on the society's behalf. This was for the *Major Barbara* production. The society still owed £20 to Wigs and Co Ltd for the hire of costumes. These two items had not been included in the Income and Expenses listed above.

Produce an Income and Expenditure Account for the membership, in such a way that the information is displayed in the most informative way.

Task 3

The Forest Vale Rugby Club's financial year ended on 31 December 19X2. It is now time for you as treasurer to produce the Club's Final Accounts for the year. The following details about the club's finances have been extracted from the books and records for the year ended 31 December 19X2.

Bar purchases £4110
Bar takings £8320
Bar stocks 31.1.X2 £530
Bar stocks 31.1.X2 £660
Stewards' wages £3100
Hire of club premises to other organisations £300.00
Rent and rates for grounds and club premises £1200
Membership subscriptions £1900
Groundsman/caretaker's wages £4600
Heating and lighting of premises £1200
Sundry administration expenses £450
Club equipment at cost £3500
Accumulated depreciation as at 31.12.X1 £1050
Balance at Bank £740
Owing for bar purchases £200
Accumulated fund as at 31.12.X1 £1300

Note the equipment is to be further depreciated by 10% of costs during year ended 31.12.X2.

Three statements are required:

1 Bar Trading Account for year ended 31.12.X2
2 Income and Expenditure Account for year ended 31.12.X2
3 a Balance Sheet as at 31.12.X2

Task 4

Your local council has estimated that it will need to raise £6.4 million by rates to meet its net expenditure during the next financial year. Rates details are shown on p 95.

Rates to be collected	**Rate in the £**	**Amount raised**
Midland District Council	20p	£6 400 000

This estimate has been based on the assumption that the Central Government block grant will be £2.1 million. If, when the block grants are announced, the basis for assessing Midland District Council's grant is changed and they only receive £1.78 million, what extra amount has to be raised by rates and to what level will the rate in the £ rise.

Task 5

After establishing the new rate in Task 4, the local authorities settle a wages claim from their manual workers at a level higher than anticipated; this will add £160 000 to the council's costs above that allowed for in the budgets. Calculate the increased rate in the £ to cover this additional cost.

14 Management accounting

INTRODUCTION

We have seen in Chapter 7 that management accounting is concerned with the provision of financial information that enables managers to efficiently organise the running of the business and to make rational predictions about future performance.

This activity can be described as planning and control; it is similar in nature to the personal planning and control of finance discussed in Chapter 4, but of course the scale is larger. As with personal finance, the monetary expression of the plans is a Budget, control takes place through the comparison of actual with budget and reacting to the difference.

THE CONTROL CYCLE

Management accountants are concerned with the critical stages in the control cycle. They participate in:

1 Planning, i.e. giving management the financial information on which planning decisions can be made; this may involve providing management with a range

Fig. 14.1 The control cycle

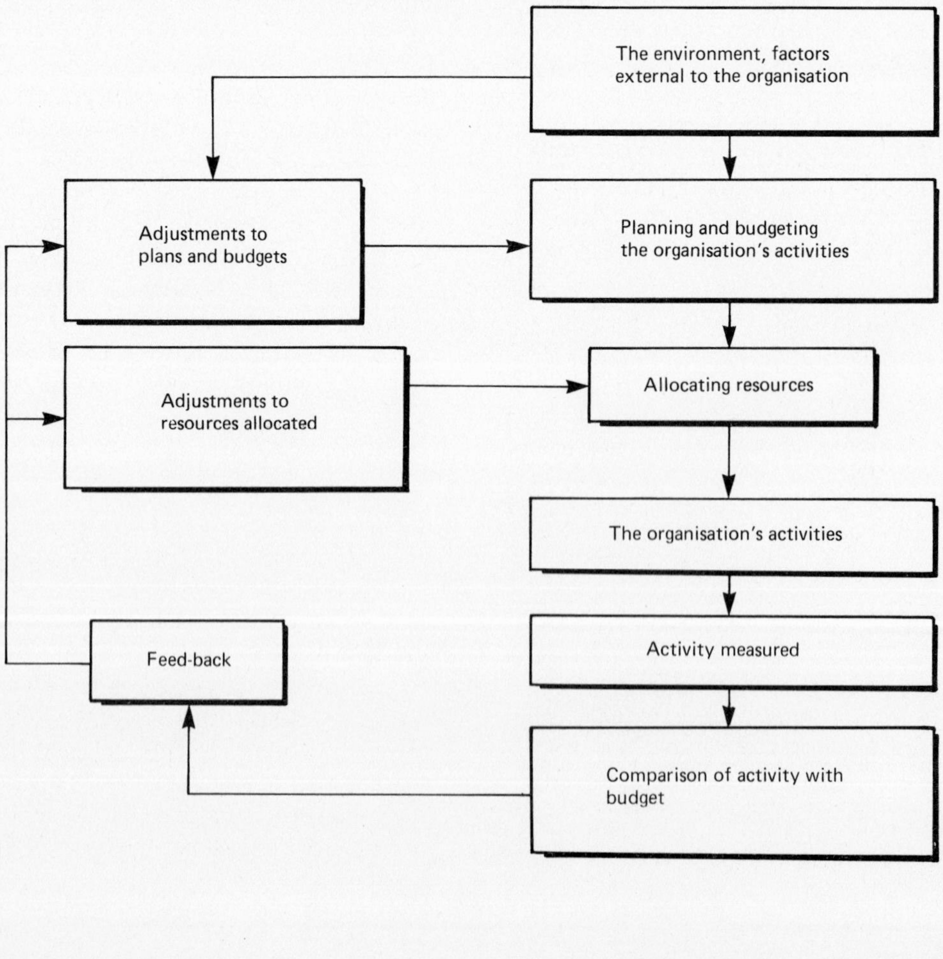

of options and their financial implications. When the plans are established, the accountants then translate them into budgets and advise management of any further adjustments required.
2 Measuring the activity of the organisation, using cost accounting techniques to provide the date required when the actual activity and its associated revenue and costs is compared with the budget.
3 Comparing actual with budget which provides the feed-back required by management to control the organisation. This feed-back often takes the format of a *Variance Report*, that is any variation between budget and actual performance is reported to management. Both under and over budget results are reported.
4 Adjusting resource allocation which requires further accounting information so that the cost implications of any changes can be assessed by management.
5 Adjusting the plans, which requires adjusted budgets to be drawn up.

BUDGETING

The controlling process revolves around the budget; this performs various functions, some of which are behavioural rather than financial in that the budget is prepared from the contributions of all managers within the organisation and can therefore be seen as a collective commitment to the organisation's objectives. There are various constraints within an organisation on its level of activity; each section manager will therefore build into that section's budget its limitations and hence the complete budget when collated should be a statement of achievable standards that all are happy to be judged against. The one constraint that overrides all others is called the *limiting factor*. Often the limiting factor lies in the area of either Sales, i.e. the number of products that can reasonably be expected to be sold in the period or Production, i.e. in a given period the production capacity of an organisation can be limited. In the long term it is possible to expand but until that occurs, production capacity will limit the sales volume.

The process of compiling individual section budgets and co-ordinating their inclusion into a *Master Budget* (a projected Profit Statement and Balance Sheet) is complicated. Figure 14.2 (page 98) outlines the procedure.

Sales, Production and Raw Material Purchase Budgets

Example

CBN Ltd can sell 10 000 of its electronic heating control systems during the next accounting period, Period 1. Included in the product is a digital display unit. The organisation has stocks of 500 finished systems and 250 digital display units at the start of the period. In anticipation of demand for the product in the next but one accounting period, Period 2, the management of the organisation plan to have doubled their current stock levels at the end of Period 1. The Sales, Production and Raw Material Purchase Budgets will be as follows:

Period 1	*Units*
Sales Budget	10 000
Production Budget	
Sales requirement	10 000
add Stock requirement	1000
	11 000
less Existing stocks	500
Actual production required	10 500
Raw Materials Purchase Budget (Digital display unit)	
Production requirement	10 500
add Stock requirement	500
	11 000
less Existing stocks	250
Purchase requirement	10 750

Notice the effect of existing and required stock levels on the Production and Purchasing Budgets. Because the stock levels are to be increased both of these budgets include an element of producing or buying for stock. Therefore a sales requirement of 10 000 complete control systems means a purchase requirement of 10 750 digital display units.

In this example, sales volume is taken to be the limiting factor, however, if on contacting the digital display unit supplier it was found that supply would be limited to 9000 units in Period 1, then this component would become the limiting factor and the sales and stock increase plans would have to be amended to take this external constraint into consideration.

Cash Budget

This important budget is used to evaluate the effect of the planned level of activity upon the organisation's Bank Account. Throughout the period under consideration, there will be a constant stream of transactions, cash inflows and outflows, passing through the account. If outflows exceed inflows then the difference must be financed in some way and the arrangements for this finance must be made in advance. Because of the credit periods given and taken in business transactions, the preparation of the Cash Budget is a complex

Fig. 14.2 How to draft the Master Budget

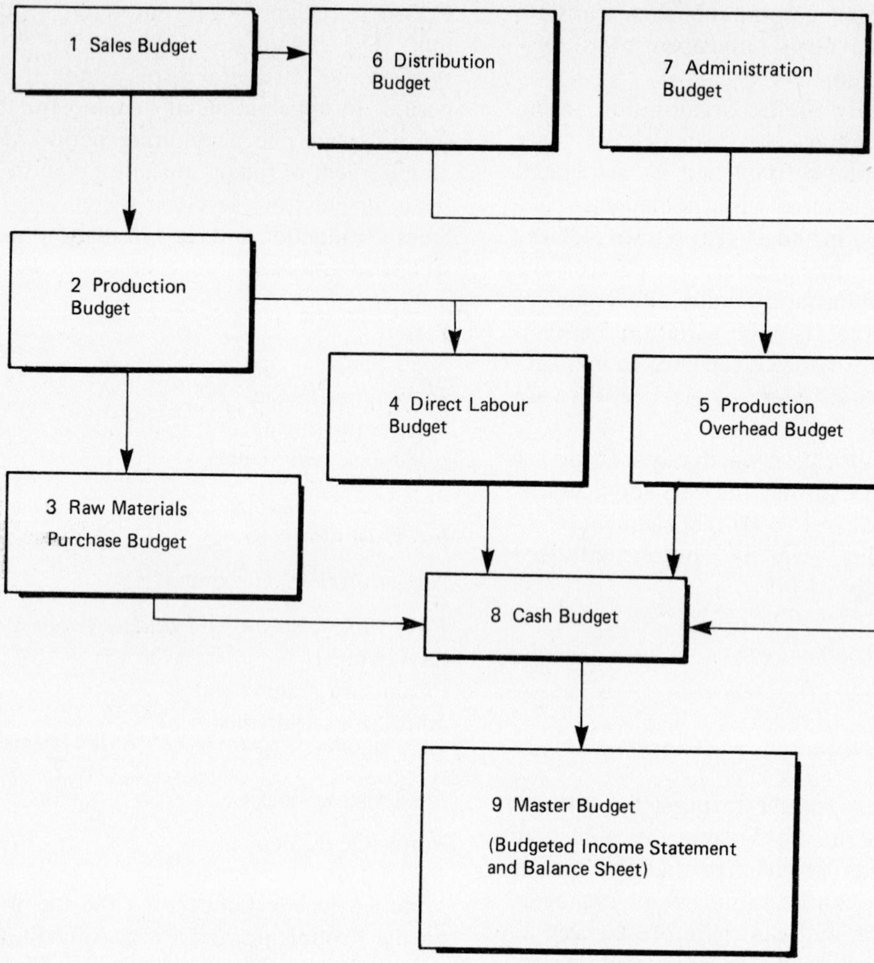

Key to items

1 Sales Budget: planned sales for the period.
2 Production Budget: production required to meet sales requirement taking into consideration stocks of finished goods.
3 Raw Materials Purchase Budget: the raw materials required for production taking into consideration stocks of raw materials.
4 Direct Labour Budget: production labour required for the budgeted production levels.
5 Production Overheads Budget: the expected level of overheads for the budgeted production level.
6 Distribution Budget: the selling and distribution expenses that will be incurred at the budgeted level of sales.
7 Administration Budget: the administration expenses for the planned level of activity.
8 Cash Budget: the net effect of all the cash inflows from sales revenue and cash outflows to pay expenses. Also included will be planned capital expenditure and any borrowing.
9 Master Budget: gives the planned profit at the end of the period and states the expected financial state of the organisation regarding assets and liabilities when the plans have been achieved.

procedure. The format of the budget is similar to that of the personal budget shown in Chapter 4. In the following examples the months in which the Bank Account will have an overdrawn balance are clearly shown and we can see if the company will achieve its objective of clearing any overdraft by the end of December.

Example

Tival Ltd is preparing its budgets for the next six months. The Cash Budget (Fig. 14.3) is to be prepared from the section budgets and these are already available:

(a) *Sales budget*: £100 000 per month, July to September;
£120 000 per month, October to December.

(b) *Raw Materials Purchase Budget*: £30 000 per month.

(c) *Direct Labour Budget*: £10 000 per month.

(d) *Production Overhead Budget*: £20 000 per month (including depreciation).

(e) *Distribution Budget*: £10 000 per month, July to September.
£15 000 per month, October to December.

(f) *Administration Budget*: £5000 per month.

Other planned expenditure:
(a) Taxation £65 000 September
(b) New equipment £25 000 December

Note

1 One month's credit is given to customers. Debtors at 1 June are expected to be £90 000.
2 Suppliers give two months' credit, creditors at 1 June £45 000 payable, £20 000 in July and £25 000 in August.
3 The year's depreciation charge is £12 000 and it has been included in the Production Overhead Budget on a monthly basis.
4 All other expenses are paid in the month incurred.
5 The company currently has a £50 000 bank overdraft which it would like to clear by the end of the year.

Fig. 14.3

Tival Ltd
Cash Budget for July to December

	July	*Aug*	*Sept*	*Oct*	*Nov*	*Dec*
Receipts	*£000*	*£000*	*£000*	*£000*	*£000*	*£000*
from Trade debtors	90	100	100	100	120	120
Payments						
to Trade creditors	20	25	30	30	30	30
Direct labour	10	10	10	10	10	10
Production overheads	19	19	19	19	19	19
Distribution	10	10	10	15	15	15
Administration	5	5	5	5	5	5
Taxation			65			
Equipment						25
	64	69	139	79	79	104
Balance b/f	(50)	(24)	7	(32)	(11)	30
Add Receipts	90	100	100	100	120	120
	40	76	107	68	109	150
Less Payments	64	69	139	79	79	104
Balance c/f	(24)	7	(32)	(11)	30	46

Note

1 Receipts from trade debtors: this section starts with the amount owed by debtors in July and then follows with the value of July's sales received in August, etc.
2 Payments to trade creditors follow a similar pattern except that in this case it starts with the amounts owed in July and August and, because suppliers allow two months' credit, the payments are made in the second month following receipt of the goods, i.e. July purchases are paid for in September.
3 Production overheads are reduced by £12 000/12 = £1000 per month for depreciation. Depreciation is a non-cash expense and therefore should not be recorded in the Cash Budget.
4 Overdrawn amounts are indicated by the use of brackets, e.g. the period started with an overdraft of £50 000 which is shown as (50) and at the end of July this had been reduced to (24).

Master Budget

The Master Budget consists of an estimated Income Statement for the budget period and an estimated Balance Sheet at the period end. These statements, although estimates of a future situation, are drawn up using the same concepts and conventions as a set of Final Accounts reporting on past events.

Example

Tival Ltd wishes to produce a Master Budget for the budget period July to December. In addition to the information in the previous example, the following is available concerning balances on the books at 1 July.
Issued share capital £250 000 in £1 ordinary shares
Profit and Loss Account balance £310 000
Fixed assets at book value £629 000
Stock of raw materials and finished goods £20 000. There is no planned change in this level of stockholding.
Note Taxation and dividends are ignored in this example.

Tival Ltd
Budgeted Income Statement for 6 months ending 31 December

	£	£
Sales		660 000
Cost of sales		360 000
Gross profit		300 000
Distribution expenses	75 000	
Administration expenses	30 000	105 00
Profit		195 000
Profit and Loss Account balance b/f		310 000
Profit and Loss Account balance c/f		505 000

Tival Ltd
Budgeted Balance Sheet as at 31 December

	£	£
Net assets employed		
Fixed assets at book value		629 000
Current assets		
Stock	20 000	
Debtors	120 000	
Bank	46 000	
	186 000	
Current liabilities		
Creditors	60 000	
Net current assets		126 000
		755 000
Capital and reserves		
Issued share capital £1 ordinary shares		250 000
Profit and Loss Account		505 000
		755 000

Workings – Income Statement

1 *Sales*

3 months × £100 000 per month	300 000
3 months × £120 000 per month	360 000
Total sales for the period	660 000

2 *Cost of sales*

The organisation described is a manufacturing business. This means that the cost of sales will not be found by simply taking the purchases figure and adjusting for stock levels but by adding together all of the production costs.

Note Stock levels are planned to be the same at the start and finish of the period, therefore the purchases figure does not need to be adjusted.

Cost of sales is found by:

Raw materials purchased:	
6 months × £30 000 per month	180 000
Direct labour costs:	
6 months × £10 000 per month	60 000
Production overhead cost:	
6 months × £20 000 per month	120 000
Total production cost of sales	360 000

3 *Distribution expenses*

3 months × £10 000 per month	30 000
3 months × £15 000 per month	45 000
Total distribution expenses	75 000

4 *Administration expenses*

6 months × £5 000 per month	30 000

Workings – Balance Sheet

1 *Fixed assets*	£
Book value on 1 June	610 000
less Depreciation 6 months @ 1000 p.m.	6000
	604 000
Plus Cost of new equipment purchased in December	25 000
Book value on 31 December	629 000

2 *Current assets*

(a) Stock as per notes

(b) Debtors £120 000 owing for December sales

(c) Bank balance as per final balance on Cash Budget

3 *Current liabilities*

Creditors: two months' raw materials purchases at £30 000 per month

4 *Profit and Loss Account balance from Income Statement*

PROJECT APPRAISAL

Management accountants can be involved in assessing the financial viability of plans that extend well beyond the next financial period. The assessment criteria for investments in future projects are associated with risk. The *risk assessment* can be expressed in a number of ways, but simply put they fall into two areas:

1 How quickly will the organisation get its money back; the quicker the better in high-risk situations.
2 Does the return on the investment match that which the organisation considers sufficient to compensate it for the risk taken.

Two methods of evaluating projects will be considered, they are not mutually exclusive and may both be employed as assessment criteria.

Pay-back period

An organisation may set a time limit on the period during which the returns from the investment should repay the sum initially invested, i.e. if £20 000 is to be invested how long will it take to get £20 000 back from the investment returns? Projects which fail to meet the desired *pay-back period* are excluded, and if a number of projects are to be considered preference is given to the project with the fastest pay back.

Example

The Delaforce Engineering Co Ltd wishes to purchase machinery in order to enter a new market providing a specialist engineering service. Two machines are on offer, details of costs and potential returns are given, below.

	Machine A	*Machine B*
	£	£
Installation cost	50 000	72 000
Cash inflow generated:		
Year 1	17 000	21 000
Year 2	18 000	23 000
Year 3	20 000	27 000
Year 4	19 000	24 000
Year 5	16 000	22 000
Totals	90 000	117 000

Machine A will pay back in two years and nine months. Machine B will pay back in three years and two weeks.

Machine A is chosen because of the shortest pay-back period even though the project would gain greater net returns from the use of Machine B if the whole five years is taken into consideration – £45 000 as opposed to £40 000. If the company had a maximum pay-back period of three years, Machine B would be excluded on those grounds as well.

Discounted cashflow

The pay-back period method of capital investment project appraisal has its merits, particularly in high-risk situations, but in assessing the returns one important factor is ignored – that is the *time value for money*.

The time value for money refers to the fact that if a certain sum is required at some time in the future, a lesser amount can be invested today and the added interest will provide the required amount in the specified time.

In project appraisal, this idea is used to 'discount' the future returns in such a way that we can establish the investment required today, at a given rate of interest, that will provide the required sum in the specified period. The investment required today is called the *present value* of the future return. Present values are found by the use of tables (*see* Fig. 14.4).

Example

You wish to invest a sum today which will have grown to £3000 in three year's time. Your building society is offering 9% p.a. for investments of this nature. Assuming investments rates remain at 9% for the full three years, then the investment required will be:

£3000.00 × 0.7722* = £2316.60

* From the table in Fig. 14.4, the present value of £1 received in three years at an interest rate of 9%

You can prove this to be correct by the use of the compound interest formula:

$$\text{Amount} = \text{Investment} \times (1 + \text{rate}/100)^{n \text{ years}}$$

$$\text{Amount} = £2316.60 \times (1 + 9/100)^{3}$$

$$= £2316.60 \times 1.29503$$

$$= £3000.07$$

The 0.7 is caused by rounding errors and is ignored.

If the example used to demonstrate pay-back periods is reassessed using this method, we find the following if a required rate of return of 12% p.a. is given.

Note that this assessment method assumes that all cashflows occur at the end of the year under consideration.

Machine A

End of year	*Cashflow* £	*12% Discount factor*	*Present value* £
1	17 000	0.8929	15 179.3
2	18 000	0.7972	14 349.6
3	20 000	0.7118	14 236.0
4	19 000	0.6355	12 074.5
5	16 000	0.5674	9078.4
		Present value of all returns	64 917.8

Machine B

End of year	*Cashflow* £	*12% Discount factor* £	*Present value* £
1	21 000	0.8929	18 750.9
2	23 000	0.7972	18 335.6
3	27 000	0.7118	19 218.6
4	24 000	0.6355	15 252.0
5	22 000	0.5674	12 482.8
		Present value of all returns	84 039.9

In the case of Machine A, it would be necessary to invest £64 917.8 today, at 12%, in order to be able to obtain from the investment the cashflows shown in years 1 to 5. However, it is proposed to invest only £50 000 in the machine so the internal investment must be generating a higher return than 12% because a

Fig. 14.4

Table of the present value of 1 received in 'n' years % rate of interest

'n' years	8	9	10	11	12	13	14	15	16	17	18	19	20
1	0.9259	0.9174	0.9091	0.9009	0.8929	0.8850	0.8772	0.8696	0.8621	0.8547	0.8475	0.8403	0.8333
2	0.8573	0.8417	0.8264	0.8116	0.7972	0.7831	0.7695	0.7561	0.7432	0.7305	0.7182	0.7062	0.6944
3	0.7938	0.7722	0.7513	0.7312	0.7118	0.6931	0.6750	0.6575	0.6407	0.6244	0.6086	0.5934	0.5787
4	0.7350	0.7084	0.6830	0.6587	0.6355	0.6133	0.5921	0.5718	0.5523	0.5337	0.5158	0.4987	0.4823
5	0.6806	0.6499	0.6209	0.5935	0.5674	0.5428	0.5194	0.4972	0.4761	0.4561	0.4371	0.4190	0.4019
6	0.6302	0.5963	0.5645	0.5346	0.5066	0.4803	0.4556	0.4323	0.4104	0.3898	0.3704	0.3521	0.3349
7	0.5835	0.5470	0.5132	0.4817	0.4523	0.4251	0.3996	0.3759	0.3538	0.3332	0.3139	0.2959	0.2791
8	0.5403	0.5019	0.4665	0.4339	0.4039	0.3762	0.3506	0.3269	0.3050	0.2848	0.2660	0.2487	0.2326
9	0.5002	0.4604	0.4241	0.3909	0.3606	0.3329	0.3075	0.2843	0.2630	0.2434	0.2255	0.2090	0.1938
10	0.4632	0.4224	0.3855	0.3522	0.3220	0.2946	0.2697	0.2472	0.2267	0.2080	0.1911	0.1756	0.1615

smaller initial investment is required to obtain the same return. The size of the extra amount required for investment externally to the organisation, to give the same return, is called the *Net Present Value*.

Thus, for Machine A Net Present Value (NPV) = £64 917.8 − £50 000 = £14 917.80
The NPV of the investment in Machine B is found by:

£84 039.90 − £72,000 = £12 039.90

Both of these alternative investments give positive NPVs and are both therefore worthwhile investments because they meet the minimum return criteria for the organisation. If one is to be chosen in preference to the other, the project with the highest positive NPV is chosen.

Projects that give a negative NPV are discarded as not giving sufficiently high returns.

Discounted cashflow can be used to assess the least cost method of acquiring an asset. Here the cash inflows and outflows are assessed and the lowest present value alternative is chosen.

Example

Dolby and Son wish to purchase a new van which is expected to last for about four years, when it will be sold for £1000. They have been offered the following methods of obtaining the van:

1 Outright purchase for cash £8000 less a discount of 7½% = £7 400
2 Hire purchase at a special offer rate, deposit £2000 then 3 payments at the end of years 1, 2 and 3 of £2300 p.a.
3 Lease the van for 4 annual payments of £2960 at the end of each year. The van would remain the property of the leasing company who would repossess it at the end of the agreement. The business could borrow money at 15% from its bankers (this is the business's *cost of capital*).

Evaluations

Note that because inflows and outflows are being assessed in the same evaluation, the NPV is automatically calculated.

1 Cash purchase

End of year	*Cash inflow (outflow)*	*15% discount factor*	*Present value*
	£		£
* 0	(7400)	1.0000	(7400)
4	1000	0.5718	571.8
		NPV	(6828.2)

* End of year '0' indicates the start of year 1. The discount factor for a sum required today is 1 if you require £x today you must invest £x today − no interest is paid on an investment immediately withdrawn.

2 Hire purchase

End of year	*Cash inflow (outflow)*	*15% Discount factor*	*Present value*
	£		£
0	(2000)	1.000	(2000.00)
1	(2300)	0.8696	(2000.08)
2	(2300)	0.7561	(1739.03)
3	(2300)	0.6575	(1512.25)
4	1000	0.5718	571.80
		NPV	(6679.56)

3 Leasing

End of year	*Cash inflow (outflow)*	*15% Discount factor*	*Present value*
	£		£
1	(2960)	0.8696	(2574.02)
2	(2960)	0.7561	(2238.06)
3	(2960)	0.6575	(1946.20)
4	(2960)	0.5718	(1692.53)
		NPV	(8450.81)

The evaluation of the alternative shows that hire purchase gives the lowest NPV and is therefore the least cost alternative if the time value of money is taken into consideration.

SUMMARY

Management accounting is the provision of financial information by which the organisation's management can make decisions about business control and planning.

The core of the business control cycle is the budgeting process which specifies the required performance levels of all of the organisation's sections and is used to assess their actual performance.

Future projects requiring capital investment are risky but the estimated returns from proposed projects can be assessed in the light of criteria which take the risk into consideration by setting a pay-back time scale or a minimum percentage rate of return.

TASKS

Task 1

Your organisation's Sales Department have estimated the sales demand for Assembly 730 at 20 000 units in the next period. You are required to prepare the Production and Purchase Budgets, in units, relating to this product. The following information is available.

Assembly 730 is made up of three components that are bought from outside suppliers, components A, B and C. The current stocks are:

Finished goods: Assembly 730 – 400 units
Components: A – 200 units
B – 400 units
C – 100 units

Management wishes to reduce the stock of finished goods to half its present level by the end of the next period and to bring component stocks to the same level as that of the finished assembly.

Task 2

The Sales Department have received an order for 100 000 units of component W7. The Production Department have 190 000 labour hours available in the next period that could be committed to this order. Component W7 takes two labour hours to produce. The raw material content of component W7 is 1 kg of CD302.

Current stocks
Finished goods: Component W7 – 7000 units
Raw materials : CD 302 – 500 kg
Minimum acceptable stock levels are 1000 units of component W7 and 100 kg of raw material CD302.

Prepare Production and Raw Material Purchase Budgets, in units, for the above order.

Task 3

A customer has asked how many units of product TL20 can be supplied in the next period. From the Production, Purchasing and Stores Departments you gather the following information:

TL20 takes three labour hours to produce.
The number of labour hours available in the next period that can be committed to TL20 production is 3600.
Raw material content: 2 kg of Chemizap per unit of TL20.
Raw material stocks: 200 kg of Chemizap. The supplier can provide 2000 kg during the next period.

You are required to:
(a) Identify the limiting factor;
(b) Write to the customer advising the maximum quantity of product TL20 that can be supplied in the next period.

Task 4

David Wilkinson has asked for your assistance in preparing a Cash Budget for a proposed business venture. He is sure that he will need overdraft finance from his bank but cannot establish how much nor the time his account will remain overdrawn. The financial details of his business for the first six months are provided below:

Receipts
1 Capital provided by David Wilkinson to start the business: £6500.

2 *Sales*	*Cash*	*Credit*
Month 1	£1000	£500
Months 2 and 3	£1500	£1000
Months 4, 5 and 6	£2000	£2000

Payment for credit sales is received in the month following the sale.

Payments
1 Payments for stock will be on a cash basis:

Month 1	£1000
Months 2 and 3	£1200
Months 4, 5 and 6	£2000

2 Rent of premises: £200 per month paid quarterly in advance.
3 General running expenses: £400 paid in month incurred.
4 Administration expenses: £200 paid in month incurred.
5 Cash withdrawn for personal use by David Wilkinson: £500 per month.
6 In the first month the following payments will be made:
(a) Purchase of fittings £3000
(b) £2000 deposit on motor van followed by monthly payment of £100 per month commencing in Month 1.

Prepare a Cash Budget for David Wilkinson's first six months in business to show him his maximum overdraft and the month during which it will be repaid.

Task 5

Briomond Ltd is preparing its budgets for the next twelve months. The individual section managers have prepared their budgets and they are now to be collated into the Cash Budget for the period 1 January to 31 December. The budget details are given below:

1 Balance at Bank on 1 January estimated to be £5000.
2 Sales budget estimates show sales in January to April at £45 000 per month inclusive, rising thereafter by £2000 per month until the end of the year. The sales are all cash sales.
3 Purchases Budget is £24 000 per month, and rising by £1000 per month from May. Payments are made one month in arrears. At 1 Jan payments due to trade creditors were £24 000, all for payment in January.
4 Direct Labour Budget is £11 000 per month January to June rising to £13 000 per month July to December.
5 Production Overhead Budget is £9000 per month (this includes depreciation at the rate of £1000 per month).

6 Administration Expenses Budget is £4000 per month.
7 Capital Expenditure Budget £10 000 in December.

Prepare a Cash Budget for Briomond Ltd for the next twelve months and establish:
(a) Balance at Bank on 31 December;
(b) Maximum overdraft required;
(c) The months during which the Bank Account will be overdrawn.

Task 6

The Managing Director of Briomond Ltd has approved the section budgets and the Cash Budget but required a budgeted Income Statement before putting the full plan for the next financial year before the Board of Directors. You are asked to prepare this statement. Note that the Purchases and Production Budgets were based on the assumption that no changes would take place in average stock levels.

Task 7

Richard Lovat is making plans for a business selling a fast-food product from a market stall. He has to purchase the machinery for making and cooking the food. Two manufacturers offer models of a size suitable for his business, they differ in purchase price, output rate, and hence earning potential. Details are given below for a four-year period. (After four years it is impossible to predict with any degree of certainty the financial situation of the business).

	Machine A (*High output rate*)	*Machine B* (*Normal output rate*)
Cost for Year 0	10 500	8500
Projected net cash inflow		
for Year 1	5000	5000
Year 2	6000	6000
Year 3	8000	6000
Year 4	8000	6000

As this product and the chosen selling site are unusual the project has a high risk of failure. In this case Richard is looking for a quick pay-back – advise him of the machine to choose.

Task 8

Richard realises that the choice of machine by pay-back criteria may limit the overall returns on the project and so he is prepared to relax his pay-back time to a maximum of two years and use an alternative method to assess the merits of the two machines.

You provide him with a calculation of the Net Present Value of the alternatives and advise which machine to purchase, taking both assessment criteria into consideration. Richard's cost of capital on a bank loan to help finance the purchase of the machine will be 15% p.a.

Task 9

Your organisation has been offered the following business investment opportunity by a company that you have previously joined in successful joint ventures. Advise the Managing Director of the acceptability of this venture, taking into consideration that the minimum acceptable return on investment projects is 18%.

Investment proposal

End of year	*Investment required* £	*Inflow generated* £	*Net inflow or (outflow)* £
0	120 000	–	(120 000)
1	50 000	20 000	(30 000)
2	–	60 000	60 000
3	–	90 000	90 000
4	–	90 000	90 000
5	20 000	80 000	60 000
6	–	40 000	40 000

You are advised to discount the net inflows or (outflows) and add the annual amounts to give a Net Present Value for the project over the six years.

Task 10

The Purchasing Department of your organisation have to purchase a new fork lift truck for use in the warehouse. A suitable model has a price of £4500, and the supplier can offer three alternative methods of paying for the vehicle (ignoring the effects of taxation):

1 Outright cash purchase at a discounted price of £4200;
2 A credit purchase arrangement which will require a deposit of £1000 and three payments at the end of years 1, 2, and 3 of £1400 p.a.
3 A leasing arrangement which would last for five years. Annual payments would be £1350 payable at the end of each year.

It is expected that the vehicle will be worn out after five years and will be disposed of for minimal scrap value.

Advise the purchasing officer of the least cost alternative of the payment methods. The company's cost of capital is 16% p.a.

15

The nature and behaviour of costs

INTRODUCTION

The costs of an organisation are assessed against two criteria:

1 How do they behave in relation to production output, are they *variable costs*, those that change in proportion to output, or are they *fixed costs*, those that are fixed for the financial period.
2 How can they be allocated to the production process, are they *direct costs*, those that can be attributed to a unit of output, or are they *indirect costs*, those that are production-related but not identifiable with a specific unit of output.

Note that these assessment criteria are not mutually exclusive, it is possible to refer to a cost as being both variable and direct and to another as being variable and indirect. Fixed costs are almost always considered to be indirect costs. (*See* Fig. 15.1.)

VARIABLE COSTS

These costs vary with output levels but not necessarily in direct proportion with output. For example, the production labour cost per unit produced may be £2, up to a certain level of output. After that level has been reached overtime working is required at, say 1½ times the normal rate, and this means that the labour cost of the extra production will be £2 × 1½ = £3 per unit.

FIXED COSTS

In the short term, say the budget period, some costs are considered to be fixed, that is the production volume has no effect on these costs and these remain a constant amount for the period. Take Rates for example, this is a standard charge which does not depend on the organisation's level of activity. In the short term it is a fixed cost, although in the medium and long term it may be varied because of Rates charge increases or changes in premises.

SEMI-VARIABLE COSTS

Some costs remain fixed until the level of activity rises above a certain level, then extra costs are incurred. This extra cost may be variable in nature or remain fixed again until a further change in activity level triggers another change in cost level.

DIRECT COSTS

If a cost can be clearly identified as arising from the production of one unit of output then that cost is known as a direct cost. For example, the production of one unit of 'WAT' requires the following direct costs:

(a) 1 kg of raw materials at £10 per kg = £10

(b) 1½ hours' work at £4 per hour for production labour = £2

Total direct cost of production = £12

Direct expenses can also be identified, e.g. royalty fees or plant hire costs.

INDIRECT COSTS

Those production costs that cannot be identified as arising from the production of a unit of output are *indirect* or *Production Overhead costs*. Indirect costs are part of the overall cost of production and must therefore be included in any production cost calculation, total production cost or unit production cost.

Fig. 15.1 Cost behaviour diagram

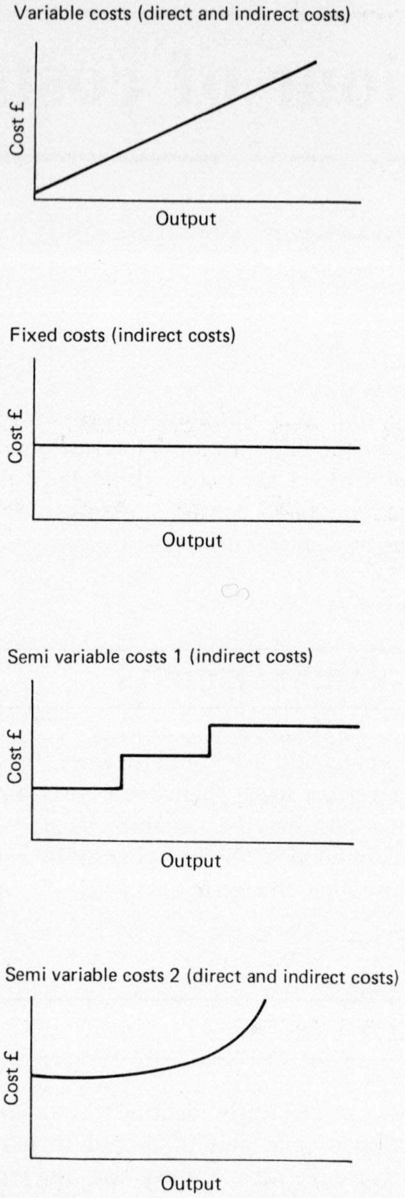

Key to diagrams in Fig. 15.1

(a) Variable costs rise in direct proportion to output, e.g. raw material cost.

(b) Fixed costs remain at the same level irrespective of the output quantity, e.g. rent of premises.

(c) The cost is fixed for a given output quantity, when this quantity is exceeded additional fixed costs are incurred. These are known as 'stepped' costs, e.g. depreciation on machinery (each new machine purchased to increase production 'steps up' the fixed cost of depreciation).

(d) Additional costs are incurred after a given output quantity, the rise in costs is proportional to output, but not necessarily in direct proportion.

- direct costs – overtime working will increase direct labour cost for additional output
- indirect costs – this can be seen in a non production cost example such as selling expenses. The greater the quantity sold the greater the selling expenses, but the expense of selling the last unit is likely to be greater than the expense of selling the first unit.

MANUFACTURING ACCOUNTS

The drawing together of all the production costs both direct and indirect can be seen in a Manufacturing Account.

The calculation can be seen as a number of steps following the manufacture of the products.

Step 1: find the cost of raw materials consumed by the factory in the financial period, this is known as the *direct cost* of raw materials.

Example

	£
Opening stock of raw materials	2400
add Purchases of raw materials	54 000
	56 400
less Closing stock of raw materials	3600
Direct cost of raw materials	52 800

Step 2: find the labour cost for the actual production process, this is known as the *direct labour cost*. Then identify any expenses that arise specifically from the production process; these are *direct expenses*.

Add direct labour cost and direct expenses to direct cost of raw materials, the total of all these direct costs is called *prime cost*.

Example

	£
Direct costs of raw materials	52 800
Direct labour cost	67 200
Direct expenses	12 000
Prime cost	132 000

Step 3: sub-total all of the non direct expenses incurred by the factory, i.e. the factory overheads. It may be necessary to separate factory and office expenses. Factory overheads are added to prime cost to give *production cost*.

Example

	£	£
Prime cost		132 000
Factory overheads:		
Factory rent	72 000	
Indirect labour cost	12 000	
Factory power	4800	
Depreciation of machines	18 000	
		42 000
Production cost		174 000

Step 4: the production cost includes the cost of unfinished goods, i.e. *work in progress*, in order to find the *production cost of finished goods*, that is the value of finished goods transferred from the factory to the warehouse for subsequent sale, an adjustment for stocks of work in progress must be made.

Example

	£
Production cost	174 000
add Opening stock of work in progress	10 800
	184 800
less Closing stock of work in progress	13 200
Production cost of finished goods	171 600

If the output of production was 60 000 finished units then the production cost of a unit can be found by £171 600/60 000 = £2.86 per unit.

Manufacturing and Trading and Profit and Loss Account

The production cost of finished goods is transferred to the Trading Account where it is substituted for 'Purchases'.

You will have noticed that although the calculation has been broken down in steps, the closing point of one step was the opening of the next step. The steps are linked together to form the Manufacturing Account. In its turn this account may be linked with the Trading and Profit and Loss Account to form a *Manufacturing and Trading Profit and Loss Account*. (*See* Fig. 15.2.)

Fig. 15.2

Manufacturing and Trading and Profit and Loss Account for period ending 31 December 19X7

		£	£
Turnover			240 000
Opening stock of raw materials		2400	
add Purchases of raw materials		54 000	
		56 400	
less Closing stock of raw materials		3600	
Direct cost of raw materials		52 800	
Direct labour cost		67 200	
Direct expenses		12 000	
Prime cost		132 000	
Factory overheads			
Factory rent	7200		
Indirect labour cost	12 000		
Factory power	4800		
Depreciation of machines	18 000		
		42 000	
Production Cost		174 000	
add Opening stock of work in progress		10 800	
		184 800	
less Closing stock of work in progress		13 200	
Production cost of finished goods		171 600	
add Opening stock of finished goods		14 400	
		186 000	
less Closing stock of finished goods		18 000	
Cost of goods sold			168 000
Gross profit			72 000
less:			
Administration expenses		12 000	
Selling and distribution expenses		18 000	
			30 000
Net profit			42 000

SUMMARY

The costs of an organisation can be classified in various ways (variable, fixed, direct or indirect costs) in order to help understand the nature and behaviour of the cost in relation to the businesses production process. All costs may be drawn together in a Manufacturing and Trading and Profit and Loss Account.

TASKS

Tasks 1 and 2

Task 1

The following figures have been extracted from the books of your company by the Accountant. You are asked to help junior members of staff understand the descriptions applied to costs by drawing up a table of production costs under the headings shown below and indicating the classifications for each production cost item.

Production cost item	Fixed cost	Variable cost	Indirect cost	Direct cost
Purchases of raw materials etc.		√		√

Task 2

The Accountant would also like to know the production cost of a completed unit in the last year when 695 000 finished units were produced.

Production Cost Information for year ended 31 March 19X7

Stocks 1 April 19X6	
Raw materials	£3000
Work in progress	£6000
Stocks 31 March 19X7	
Raw materials	£4000
Work in progress	£5000
Production costs	
Purchases of raw materials	£42 000
Manufacturing labour	£56 000
Factory rent	£8000
Supervision	£14 000
Depreciation of machine	£4000
Heat and light	£5000
Factory power	£10 000

Tasks 3 and 4

You are sent by your supervisor to visit a client who wishes to have a Manufacturing and Trading and Profit and Loss Account drawn up. After extracting the figures set out below, the client asks you to use the account to show him what is meant by fixed, variable, direct and indirect costs.

	£
Stocks at 1 Jan 19X7	
Raw materials	1800
Work in progress	4200
Finished goods	4800
Stocks at 31 Dec 19X7	
Raw materials	2400
Work in progress	3600
Finished goods	3000
Production costs:	
Purchases of raw materials	21 600
Manufacturing labour	72 000
Manufacturing licence fee	6000
Factory rent	3000
General factory labour	24 000
Depreciation of factory plant and machinery	8400
Factory power	6000
Administration expense	12 000
Distribution expense	30 000
Turnover	240 000

Task 3

Draw up the client's Manufacturing and Trading and Profit and Loss Account.

Task 4

Draw up a table of production costs for the client, and classify them according to their nature and behaviour. Set the table out under the following headings.

Production cost item	Fixed cost	Variable cost	Indirect cost	Direct cost

16

Costs, profit, volume analysis

INTRODUCTION

The profit or loss for a particular business activity will depend upon the revenue received and the costs incurred at a given level of output. The calculation of profit is complicated by the fact that costs may be fixed or variable. It is, therefore, necessary to explore the relationship between these costs, revenue, and output volume in order to establish the profit or loss at a planned level of output.

The critical output level is the *break-even point*. This is where the output volume is at such a level that the revenue generated is sufficient to cover all costs. At the break-even output neither a profit or a loss occurs, i.e. Total costs = Total revenue.

Total costs are, of course, made up from *fixed* and *variable* costs. Assuming that the selling price of a product is greater than its variable cost we find that it is the level of fixed cost incurred in production which is the factor determining the break-even point and hence the output required to achieve a profit.

BREAK-EVEN THEORY

Consider a simple business that has one overhead expense, rent, which is £56 per week. The goods sold at £10 each by the business are purchased for £6, hence a gross profit of £4 on each transaction. This means that a number of transactions must take place before sufficient gross profit is accumulated to cover the overhead of rent.

Rent £56 ÷ gross profit £4 per sale = 14 sales required per week to pay for rent

This is known as *break-even* position, i.e. any situation in which neither a profit nor a loss is made. The 15th sale will mean a net profit of £4.

For example:

Trading and Profit and Loss Account for Week 1

	£
Sales 15 × £10	150
less Cost of sales 15 × £6	90
Gross profit	60
less Expenses	
Rent	56
Net profit	4

The cost of sales, i.e. the purchase price of the goods sold, is a variable cost and rises in proportion to sales.

Rent is a fixed cost, it is static in the short term, and is not affected by changes in sales volume.

The net profit was obtained when sales volume was such that the revenue generated was greater than fixed and variable costs combined:

		£
Sales revenue		150
less Variable cost	90	
Fixed cost	56	146
Profit		4

Obviously this profit can be increased by an increase in sales volume and the rise in profits will be £4 per extra unit sold:

	£
Sales revenue 20 units × £10 each	200
Cost of sales, variable cost, 20 units × £6	120
Gross profit	80
less Rent, fixed cost	56
Net profit	24

which means a £20 increase in profit (£24 – £4).
Alternatively:
5 extra units at £4 profit per unit = £20 extra profit

The break-even chart

This relationship between fixed and variable costs, sales volume and profitability can be shown in a *break-even chart* (*See* Fig. 16.1).

Fig. 16.1 Break-even graph for one week

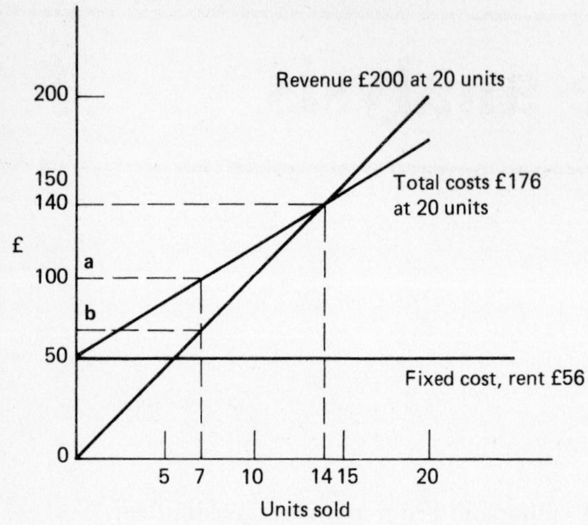

Key to graph construction

1 The vertical scale range is set by the maximum revenue expected in the period for which the graph is drawn. In this case it is £200, generated by the scale of 20 units at £10 each. It is used to measure costs as well as revenue.

2 The horizontal scale measures units of output sold. In this case the range is determined by the maximum number of units sold in the period, i.e. 20.

3 Fixed costs are drawn on the graph by means of a line cutting the vertical scale at the value of fixed costs and extending a line from that point parallel to the horizontal scale over its whole range.

The line runs parallel to the units scale because the magnitude of fixed costs is unchanged over the range of output. Thus, from the graph we can see that at zero output, fixed costs are £56 and at maximum output, fixed costs are £56.

4 The total costs line runs from the intercept between fixed costs line and the vertical scale, to a point above maximum output, 20 units, that represents the total costs at that output. This is found by:

Variable costs 20 units × £6 =	£120
Fixed costs	£ 56
Total costs	£176

The total costs line is effectively a line representing variable costs drawn on the graph using fixed costs as a base line. This is because fixed costs are incurred before any activity takes place and therefore variable costs are *additional* costs.

5 Revenue is shown as a line running from the origin of the graph, (i.e. the intersection of the scales, zero output means zero revenue) to a point above the maximum output which represents sales revenue for that output, 20 units × £10 = £200 revenue.

Note that (a) all lines are straight lines, in the short term all relationships are assumed to be linear. (b) The plotting points given in 1 to 5 are at maximum and minimum points on the scales in order to obtain as high a degree of accuracy as possible.

Reading the graph

1 The point at which the revenue line cuts the total cost line is the *break-even point*. The break-even point can be measured in terms of units by reading from the horizontal scale, 14 units, or in terms of sales revenue by reading from the vertical scale, £140. From inspection of the graph the location of the break-even point is obvious because

(a) below the break-even point the revenue line is underneath the total cost line, i.e. at these levels of output costs exceed revenue and the business makes a loss.

(b) above this point the revenue line is higher than the total costs and the business is profitable.

2 The profit or loss at any level of output can be found by measuring vertically between the total cost and revenue lines above the required output level on the horizontal scale.

For example, the loss at 7 units sold is found by reading the vertical scale to find the difference between points **a** and **b** on the graph.

Example 1

Bramble & Co Ltd are considering selling a product, 'X', which they believe will have a market of 100 units per financial period.

The product will be sold for £45 per unit and the variable costs of production are estimated at £20 per unit. The fixed costs incurred will total £100 per period.

A break-even graph (*see* Fig. 16.2) for the period is drawn up to find:

(a) profit if the project is completely successful;

(b) profit or loss if only 75% of the planned sales are achieved;

(c) the break-even point.

From Fig. 16.2. We can see that:

(a) profit, if completely successful, will be £4500 – £2900 = £1600

Fig. 16.2 Break-even graph for Bramble and Co Ltd

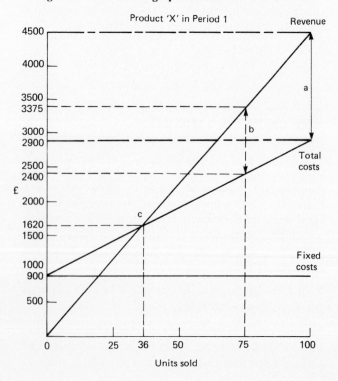

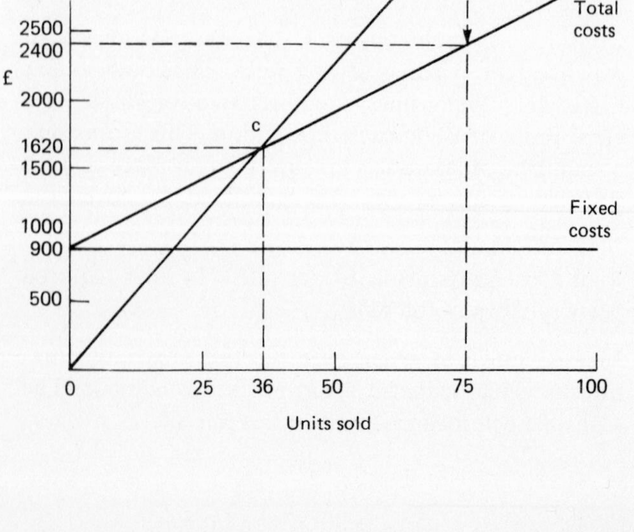

(b) profit, if only 75% successful, will be £3375 – £2400 = £975

(c) break-even point, 36 units sold, sales revenue £1620.

In Example 1 the break-even graph was used not only to find a break-even point and the profit and planned output, but to assess the profit or loss if the plans were not achieved. In this case it was established that the project would still be profitable if the sales achieved were only 75% of forecast.

Break-even graphs can be used to assess alternatives by drawing a graph for each proposal or superimposing one graph upon another.

Example 2

Susan Holder produces a product which sells for £5 per unit. Susan is currently making the product by hand in a small workshop but the production method is slow and demand exceeds supply. There are three alternatives open to Susan. Figures 16.3, 16.4 and 16.5 show the break-even graph for each alternative respectively to find the most profitable one.

1 In Alternative 1 production continues in the current way, but excess demand is exploited by increasing the price to £6 per unit.
Fixed cost of production: £1000 per period. Variable cost of production: £2. Current output level: 500 units per period.
2 In alternative 2 Susan purchases machinery to speed up production, allowing an increase in output to 700 units per period. Variable costs would fall to £1.80 per unit, but fixed costs would rise by £100 per period. The price would remain at £5 per unit.
3 In alternative 3 production is sub-contracted to a specialist producer. Output would be sufficient to meet Susan's estimate of maximum demand, 800 per period. Variable cost of production would rise to £2.50 per unit, current fixed costs would be halved. Price remains at £5 per unit.

The most profitable alternative is Alternative 3, sub-contracting the production. This option is also favoured because of the break-even point (shown in Fig. 16.5), it is the lowest of the three alternatives, which means production can fall to this level before losses are made. Assuming that there are no overwhelming non-financial criteria for rejecting the sub-contracting alternative, Susan is recommended to choose this option.

The margin of safety

Notice how, in Example 2, as the fixed costs rose so the break-even point became higher and when fixed costs fell the break-even point became much lower. We can

Fig. 16.3 Break-even graph – Alternative 1

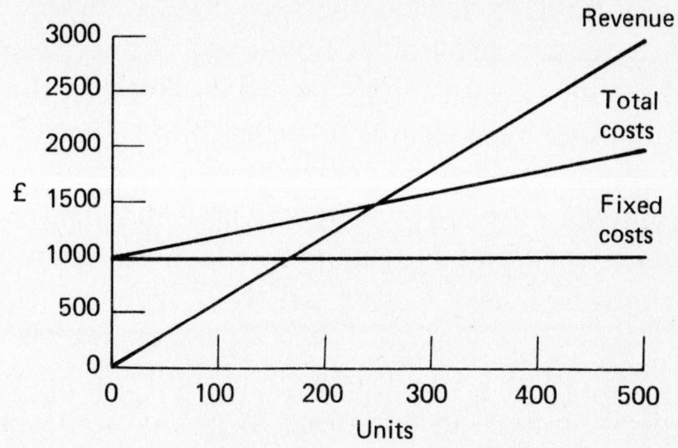

Profit at 500 units of output £1000.
Break-even point 250 units.

Fig. 16.4 Break-even graph – Alternative 2

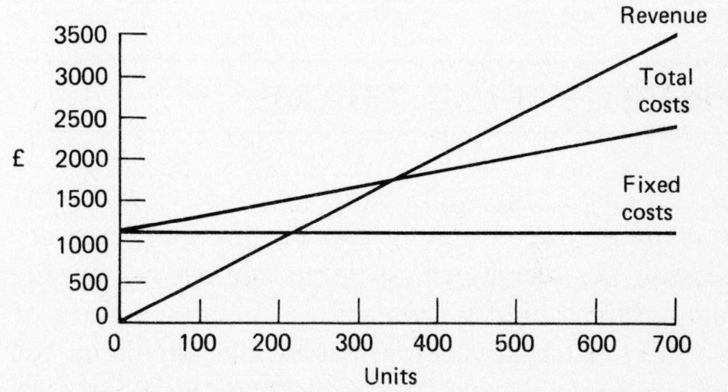

Profit at 700 units of output £1140. Break-even point 344 units.

Fig. 16.5 Break-even graph – Alternative 3

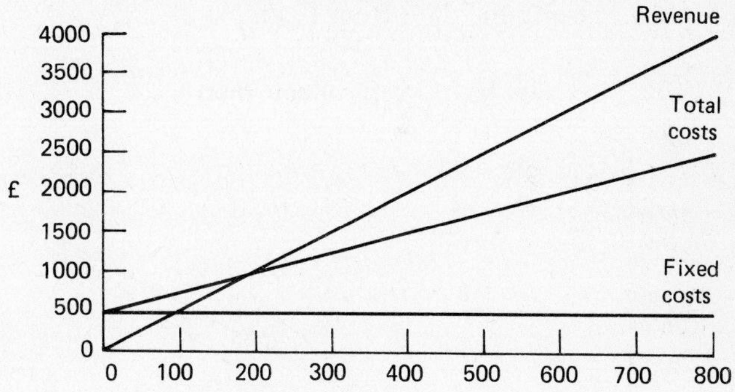

Profit at 800 units of output £1500. Break-even point 200 units.

Fig. 16.6 Margin of safety

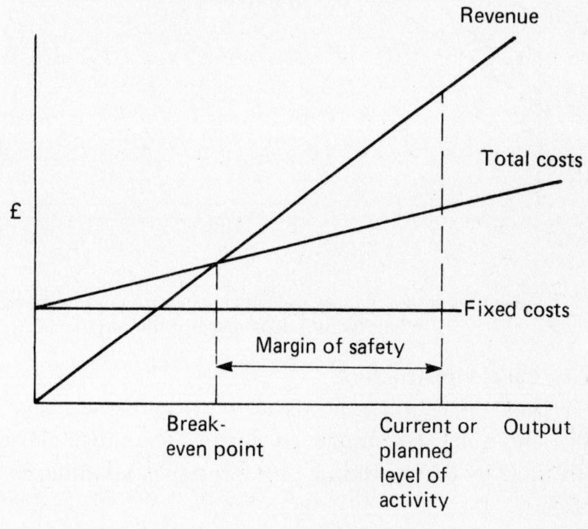

see from this that when a business has high-fixed costs it is important to achieve the sales level budgeted in order to remain profitable. Low-fixed cost organisations are able to withstand a large fall in sales volume while maintaining a degree of profitability.

The number of units of output between break-even point and the expected level of activity is the *margin of safety*, i.e. the number of units by which sales can fall from budgeted level before a loss is incurred (Fig. 16.6).

The margin of safety is important, and can be used as a decision-making criterion. In a situation where alternatives have the same or similar profit levels at the budgeted output, all other things being equal, the option with the greatest margin of safety is preferred.

PROFIT VOLUME CHART

In Example 2, three alternatives were assessed by the drawing of three different graphs, this was necessary because the display of all three alternatives on the same graph would be confusing. The presentation of all three alternatives together would highlight the differences and assist in the explanation of the conclusions to non-financial staff. An alternative presentation is the *profit volume chart*. This is shown in Fig. 16.7, using the data from Example 2.

Fig. 16.7 Profit volume chart

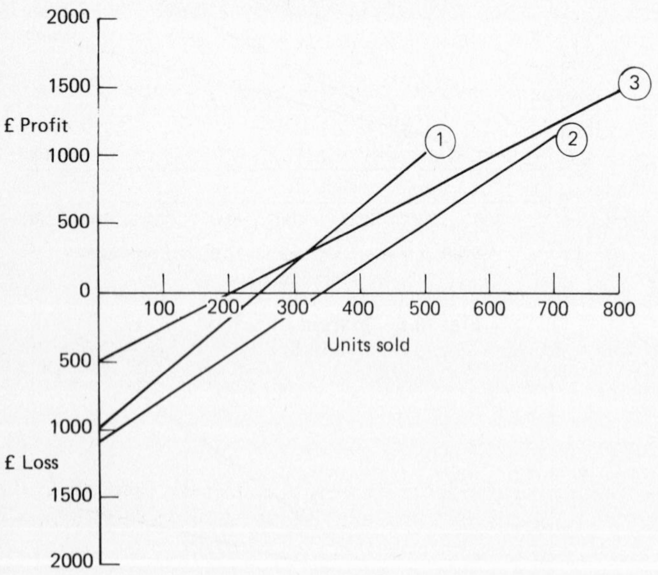

The numbers above the lines refer to the alternatives being assessed. Each line is independent of the others.

Key to chart construction

1 The scale on the vertical axis has both a positive range, for profit, and a negative range, for losses. The range chosen is determined by the maximum profit and the maximum loss to be shown.

2 The horizontal axis scale records output level.

3 Lines on the chart are independent of each other, they run from maximum loss for a process, i.e. no output but fixed costs to be paid, to maximum profit at maximum output. A straight line joins the two extremes, where it crosses the horizontal axis is the break-even point, i.e. neither profit nor loss.

Reading the chart

1 Each line represents an alternative in Example 2, they are numbered as such.

2 The profit or loss at any output level may be found by measuring vertically up from the horizontal axis until the appropriate line is reached. Measure upwards for profit and down from the axis for losses. Break-even is where the horizontal axis is cut.

This chart clearly demonstrates that Alternative 3, the sub-contracting, is the superior option, (the highest profit and lowest break-even point are found in this alternative). Note that even with just three lines on the chart, it is beginning to look cluttered, which is not good for conveying information. If a fourth option existed, it would be better to construct two charts with two options displayed on each.

CALCULATION OF BREAK-EVEN POINT

We have already calculated a break-even point at the start of this chapter. In the simple organisation described, it was said that 14 transactions per week were required, each giving a gross profit of £4, in order to pay the only overhead of £56. This type of calculation can be used to establish the break-even point in any situation where the following information is available:

(a) fixed costs for the period under consideration;
(b) selling price per unit of output;
(c) variable cost per unit of output;

(The total fixed and total variable costs may be made up of a number of constituent parts, unlike the simple business referred to above.)

First, the *contribution* per unit must be found. Contribution is the difference between selling price and variable costs.

Example

	£	£
Selling price per unit		20
less Variable cost per unit		
Materials	4	
Labour	10	
Expenses	2	16
Contribution per unit		4

This sum is *contribution* towards:

(a) fixed costs;

(b) profits.

When a sufficient number of units of output have been sold such that the accumulated contribution equals fixed costs then the break-even point has been reached and any additional sales volume will generate contribution towards profits. We can see therefore that the break-even point may be found by:

Break-even point in units of output

$$= \frac{\text{fixed costs}}{\text{contribution per unit of output}}$$

Furthermore if a certain level of profits are required then the level of output that will achieve it can be found by:

Units of output required

$$= \frac{\text{fixed costs + required profit}}{\text{contribution per unit of output}}$$

Example

The directors of Zeta Ltd are considering a project that will require an investment of £100 000. It is company policy to only invest in projects that can provide a return of 20% p.a. The fixed costs are estimated at £25 000 p.a. and the unit variable cost at £4. The product will be sold for £8 per unit and the expected sales volume is 12 000 units per annum.

Before proceeding the directors would like to know:

(a) the break-even point in units of output;

(b) the output required to obtain the required return.

Answers

(a) *Step 1* Calculate contribution per unit:

Selling price £8 – variable costs £4 = contribution £4

Step 2 Calculate break-even point:

Break-even point in units of output

$$= \frac{\text{Fixed costs}}{\text{contribution per unit of output}}$$

$$= \frac{£25\ 000}{£4}$$

= 6250 units

(b) *Step 1* Calculate profit required to give a 20% return on the investment:

£100 000 investment × 20% = profit of £20 000

Step 2 Calculate output required to give that level of profit:

Units of output required

$$= \frac{\text{fixed costs + required profit}}{\text{contribution per unit of output}}$$

$$= \frac{£25\ 000 + £20\ 000}{£4}$$

= 11 250 units

The directors can be satisfied with this project – it will provide them with the required return on the investment made at 11 250 units sold; this is below the expected sales volume and should therefore be achievable.

USE AND LIMITATIONS OF COST, VOLUME, PROFIT ANALYSIS

Management accountants use the term *cost, volume, profit* (*CVP*) analysis to describe this study of relationships between activity levels, costs, profit and losses. In the short term and within a clearly defined range of values, CVP analysis is an important method for assessing alternatives. It also allows the significance of slight variations from the existing relationships to be established.

The use of a graphical presentation of the relationships can be of use when explaining the significance of the accounting information to non accountants, when a simple overview is often sufficient. Certain assumptions are made in the construction of break-even charts and the calculation of break-even points:

1 All costs can be resolved into fixed and variable categories and that these costs, as well as revenue, have a linear behaviour pattern over the range of values being considered.

2 All environmental and organisational factors that may effect costs, volume or profit remain constant for the period under consideration.

3 The analysis is for one product company/project or the assumption that the sales mix remains constant over the range of activity and for the period under consideration.

These assumptions are made to simplify a situation so that decisions can be based on the essential, influencing factors effecting the alternative outcomes. However, the following limitations should be borne in mind:

1 The relationships shown are only true within the short term and this makes the maximum period for a realistic assessment one financial year;

2 The relationships are only true for a known range of activity levels, say, 25% above and below the normal activity level;

3 Fixed costs are likely to change with activity level changes and if necessary this must be shown on the break-even graph;
4 Variable costs are unlikely to be linear over the whole of the activity range, e.g. if overtime working is required to achieve the highest levels of activity, labour costs will change at some point with the range under consideration.

SUMMARY

Cost, volume, profit analysis allows the relationship between these factors to be considered by management in order to choose the most appropriate of the alternatives before them. Graphical presentations of the relationships are suitable for a non accounting reader.

Assumptions are made in the CVP analysis which lead to limitations upon its usefulness. These must always be considered when assessing the results of CVP analysis.

TASKS

Task 1

You plan to start a business delivering eggs to the consumers' door. This will be a once a week delivery on the Saturday morning following a Friday night collection of eggs. The eggs will be purchased in bulk from a farm at 45 pence per dozen and sold for 80 pence per dozen. The eggs will be collected, stored and delivered in a small van, the running of which will be the only overhead of the business. These costs include lease payments, tax, insurance and running expenses and are considered to be the equivalent of a weekly fixed cost of £35. The maximum capacity of the van for a single collection of eggs is 250 dozen eggs.
Draw a break-even graph to find the weekly break-even point for the business, in dozens of eggs sold.

Task 2

Your employer is considering two alternative production methods for a new product that has been developed. Whatever the production method, the selling price of the product will be £12 per unit, at an expected sales volume of 2000 units per period.

Method 1
A largely automated process with a capacity of 4000 units per period, allowing expansion if required. The fixed costs associated with this process are £12 000 per period.

Variable costs are:

Raw materials	£2.00 per unit
Labour	£1.50 per unit
Variable expenses	£0.50 per unit

Method 2
The traditional method for products of this nature – it has low fixed costs at £4500 per period but requires more expensive raw materials and is labour intensive.
Variable costs are:

Raw materials	£2.50 per unit
Labour	£3.50 per unit

Time constraints prevent this production method having an output of more than 2500 units per period with the currently available facilities.

Draw a break-even graph to show the two alternatives and indicate to your employer the expected profit from the alternatives at the planned level of activity.

Task 3

Three suppliers are attempting to secure your business for the supply, installation and maintenance of an automatic vending machine supplying a product to persons visiting your premises. The supplier will charge an annual rental for the machine which will include all costs but the restocking of the machine and collection of the takings. Restocking will take place using products supplied to you by the machine owner at wholesale prices.
Details of the alternatives are

Supplier J
Annual rental £500
Price of product: (a) Retail £0.25 each
(b) Wholesale £0.20 each
Supplier's estimate of annual demand for their version of the product is 30 000 units.

Supplier K
Annual rental £600
Price of product (a) Retail £0.22 each
(b) Wholesale £0.18 each
Supplier's estimate of annual demand for their version of the product is 40 000 units.

Supplier L
Annual rental £200
Price of product (a) Retail £0.20 each
(b) Wholesale £0.175
Supplier's estimate of annual demand for their version of the product is 48 000 units.

Draw break-even charts to find the best of the alternatives offered to you and make a decision on which supplier to choose.

Task 4

The company you work for is experiencing a lot of

competition from rival producers of one of its products, 'DIAM', and in order to remain competitive the company has decided to cut the price of DIAM to £5 each. The management want to convey to the sales force the need to increase the volume of sales at this lower price in order to remain profitable.

You have been asked by the Sales Manager to produce a profit volume chart to illustrate this need for increased volume for use at the next monthly sales meeting.

The following information is available on the production costs of DIAM:

Fixed costs allocated to DIAM	£300 000 p.a.
Variable cost of production and distribution	£3.50 per unit
Plant capacity allocated to DIAM	500 000 units per year

Task 5

Having cut the price of 'DIAM' in an attempt to maintain market share, the directors of your company are looking for ways of reducing costs so that the profit per unit sold can be restored to its former level. An alternative production method is available which will allow the variable costs to fall by £0.10 per unit, but at the penalty of a 12% rise in fixed costs. Sales and production volumes would remain the same.

Produce a PV chart to show this alternative method of production and the situation described in Task 4 so that you can recommend to management which of the production methods is the best under various market conditions.

Task 6

During a meeting with a supplier, the following statement is made: 'As your fixed costs are in the order of £100 000 per annum, and the use of our materials will reduce your variable costs to approximately £2.00 per unit, on your current selling price of £4 each your break-even point will be halved from its current 80 000 units per year'.

The supplier's estimates of your costs are remarkably accurate but is he correct about the effect of his product's price on your break-even point?

Do a calculation to check his assumption.

Task 7

The cost breakdown for two products is shown below. Calculate the break-even point of both and then recommend to management which of the two should be produced in the limited capacity available, 20 000 units capacity, in this financial period.

	Product M	*Product N*
Fixed costs of the capacity available this period	£50 000	£50 000
Additional fixed costs incurred to produce the products	–	£10 000
Selling price of product	£12.00	£7.25
Variable cost of production		
Raw materials	£4.00	£2.00
Labour	£3.50	
Expenses	£2.00	–

Task 8

You are considering investing in a business project that is complementary to your existing business interests. The investment required is £50 000 and a minimum return on that investment should be 15% per annum otherwise the investment would not be considered worthwhile.

Project details

Selling price of product	£15.00 each
Fixed costs total	£48 000 p.a.
Variable costs, per unit:	
Raw materials	£4.00
Labour	£5.00
Expenses	£2.00
Expected sales per year	18 000 units

At what level of output is this project going to provide the required profit?

Task 9

Your employer wishes to offer a particular product for sale. Two suppliers are offering the product but the market at which these suppliers are aiming their products are different.

Supplier W
This version of the product is aimed at a mass market, it is priced at £4.00 each retail, the shopkeeper receiving a 25% discount from that price. The supplier estimates an annual demand of 12 000 units and the shelf space that would be allocated to the product would have fixed costs of £6000 per annum.

Supplier X
This product is marketed as a quality product and is sold at a premium price of £6 each retail. The supplier allows the retailer a 20% discount from retail price. At an estimated annual sales volume of 8000 the shelf space required is less and therefore the allocation of fixed costs is lower than for the alternative, at £4500 per annum.

A friend who works for a similar business is of the opinion that the supplier's sales figures can only be achieved if a considerable amount of effort is given to selling these products. She suggests that 50% of the supplier's estimates is a more realistic figure.

Draw graphs of these alternatives and establish:

(a) Profit at the suppliers' estimated annual sales;

(b) The profit at 75% of the suppliers' estimates;

(c) The profit at 50% of the suppliers' estimates.

Which supplier would you recommend to your employer? Write a short memorandum referring to the graphs and giving the reasons for your recommendation.

17
Marginal costing and decision making

INTRODUCTION

In Chapters 15 and 16 we have seen how costs are separated into their fixed and variable elements and that the consideration of costs in this manner allows us to observe their effect upon profits at various levels of activity. We have also looked at the concept of *contribution* and seen how, once sufficient contribution is generated to cover fixed costs, then it provides profit as the activity level increases.

Contribution is the key element in *marginal costing*, it is used to evaluate business situations and establish the profitability of those situations.

MARGINAL COST

The marginal cost of production can be explained as: *the cost of producing one extra unit of output*. This means that *marginal cost = variable production cost*. As fixed costs will have been borne by the previous production output, only the variable costs (prime cost) of the extra unit are new costs incurred specifically because of making the extra unit.

Example

	£
Direct materials	6
Direct labour	12
Direct expense	1
Marginal cost	19

The fixed costs of the production plant may have been £1 000 000, but this is irrelevant when considering the cost of producing a unit of output extra to the normal production level.

It can be seen then that the calculation of contribution as shown in Chapter 16 can be restated in marginal costing terms as:

Selling price – marginal cost = contribution

CONTRIBUTION ANALYSIS

Contribution can be used as a basis for decision making. The contribution is calculated for a given situation and, in general, management will look for a minimum level of contribution or the highest contribution in a series of alternatives.

These are examples of *short-run tactical decisions* using contribution as the assessment criteria.

Decision making 1 – to accept a special contract

Businesses can often be faced with a situation where an additional order can be obtained but the selling price of the goods or services to be provided must be lower than the normal selling price. In some cases, the special price may appear to be lower than cost, e.g. if cost is assessed using all direct and indirect costs of production, i.e. as per Manufacturing Account. The additional order is accepted or rejected on the basis of the contribution it provides.

For example, a special one-off order is offered at £10 each selling price. The normal selling price is £12 each. Marginal cost of production is £8. Can the order be accepted? Yes, the order can be accepted because it provides some contribution:

	£
Special selling price	10
Marginal cost	8
Contribution	2

Note There are other important factors to consider:

1 The lower than normal price accepted must not jeopardise the firm's ability to obtain its usual price in normal trading.
2 The order must be accommodated in spare capacity, i.e. not interrupt normal production.
3 Acceptance of the order must not prevent the business taking on other work that would provide greater contribution.

Decision making 2 – which product to make if there is a shortage of the inputs to the production process (limiting factor).

When production output is limited by a shortage of one of the inputs then care must be taken to ensure that this commodity in short supply is used in the most profitable way. The analysis focuses on the contribution that each unit of shortage input can generate from its inclusion in particular products. This is not necessarily the product with the highest contribution but the product which has the highest contribution to consumption of scarce input ratio.

Example

A business makes three products from two ingredients. Details are shown below:

	Products *1*	*2*	*3*
Ingredient 1	100 kg	80 kg	90 kg
Ingredient 2	80 kg	120 kg	100 kg
Contribution per unit sold:	£180	£220	£210

There is a shortage of Ingredient 2, production will have to be limited to two products only. Which two? The problem can be solved by assessing the contribution per unit of ingredient for each product.

	Products *1*	*2*	*3*
Contribution	£180	£220	£210
Ingredient usage	80 kg	120 kg	100 kg

Contribution per kg of ingredient:

Product 1	£180/80 kg	= £2.25/kg
Product 2	£220/120 kg	= £1.83/kg
Product 3	£210/100 kg	= £2.10/kg

The products chosen are those with the highest contribution per kg of ingredient – 1 and 3.

Note There may be commercial criteria that override choices made by this method.

Decision making 3 – the 'Make or Buy' decision

A business may be quoted a price for a component that it currently produces 'in house' by an outside supplier. The price of this component from the outside supplier may appear to be lower than the internal production cost. Before deciding to purchase from the outside supplier, the marginal cost of the alternatives must be assessed.

The decision should be made by comparing:

(a) marginal cost of production;

(b) marginal cost of buying in.

Example

A firm produces a component 'X' for incorporation in one of its finished products. The cost of production is calculated to be £14.00. An outside supplier can provide the same component for £10.50, this appears to be a saving of £3.50 per unit used. However, if the make up of the costs for the internally produced component are examined closely a different view is formed.

Costs	**Component X** *In house* £	*Bought out* £
Raw materials	5.00	–
Direct labour	2.00	–
Variable overhead	1.50	–
Purchase price	–	10.50
Marginal cost	8.50	10.50
Fixed overhead allocated	5.50	–
Total unit cost	14.00	10.50

Comparison of the marginal costs of the alternatives shows that to buy the component would mean a loss of contribution. This is because the marginal cost of buying in is greater than that of internally producing. Therefore the marginal cost of the *complete* product would rise if the bought in component were used and, assuming that the selling price cannot change, the contribution will fall to accommodate the rise in marginal cost. Hence profits will fall if the bought out component is used in this case.

Note There may be internal factors of a non-financial nature that can affect the decision.

Decision making 4 – to stop making unprofitable products

A business may manufacture a number of products, not all of which are profitable. The decision to stop production of the unprofitable products will depend on the effect of this action on total contribution.

Example

	Products *A* £	*B* £	*C* £	*D* £
Selling price	12	15	8	13
less Variable costs	3	6	9	5
Fixed costs allocated	4	10	4	4
Profit/(loss)	5	(1)	(5)	4

Products B and C are making a loss, should manufacture of both be stopped? Consider the contribution:

	A	*B*	*C*	*D*
Contribution (selling price – variable cost)	£9	£9	(£1)	£8

Notice that the unprofitable Product B provides a contribution while the other unprofitable Product C has a negative contribution.

Only C fails to provide any contribution and production of this item should be stopped if possible. If B were to be withdrawn there would be a significant loss of contribution, this product should continue to be manufactured even though it makes a loss.

Consider the production and sale of 1000 each of the above items in a period, the fixed costs for which were £22 000.

			£
Contribution:	A 1000 × £9	=	9000
	B 1000 × £9	=	9000
	C 1000 × (£1)	=	(1000)
	D 1000 × £8	=	8000
Total contribution			25 000
Fixed costs			22 000
Profit			3000

Withdrawing C from sale will improve profits:

		£
Contribution:	A	9000
	B	9000
	D	8000
Total contribution		26 000
Fixed costs		22 000
Profit		4000

However, withdrawal of B as well can be shown to have an adverse effect on profit:

		£
Contribution:	A	9000
	D	8000
Total contribution		17 000
Fixed costs		22 000
Loss		(5000)

The loss occurs because the fixed costs have to be covered by few contribution providing products.

The conclusions that can be drawn are:

(a) if no contribution can be obtained from the sale of a product it should be withdrawn;

(b) any product that provides contribution should continue to be produced for sale.

Note *Some products may be dependent upon each other. Therefore to withdraw a non-contributing product may reduce sales of a contributing item.*

For example, the price of a dining table may be set at such a low level that no contribution is obtained, but a dining table must be sold in order to sell a set of dining chairs which provide considerable contribution.

SUMMARY

Marginal cost is the cost of producing one extra unit of output. Provided that the selling price is greater than the marginal cost, each extra unit provides extra contribution.

Marginal costing is not an accepted method for use in reporting profits and stock values but it is a powerful analytical tool for use in assessing business situations. The key to this type of analysis is contribution. In general terms, contribution should be maximised in short-run tactical decisions.

TASKS

Task 1

The cost of producing the product manufactured by your organisation is given by the cost accountant as:

		Per unit
Raw Materials:	A	£4.00
	B	£2.00
Production labour		£5.00
Production licence fee		£1.00
Production overhead allocated		£3.00
Total production cost		£15.00

In order to provide the sales force with a minimum acceptable price under special conditions, extract from these figures the marginal cost.

Task 2

A sales representative has received an enquiry for a small batch of product 'T'. You are to prepare a price to quote from the cost information shown below.

This is the first enquiry from this source. The potential for future business is considerable if this order can be obtained and a good product supplied at a competitive price. In order that negotiation can take place, you should also advise the representative of the marginal cost of this product.

1 Raw materials: 20 kg at £1.20 per kg;
2 Direct labour: 2 hours at £4.00 per hour;
3 The product is allocated a share of total overheads on the basis of £3.00 for every direct labour hour;
4 Profit is added at 10% of total cost.

Task 3

One of the products produced by your organisation has a selling price of £16.00 each. It costs £12 to produce, made up of £4.00 for materials, £5.00 for production labour and an allocation of overheads at £3.00 per unit. Calculate the contribution provided by this product.

To what extent would an increase in the allocation of overheads to the product by £1 per unit affect the contribution?

Task 4

The Costing Department has just been advised of a new pay award to production workers. Their hourly rate has been increased and this means that the labour cost included in your product costs has to be changed:

1 Production labour cost rises from £4.00 per hour to £4.20 per hour.
2 Indirect labour costs included in the overhead costs will increase the overhead costs by 1%.

Because of the market competition, the selling price of the product cannot be increased to compensate for these changes.

Calculate the contribution per unit of product 'Z' before and after the labour cost increase.

Cost data for a unit of product 'Z' prior to change in labour cost:

1 Materials: £10.00;
2 Direct Expenses: £2.00;
3 Direct labour: 2 hours;
4 Overheads allocated at £5 per direct labour hour;
5 Selling price: £36 each.

Task 5

You have been offered a special contract for the supply of your product 'M' at a price of £7 each – you normally charge £9 each. The cost of production is:

1 Materials: £3.00;
2 Labour: £2.50;
3 Allocated overhead: £2.00.

Is this special contract acceptable to you?

Task 6

Because your company's production capacity is under utilized at the moment, the Sales Representatives have been looking for special contracts on which you will accept a lower sales price. Two contracts are offered but only one of them can be accepted.

1 375 units at a selling price of £24;
2 450 units at a selling price of £22.50.

The cost details for a unit of the product are:

1 Direct materials: £7.50;
2 Direct labour: £6.00;
3 Normal selling price: £30.00.

Which one will you accept?

Task 7

The organisation for which you work produces and sells two products A and B. Both products use raw material 'AAA'.

Details are:

	Product	
	A	*B*
Material AAA	5 kg	8 kg
Contribution achieved	£10	£12

The supplier of raw material AAA has notified you of a hold up in supply which means that you have insufficient stocks of AAA to produce both products.

Advise the Production Manager of the product to produce in these circumstances.

Write a memorandum to the Sales Manager explaining the grounds on which you have made this decision.

Task 8

Four products are made and sold by Delaware Ltd. They are R, S, T and U. Because of a labour shortage, it is not possible to complete all of the orders received and management need to know which of the products should have its output restricted in order to maximise the profitability of Delaware Ltd during this shortage.

Product details

	R	*S*	*T*	*U*
Labour content of products	4 hrs	3 hrs	2½ hrs	2 hrs
Contribution achieved per product sold	£10.00	£8.25	£4.25	£6.00
Orders received	1000	800	1200	1300

Advise management which product should have its output restricted and calculate the number that can be produced given that the maximum hours available in the period under consideration is 10 000 hours.

Task 9

Management are attempting to cut costs and as part of this exercise the Purchasing Department have invited outside suppliers to quote prices for components currently produced in the company's workshops.

Components under investigation

	A742	*T391*	*VO42*
Raw materials at £2 per kg	2.5 kg	2 kg	1 kg
Labour cost at £3 per hour	2 hrs	3 hrs	1 hr
Direct expense	£1	£3	–
Fixed costs allocated	£4	£3	£3

	A742	*T391*	*VO42*
Total cost of internal production per unit	£16	£18	£8
Outside supplies quotation per unit	£14	£13	£7

Evaluate the quotations received and send a memorandum to the purchasing office to tell them which of the quotations are acceptable. Give your reasons for accepting or rejecting the quotations.

Task 10

As part of a review of the current product line up, management have asked for an evaluation of current profit per unit of the products sold. The following information has been extracted from the budgets for the next period.

	Products				
	V	*W*	*X*	*Y*	*Z*
Selling price per unit	£21	£15	£18	£21	£18
Variable cost of production per unit	£10	£16	£15	£12	£20
Fixed costs allocated	£ 5	£ 2	£ 4	£ 3	£ 2

It is planned to produce and sell 1000 units of each product in the next period. The total fixed costs for this period are expected to be £16 000, all of which have been allocated to the products.

1 Report to the General Manager the profitability of each product on a unit basis and calculate the total budgeted profit for the period.
2 As a result of your report, the General Manager insists that all of the loss making products should be dropped. Advise him if this approach is sensible and make your own recommendations as to which products should be taken out of production. Show the effect on profit of the two approaches.
3 Your recommendations are put to the monthly management meeting at which the Sales Manager states that the sales of product V are dependent upon the continued production and sale of product W. Does this change your recommendations? If so, recalculate the profit taking the Sales Manager's statement into consideration.

18 Analysing financial information

INTRODUCTION

In Chapter 7 we saw that the purpose of accounting was, in part, to report the financial affairs of the organisation to its members and other interested parties. The management of the organisation will of course be using more detailed information for the control of the business.

Financial reports on their own do not reveal a lot about an organisation, e.g. value of assets, liabilities, the amount of profit or loss, etc. These absolute values do not set the organisation's financial situation in any particular context and so ways of measuring the values relatively have been developed. These are generally known as *accounting ratios*.

Accounting ratios are used to evaluate the performance of a business. It must be understood that ratios on their own are usually meaningless and there is no such thing as the ideal ratio. The proper use of ratios entails:

(a) comparison with past performance to detect trends, and/or;

(b) comparison with predetermined standards, and/or;

(c) comparison with industry norms.

Notice that it is by comparison that ratios reveal useful information.

Ratios can be divided into four broad areas. The main ratios in each category are discussed below, but please note that you are not limited to the ratios given, if a particular relationship within the accounts is of importance to you, then a ratio may be devised to measure it.

PROFITABILITY RATIOS

Return on Capital Employed (ROCE)

This ratio is obtained by using the following formula:

$$ROCE = \frac{\text{Net profit} \times 100}{\text{Capital invested}}$$

Note There are a number of variations on this ratio, but as given here, *net profit* is for the period under consideration and *capital invested* refers to the capital at the start of the period. For company accounts use Capital and Reserves at the start of the period, i.e. closing total in *last* period's balance sheet. It is important to ensure that any other ROCE percentages used in comparisons have been calculated in the same way.

This percentage measures the return the owner/s are getting on the funds they have invested in the business. Comparison with alternative investments will be an indication of the business's success:

(a) Are similar firms doing better?

(b) Would a higher return be obtained from a bank or building society?

(c) Has the planned return been achieved?

Gross profit as a percentage of sales (gross profit percentage)

This ratio can be obtained using:

$$\frac{\text{Gross profit}}{\text{Sales turnover}} \times \frac{100}{1}$$

This is a predetermined percentage that would not be expected to vary much from year to year unless the sales mix changes. An unexpected fall in the ratio could indicate stock being lost, damaged or stolen. When an unplanned fall occurs the cause should be investigated and corrective action taken.

Net profit as a percentage of sales

The formula is as follows:

$$\frac{\text{Net profit}}{\text{Sales turnover}} \times \frac{100}{1}$$

This measures how many pence in the pound the business finally takes as pre-tax profit after all of the expenses have been paid. It can be a measure of the efficiency with which a firm controls its overheads. If overheads are rising at a faster rate than sales revenue, then the net profit as a percentage of sales will fall. The reverse will be true if sales revenue is increasing faster than overhead costs. The individual elements of total overheads can be examined as a percentage of sales to establish those overheads that have the most significant effect on profitability. Management can then concentrate on controlling those costs.

OPERATING RATIOS

Rate of stock turnover

Use the following formula:

$$\frac{\text{Cost of sales}}{\text{Average stock at cost}}$$

Note

$$\text{Average stock} = \frac{\text{Opening stock} + \text{Closing stock}}{2}$$

This measures the number of times stock is replaced during the period. It is to be expected that a business selling perishable goods will show a high rate of stock turnover.

Average debtors collection period, in days

This is obtained using:

$$\frac{\text{Trade debtors}}{\text{Credit sales for the year}} \times 365 \text{ days}$$

This gives the average number of days taken by debtors to settle their accounts. Any significant deviation from the normal credit period could indicate poor credit control.

Average creditors payment period, in days

This is obtained using:

$$\frac{\text{Trade creditors}}{\text{Credit purchases for the year}} \times 365 \text{ days}$$

This measures the time taken by an organisation to pay its creditors. The actual time established will be a combination of the various credit periods allowed and cash discounts taken, which makes the setting of a normal payment period difficult. However, a very short period may show that payments are being made before absolutely necessary and a long period could indicate problems for a potential supplier.

LIQUIDITY RATIOS

These ratios examine the organisation's ability to continue trading. Working capital (Current assets – Current liabilities) is necessary to enable a business to engage in its day-to-day trading activities. This capital is required to:

(a) hold stock to meet production or customer requirements;
(b) allow debtors the normal credit period;
(c) settle creditors accounts when they fall due;
(d) pay wages;
(e) pay all other organisational expenses as they fall due.

Current ratio (working capital ratio)

The current ratio can be obtained by:

$$\frac{\text{Current assets}}{\text{Current liabilities}}$$

This measures the number of times current liabilities are covered by current assets. This may be expressed as a ratio, the traditional safe level being 2 : 1. It may be possible to operate without danger at a lower ratio, e.g. 1.5 : 1 where a business generates a large cash flow.

Acid test or quick assets ratio

Use the following formula to obtain the quick assets ratio:

$$\frac{\text{Current assets} - \text{Stock}}{\text{Current liabilities}}$$

By removing stock from the analysis we are left with the *liquid current assets*, or those current assets that can easily be converted into *cash*. The minimum ratio is 1 : 1, i.e. £1 of liquid asset to cover every £1 of current liability. Thus the organisation's obligations can be met as they fall due.

FINANCIAL STRUCTURE

Gearing ratio

Use the following formula to obtain the gearing rate:

$$\frac{\text{Interest bearing finance}}{\text{Interest bearing finance} + \text{Ordinary share capital}} \times \frac{100}{1}$$

The gearing ratio measures the proportion of business funding from interest bearing finance. A business with a high proportion of long-term loans is said to be *high geared*. High gearing can be a problem if profits are falling as an increasingly high percentage of the profit must be allocated to interest payments leaving less each period for the owner/s. (*See* Chapter 5.)

For the purpose of gearing calculations, *preference share capital* is included in *interest bearing finance* because it has a fixed rate of dividend.

There are other methods of measuring gearing, so it is important to ensure that comparisons are made using the same basis of calculation. The method of calculation given will show high gearing as being above 50%.

Interpretation of ratios

Ratios have complex interactions and therefore it is impossible to give rules as to what is a good or bad set of ratios. The environment of the organisation must be taken into consideration as well as bare figures when making a judgement.

For example, two firms operating in the same industry – one may have a low gross profit percentage and a high rate of stock turnover and the other's ratios show the reverse situation. Which firm has the best ratios?

Answer: it is not a matter of best ratios in direct comparison, rather one of establishing if the ratios are appropriate to the individual firm's situation. The first may be a supermarket where low gross profit margins but very high rates of stock turnover lead to substantial profits, while the other business could be a corner shop earning a good profit from a high gross profit margin on its comparatively low stock turnover.

The following example will help to show the use of ratios in the interpretation of accounts.

The following are the accounts of Turners Ltd for the first three years. The business gives and receives one month's credit.

Profit and Loss Accounts for

	Year 1 £000's	*Year 2* £000's	*Year 3* £000's
Turnover	300	360	450
Cost of sales	240	288	375
Gross profit	60	72	75
Expenses	45	57	57
Pretax profit (net profit)	15	15	18
Tax	6	6	6
Retained profit	9	9	12
Profit and Loss a/c bal b/f	30	39	48
Profit and Loss a/c bal c/f	39	48	60

Balance Sheets as at end of

	Year 1 £000's	*Year 2* £000's	*Year 3* £000's
Fixed assets at book value	600	606	597
Current assets			
Stock	30	24	30
Debtors	45	39	48
Cash	—	9	15
	75	72	93
Creditors, amounts falling due within one year			
Trade creditors	48	48	48
Bank overdraft	6	–	–
	54	48	48
Net current assets (working capital)	21	24	45
Net assets employed	621	630	642
Financed by			
Issued ordinary share capital	582	582	582
Reserves: Profit and Loss a/c	39	48	60
	621	630	642

The ratios opposite (page 125) were calculated for the first three years of Turners Ltd.

Comments

By any standard, the return on capital employed is a very low return on the investment although a slight upturn is seen in Year 3. However, the fact that these are the first three years of trading may be a significant fact.

The gross profit percentage is considerably reduced in Year 3. A fall of this order suggests a change in pricing policy, i.e. profit margin has been cut in order to stimulate an increase in sales volume in the hope of an increase in total profits. This is borne out by an increase in turnover, a fall in net profit percentage and more particularly the marked increase in rate of stock turnover.

Increased management efficiency is indicated by three facts:

1 The average debtors collection period has fallen to 39 days, much closer to the credit period given, 30 days (1 month).

2 Average creditor payment period has fallen to 46 days, much nearer to the 30 days (one month) allowed.

3 The initial liquidity problems have been resolved. Although the current ratio was low in the first year, it was the acid test ratio that showed possible danger. A ratio of 0.8 : 1 means that only 80 pence was available to meet every £1 of liability, and a business cannot survive long in this situation. However, the ratio in the third year shows that there is no longer a liquidity problem.

Accounting ratios

	Year 1	*Year 2*	*Year 3*
Return on capital employed	$\frac{15}{582} \times \frac{100}{1} = 2.6\%$	$\frac{15}{621} \times \frac{100}{1} = 2.4\%$	$\frac{18}{630} \times \frac{100}{1} = 2.9\%$
Gross profit percentage	$\frac{60}{300} \times \frac{100}{1} = 20\%$	$\frac{72}{360} \times \frac{100}{1} = 20\%$	$\frac{75}{450} \times \frac{100}{1} = 16.7\%$
Net profit percentage	$\frac{15}{300} \times \frac{100}{1} = 5\%$	$\frac{15}{360} \times \frac{100}{1} = 4.2\%$	$\frac{18}{450} \times \frac{100}{1} = 1.7\%$
Rate of stock turnover*	$\frac{240}{30} = 8$ times	$\frac{288}{\frac{(30+24)}{2}} = 10.7$ times	$\frac{375}{\frac{(24+30)}{2}} = 13.9$ times
Average debtor collection period	$\frac{45}{300} \times 365 = 55$ days	$\frac{39}{360} \times 365 = 40$ days	$\frac{48}{450} \times 365 = 39$ days
Average creditor payment period**	$\frac{48}{270} \times 365 = 65$ days	$\frac{48}{282} \times 365 = 62$ days	$\frac{48}{381} \times 365 = 46$ days
Current ratio	$\frac{75}{54} = 1.4:1$	$\frac{72}{48} = 1.5:1$	$\frac{93}{48} = 1.9:1$
Acid test	$\frac{75-30}{54} = 0.8:1$	$\frac{72-24}{48} = 1:1$	$\frac{93-30}{48} = 1.3:1$

Gearing: There is no gearing for Turners Ltd as its only capital is ordinary share capital.

* For the calculation of Year 1's figure the Balance Sheet stock figure was assumed to represent the average value of stock; there being no opening stock to use in the calculation of average stock. You will have realised that in subsequent years average stock is calculated by using the previous and current years' Balance Sheet value of stock.

** Purchases were calculated by working backwards from cost of sales, taking the stock levels into consideration.

	Year 1 £000's	*Year 2* £000's	*Year 3* £000's
Cost of sales	240	288	375
add Back closing stock	30	24	30
	270	312	405
Less Opening stock (last year's closing stock)	—	30	24
Purchases for the year	270	282	381

Parties interested in these ratios will include:

1 *Management*
The satisfaction in these results expressed by management will depend upon the targets set and the degree to which they have been met. An increase in the profit from £15 000 p.a. to £18 000 p.a. was achieved in Year 3, although the net profit percentage fell, presumably as a result of the cut in sales price. This profit is presumably still too low and a dividend has not been declared in any of the three years. With the possible exception of profitability, management appear to have control of the business.

2 *Creditors*
Creditors, had they checked the figures, should have been worried in Years 1 and 2 because of the liquidity situation of the business and the time taken to receive payments from Turners Ltd. However, Year 3 shows an improvement in both areas – Turners Ltd have the liquidity to ensure that payment can be made and an improvement in the payment period can be expected in the future.

3 *Employees/trade unions*
The payment of wages seems to be ensured with the liquidity ratios being much improved in Year 3, but they should not hold out any hopes of a pay increase unless profitability improves.

4 *Potential lenders*
Lenders of finance to the business must assess two basic things:

(a) What security is offered? The Balance Sheet shows fixed assets without any other lending secured on them and therefore, assuming realistic Balance Sheet values for the fixed assets, this aspect is satisfactory.

(b) Can the borrower make repayments of interest and capital? In this case the profitability is low, which will limit the borrowing capacity of the business. Turners Ltd cannot afford to pay a dividend, which shows a need to reinvest all of the profit obtained at the current time and the prospect of being able to afford interest payments does not look good. However, if it could be shown that the borrowing would be used to increase profitability to a satisfactory level then loan approval could be forthcoming from a lending institution.

5 *Shareholders*
Turners Ltd has not paid a dividend since it commenced trading, because the low profits have had to be reinvested in the business. This is fine if the shareholders are all employed in the business and therefore receiving an income by way of a salary, but other shareholders will not be so happy. This is a small private limited company where the investors are likely to be directors of the company and the level of dividend may not be important to them in its early years. However, in the case of public limited companies, shareholders will be considering the dividends carefully as it is a factor in assessing the share price.

INVESTMENT RATIOS

There are a number of ratios calculated by those investing in shares in an attempt to assess the worth of a particular share or to measure the return on their investment in shares. The picture is complicated by the fact that shares are bought and sold at market prices rather than nominal value and this market price is determined by investors' perception of the shares' future performance in terms of dividends received and changes in the price level. We will confine ourselves to two ratios, as they give different views of the organisations's financial performance.

Price earnings ratio (P/E ratio)

The P/E ratio is an expression of investors' perception of the growth potential for the company and the risk of not achieving that growth. A high P/E ratio indicates that investors have high expectations for the company's growth. The P/E ratio is found by:

$$\frac{\text{Market price per share}}{\text{Earnings per share}}$$

The market price is obviously determined by trading activity on the Stock Market, but earnings per share is calculated and published by the company. SSAP 3 standardises the calculation of earnings per share so that the P/E ratio of companies can be compared. Earnings per share is calculated by:

$$\frac{\text{Earnings from ordinary activities after tax and preference share dividends}}{\text{The number of issued ordinary shares}}$$

You will find this ratio underneath the Income Statement in a set of published accounts with a note explaining the calculation.

Dividend yield

Small investors may be more interested in the income obtained from their investment than increases in market price. Dividend yield allows comparison with other forms of investment, e.g. bank deposits, and it is found by:

$$\frac{\text{Gross dividend}}{\text{Share price}} \times \frac{100}{1}$$

The gross dividend must be used because most investments have their rates of return quoted gross, i.e. before deduction of Income Tax. Dividends on shares are paid net of Income Tax and so to obtain the gross figure for the calculation, the tax must be added back.

Example

Apex plc paid a dividend for the year of 10.22 pence per share. The current market price for the shares of Apex is 200 pence.

The current standard rate of Income Tax is 27%. The gross dividend can be found by:

$$\frac{\text{Net dividend}}{(100\% - 27\%)} = \frac{10.22}{100\% - 27\%}$$

$$= \frac{10.22}{73\%} \text{ or } \frac{10.22}{.73}$$

$$= 14 \text{ pence per share}$$

The dividend yield is then found by:

$$\frac{\text{Gross dividend}}{\text{Market price of share}} = \frac{14\text{p}}{200\text{p}} \times \frac{100}{1}$$

$$= 7\%$$

This yield can then be compared with other forms of investments. It must not be forgotten that the yield is calculated on the current market price, but the investor may not have paid that price. This makes the comparison with other investments difficult. A low dividend yield suggests that investors are paying a high price for the shares in expectation of higher dividends in the future.

GUIDELINES FOR USING RATIOS

1 Try to compare like with like. Any variation in the basis on which the accounts are prepared will distort

the ratios calculated and make comparison difficult. This is a particular problem when comparing different companies who may have different accounting policies.
2 Do not use past performance as a foolproof guide to future performance. Past trends may be projected into the future, but the degree of confidence in future performance assessments based on past data must diminish rapidly outside of the short term.
3 Published accounts only show what the company is forced or wishes to show. It is the concealed information which is probably the most important.
4 Inflation has made past data unreliable, in that the values of five years ago are unsuitable for the calculation of ratios for use in analysing today's situation.

SUMMARY

1 Accounting ratios allow those with an interest in the business's performance to go behind the bare figures and analyse the financial situation.
2 Accounting ratios on their own mean very little, they must be used for comparison with similar companies or establishing trends in an individual company.
3 The environment in which the ratios were calculated and the business operates must be considered when evaluating the ratios.
4 The traditional accounting ratios should be seen as a framework for ratio analysis – other ratios may be devised to measure some aspect of the business under consideration that appears to be important in the context of the investigation.

TASKS

Task 1

Exxton Manufacturing Ltd changed its price structure at the start of 19X5 in order to meet a more aggressive sales drive from its major competitor. The Income Statements for the past three years are shown. Calculate the gross profit percentage and the net profit percentage for the three years and comment on your findings.

	19X3	*19X4*	*19X5*
	£000	*£000*	*£000*
Sales turnover	3750	4000	5000
Cost of sales	3000	3200	4125
Gross profit	750	800	875
Expenses	550	585	675
Net profit	200	215	200

Task 2

At the end of 19X7 the Exxton company reported the following profits – 19X6 is included for comparison purposes.

	19X6	*19X7*
	£000	*£000*
Sales turnover	6400	8500
Cost of sales	5280	7000
Gross profit	1120	1500
Expenses	870	1160
Net profit	250	340

Calculate the gross profit percentage and the net profit percentage, and compare your findings with those in the period 19X3 to 19X5. Do your comments made in 19X5 regarding the change in pricing policy still stand in the light of the 19X7 results?

Task 3

You have been looking at the accounts of various businesses, because you wish to buy a small retail business. The rate of stock turnover suggests itself to you as a reasonable measure of the efficiency with which the business is currently run.

Calculate the rate of stock turnover for the two businesses shown and indicate which one you consider to be the better managed.

Income Statements

	Business A		*Business B*	
	£	£	£	£
Sales turnover		150 000		150 000
Cost of Sales				
Opening stock	18 000		5000	
add Purchases	109 000		106 000	
	127 000		111 000	
less Closing stock	22 000		6000	
		105 000		105 000
Gross profit		45 000		45 000

Task 4

As Credit Controller it is your responsibility to establish the credit worthiness of new customers and decide if your organisation is prepared to do business with them on a credit basis. Before making further enquiries, you look at their accounts and calculate their average creditors payment period in order to establish which, if any, could prove to be a poor payer. The accounts are shown below:

Income Statements

	Company A	Company B	Company C
	£	£	£
Turnover	480 000	1 200 000	750 000
Cost of sales	360 000	1 020 000	600 000
Gross Profit	120 000	180 000	150 000
Expenses	50 000	100 000	50 000
Net Profit	70 000	80 000	100 000

Balance Sheets

	Company A	Company B	Company C
	£	£	£
Fixed assets	260 000	600 000	430 000
add			
Current assets			
Stock	20 000	240 000	80 000
Debtors	30 000	150 000	40 000
Cash	10 000	10 000	30 000
	60 000	400 000	150 000
less			
Current liabilities			
Trade creditors	30 000	170 000	60 000
Others	10 000	30 000	20 000
	40 000	200 000	80 000
	280 000	800 000	500 000
Capital	£280 000	£800 000	£500 000

For the purpose of this analysis assume that cost of sales equals purchases and that one month's credit is allowed.

Task 5

Establishing the time taken for creditors to pay is not the only analysis that can help the Credit Controller's assessment of a business's credit worthiness. Calculate the liquidity ratios for the companies in Task 4 and comment on them in the light of the ratios established in Tasks 4 and 5. Are there any companies you would have doubts allowing credit to?

Task 6

Credit Controllers like to compare the debtors collection period for other companies. Check the periods for Companies A, B and C in Task 4. Do they achieve the industry norm of 30 days? Do any of them do better than this? If so, can you suggest why?

Task 7

Tayoid Ltd have approached the bank with a request for loan finance. The Manager has asked you to draw up a report on Tayoid Ltd for use in assessing their loan application. In your report you may make any recommendations about granting a loan, and the management of the company if the loan were granted, that you think appropriate for the protection of the bank's interests. The accounts for the last three years of Tayoid are given:

Tayoid Limited
Income Statements

	Year 1	Year 2	Year 3
	£000's	£000's	£000's
Turnover	780	765	720
Cost of sales	624	622	555
Gross profit	156	143	165
Expenses	73	84	108
Pretax profit	83	59	57
Tax	38	30	23
Retained profit	45	29	34
Profit and Loss a/c bal b/f	15	60	89
Profit and Loss a/c bal c/f	60	89	123

Balance Sheets as at end of

	Year 1	Year 2	Year 3
	£000's	£000's	£000's
Fixed assets at book value	900	931	964
Current assets	90	102	114
Debtors	108	120	120
Cash	14	7	3
	212	229	237
Creditors, amounts falling due within one year			
Trade creditors	121	138	147
Net current assets	91	91	90
Net assets employed	991	1020	1054
Financed by:			
Issued share capital	931	931	931
Reserves: profit and Loss Account	60	89	123
	991	1020	1054

Note Assume that the stock shown in the Balance Sheet as at end of Year 1 represents average stock.

Task 8

The organisation for which you work is a public limited company with shares quoted on the Stock Exchange. Extracts from the last three years' company reports are given. From these, establish the trends in performance from the point of view of investors in your company's shares and comment upon them.

You should calculate:

(a) Earnings per share;
(b) P/E ratio;
(c) Dividend yield.

Extracts from the Final Accounts of a plc

	19X4	19X5	19X6
Issued share capital:			
Ordinary share of 50p each	£1 500 000	£1 500 000	£2 000 000
	£	£	£
Profit on ordinary activities after tax	900 000	1 050 000	1 680 000
Ordinary share dividend	360 000	420 000	600 000
Retained profit	540 000	630 000	1 080 000
Market price of shares on declaration of results	150p	210p	252p

19

The business plan

INTRODUCTION

We have seen that it is necessary to establish objectives for a business in order to control it. The objectives are the required achievements and control action is stimulated when the actual achievement differs from that required. In this chapter, we will discuss how a business plan can be established.

THE NEED FOR A PLAN

1 As seen before, if a plan is not set out then business performance cannot be measured.
2 If the business venture requires finance from outside sources, the potential lenders will wish to assess the proposal to check its viability.
3 A plan is not set down without going through a process of researching and evaluation of information which enables the business's objectives to be refined as part of the planning process. It is unlikely that the original idea will be continued with if research suggests that it is not viable.

THE CONTENTS OF THE PLAN

A full plan for presentation to a bank or other lender will contain many details on the organisation, its management, the product and markets, history of the organisation as well as the new proposal. This is in order to give an overall view of the organisation and to set the new proposals in context. It may be that these non-financial details reveal weaknesses in the organisation that must be rectified before the plan is put into effect.

The financial details of the plan will include:
(a) existing financial situation;
(b) realistic sales projections for the product in the next period followed by estimates for the following periods;
(c) capital expenditure required and the expected depreciation rate associated with this expenditure;
(d) how this expenditure will be financed;
(e) what working capital is required, taking into consideration stock requirement, credit periods given and received;
(f) cashflow forecast (Cash Budget);
(g) a Budgeted Income Statement for the first period in some detail;
(h) analysis of the break-even point;
(i) a Budgeted Balance Sheet for the end of the first period in some detail.

DRAWING UP THE PLAN

The Business Plan is going to be a document vital to the success of the business. It is therefore important that the financial projections are based on accurate and reasonable assessments of the business's performance in the periods under consideration. This means doing market research to establish:
(a) the existence of a market;
(b) the size of the market;
(c) the suitability of the product for the market;
(d) the price the market is prepared to accept;
(e) the projected sales in the next period and estimates for the following periods.

It is impossible to produce the financial plans until these matters are settled and to produce realistic estimates may require the services of a specialist market research organisation. However, for the small business, personal enquiries will probably produce reasonable estimates which, if treated conservatively, will be satisfactory.

The production of the financial aspects of the plan may also require specialist work. The organisation's accountant is obviously the most suitable person to carry out this work. If the proposal is for a new business it is advisable to engage an accountant at this stage so that the accountant is available to advise on the plan and assist in the monitoring of the business's progress.

The banks and other lending institutions provide advice for their clients. Many publish books and leaflets on business planning and presenting your case for finance to the lender, e.g. Midland Bank's 'The Business Plan'.

THE FINANCIAL PLAN

A plan is to be produced for a new business venture and after market research, the sales estimates are available, so detailed planning can now take place.

Stage 1

Establish the total capital required for the business; this is found from:

(a) capital expenditure requirements;
(b) working capital requirements;
(c) start-up expenses.

Capital expenditure requirements can be found by the total cost of premises, fittings, equipment, installation costs, etc. Working capital requirements are more difficult to assess and the concept of the operating cycle is of use here. The operating cycle starts with the purchase of materials or goods for resale and ends when debtors settle their accounts. It is a measure of the time between these events and this can be used to estimate the finance required to fill the financial gap between the two events.

Example

A business purchases stock on one month's credit, which usually takes two months to process and sell to debtors, who are allowed a further month in which to pay.

The operating cycle would be:

Time between receipt of goods and sale to customers	2 months
Credit period allowed to customers	1 month
	3 months
less Credit period allowed by suppliers	1 month
Operating cycle	2 months

This shows that there is a need for working capital to cover the cost of goods sold for two months.

Thus, if cost of sales is £2000 per month, the working capital required to cover the operating cycle time is £2000 × 2 months = £4000. To this must be added the expenses which will be incurred in that two month period, say £1000 per month. Therefore the total working capital is found by:

2 months' cost of sales £2000 × 2 months	£4000
2 months' expenses £1000 × 2 months	£2000
Total working capital required	£6000

Start-up expenses are the initial expenses associated with the launch of a new business or new venture for an existing business. They may include legal and accounting professional fees, advertising and other marketing expenses. They should not be confused with start-up *costs* which refer to the total starting costs, capital and revenue, of the new project.

Stage 2

Sources of suitable capital should now be sought for the business's financial requirements (*see* Chapter 5 on sources of finance). It is important to match the source with the requirement, i.e. long-term investments require long-term finance, and short-term requirements such as working capital need short-term finance like bank overdraft facilities.

Stage 3

The cashflow forecast for the first year can now be prepared. It should be remembered that it deals in *cash* flows, therefore credit periods must be taken into consideration and any non-cash expenses excluded.

The forecast includes capital to be invested and any borrowing, with the exception of bank overdrafts as they show up as an overdrawn balance in the appropriate periods.

The first six months should be in as much detail as possible with less detail necessary for the rest of the year. The overdrawn balances shown should be as predicted by the estimates of types of finance required. If not, check the previous workings as perhaps not all of the expenses have been included or the timing of payments might need clarification.

Stage 4

A Budgeted Income Statement can now be drawn up for the first year. At this stage, some analysis on the plan can start, e.g. net present value of the returns, gross profit and net profit percentages and ROCE of the proposed capital investment (*see* Chapters 14 and 18). If these are satisfactory, we can proceed to Stage 5.

Stage 5

It is always worthwhile knowing the break-even point for a project and so this is drawn up graphically or by calculation for a specified period. In order to do this, the organisation's costs must be categorised as fixed or variable costs (*see* Chapter 16). If the break-even point is higher than expected a revision of the plans may be necessary.

Stage 6

Draw up a Budgeted Balance Sheet as a statement of the organisation's planned financial situation at the end of the first year.

A worked example

In this example, the situation is simplified in order to show clearly the steps in preparing the financial parts of the Business Plan. (VAT has been ignored.)

David Matthews has identified a market in his home town for a product 'TURMOD'. He has agreed with the supplier that he will have the sole agency for the product in his area.

The product will be supplied in bulk to David at a price of £3.50 each wholesale – the recommended retail price is £5 – in monthly batches with the first delivery being twice the normal amount to provide a buffer stock which will be maintained. The supplier's market research suggests an annual sales volume of 40 000 units but David's own research indicates that in the first year 60% of this sales volume is a more realistic basis on which to plan, i.e. sales of 24 000 units in the first year. Suitable premises have been found at a rent of £5000 p.a. payable quarterly in advance. The other regular expenses are estimated at:

- Rates – £1200 per year payable half-yearly in advance;
- Light and heating of premises – £200 per quarter in arrears;
- Telephone, postage and other administration costs – £2000 p.a. payable telephone £200 per quarter in arrears and the balance on a monthly basis. Administration costs include any bank charges.
- Various insurance premiums – £1000 p.a. payable in advance;
- Staff costs – £10 200 p.a. payable monthly;
- Depreciation of fixtures and fittings – 20% p.a. on a cost of £10 000 which will be invoiced and paid for in the first month;
- Advertising – £1800 p.a. payable monthly;
- Equipment rental – £3000 p.a. payable monthly;
- David expects to pay himself £600 per month in the first year of business. (*Note* This is not a business expense but is considered to be an advance of profits and is known as *drawings*.)

There will be various start-up expenses:

- Professional fees and disbursements – £1000;
- Launch advertising and other promotions – £2000;
- Redecoration of premises, signwriting, etc. – £1500.

The financial plans can be prepared from this information:

Stage 1 Capital requirements

(a) Capital expenditure on fixtures and fittings – £10 000.

(b) Working capital, as this is a retail organisation the customers will be paying cash, thus reducing the working capital requirements.

Initial working capital needs will be established by the cashflow forecast.

(c) Start-up expenses totalling £4500.

Stage 2 Sources of capital

David has investments of £12 000, therefore he has sufficient funds to meet the capital expenditure and part of the start-up expenses, but must borrow to finance the balance of start-up expenses and any working capital requirements. The actual amount will be revealed in the cashflow forecast and as it is assumed to be short-term requirements, the bank will be approached for an overdraft.

Stage 3 Cashflow forecast

All *cash* inflows and outflows are shown for the first year (see opposite).

The cashflow forecast reveals that the overdraft required is £3250, say, a limit of £4000, which will be repaid by the end of the first year.

	Month 1 £	*Month 2* £	*Month 3* £	*Month 4* £	*Month 5* £	*Month 6* £	*Qtr 3* £	*Qtr 4* £
Receipts								
Sales revenue	10 000	10 000	10 000	10 000	10 000	10 000	30 000	30 000
Capital invested	12 000							
Total receipts	22 000	10 000	10 000	10 000	10 000	10 000	30 000	30 000
Payments								
Rent	1250			1250			1250	1250
Rates	600						600	
Light and heat			200			200	200	200
Telephone			200			200	200	200
Administration	100	100	100	100	100	100	300	300
Insurances	1000							
Staff costs	850	850	850	850	850	850	2550	2550
Advertising	150	150	150	150	150	150	450	450
Equipment rental	250	250	250	250	250	250	750	750
Drawings	600	600	600	600	600	600	1800	1800
Purchases (one month's credit)		14 000*	7000	7000	7000	7000	21 000	21 000
Fixtures and fittings	10 000							
Start-up expenses	4500							
Total payments	19 300	15 950	9350	10 200	8950	9350	29 100	28 500
Balance b/f	NIL	2700	(3250)	(2600)	(2800)	(1750)	(1100)	(200)
Add receipts	22 000	10 000	10 000	10 000	10 000	10 000	30 000	30 000
	22 000	12 700	6750	7400	7200	8250	28 900	29 800
less payments	19 300	15 950	9350	10 200	8950	9350	29 100	28 500
Balance b/f	2700	(3250)	(2600)	(2800)	(1750)	(1100)	(200)	1300

* This is for the initial delivery of stock and one month's normal supply

Stage 4 Budgeted Income Statement for the first year

	£	£
Sales (24 000 units × £5 per unit)		120 000
less Cost of sales		
Opening stock	NIL	
Purchases (24 000 + 2000 units @ £3.50)	91 000	
less Closing stock (2000 units @ £3.50)	7000	
		84 000
Gross profit		36 000
less Expenses		
Rent	5000	
Rates	1200	
Light and heat	800	
Telephone	800	
Administration	1200	
Insurance	1000	
Staff costs	10 200	
Advertising	1800	
Equipment rental	3000	
Depreciation of fixtures and fittings (10 000 × 20%)	2000	
Start-up expenses**	4500	
		31 500
Net profit		£4500

** These are first-year expenses only and should not be included in any assessment of the business's underlying profitability. Adding back these special expenses of £4500 to the net profit of £4500 reveals a normal profit level of £9000 at this sales volume.

Stage 5 Break-even point

To establish the break-even point it is necessary to establish the variable costs and the fixed costs. In this case, it is reasonable to assume that the cost of sales is a variable cost and that the 'Expenses' are fixed in the period under consideration. Therefore, unit variable cost is £3.50 (i.e. wholesale price of product sold) and the fixed costs were £31 500 (total of expenses).

Unit contribution must also be calculated:

Selling price per unit	£5.00
less Variable cost per unit	£3.50
Contribution per unit	£1.50

$$\text{Break-even point} = \frac{\text{Fixed costs}}{\text{Unit contribution}}$$

$$= \frac{£31\,500}{£1.50}$$

= 21 000 units in the first year

The normal expenses for this level of sales would be £31 500 *less* £4500 start-up expenses = £27 000

Under these circumstances, the break-even point would be:

$$\frac{£27\ 000}{£1.50} = 18\ 000 \text{ units per year}$$

or 1500 units per month

Stage 6 Budgeted Balance Sheet as at end of first year

	£	£
Fixed assets		
Fixtures and Fittings at cost		10 000
less Depreciation		2000
		8000
Current assets		
Stock	7000	
Cash at bank	1300	
	8300	
Current liabilities		
Trade creditors	7000	
		1300
Net assets employed		9300
Financed by:		
Capital invested at start of first year		12 000
Net profit		4500
		16 500
Drawings (£600 × 12 months)		7200
Capital at close of first year		9300

Evaluation

The financial part of the Business Plan is now complete, but what does it reveal?

1 A small overdraft is required which will be repaid within the first year.

2 A small profit is achieved, but not sufficient to meet David's requirements for drawings of £7200 p.a., however, this situation is not unusual for the first year of a new business.

3 Break-even point is artificially high in this year and the underlying break-even point gives a reasonable margin of safety for the expected level of activity, i.e. 3000 units.

4 The Balance Sheet shows a poor liquidity situation, but when the fact that the stock will be sold for cash before the payment to creditors falls due is taken into consideration, there is no immediate danger.

SUMMARY

The Business Plan assists the management in its control of the business and provides assessment material for potential lenders. It must be carefully drawn up, usually with the assistance of an accountant. The financial aspects of the plan need to be based on good market research if they are to be meaningful.

TASKS

Task 1

Delta Ltd allow their customers two months' credit, receiving one month from their suppliers. In order to maintain sufficient stocks for the production process and provide their product to customers' exstock, they maintain one month's stock of materials, and two weeks' stock of finished goods.

The production process takes about one week. Advise the management of Delta Ltd of the length of their operating cycle, in weeks (1 month = 4 weeks).

Task 2

On visiting Delta Ltd as part of the audit team, you observe the real situation which appears to be:

(a) customers take about three months to pay;

(b) raw material stocks are sufficient for six weeks;

(c) finished goods stocks are sufficient for three weeks;

(d) because of production delays, materials are spending an average of two weeks in the production process;

(e) creditors' accounts are settled late, on average it takes seven weeks to pay suppliers' bills.

What is DELTA Ltd's true operating cycle?

Task 3

Linda Thompson has savings of £4000 which she wishes to invest in a business providing a reprographics service to local businesses. Linda would only expect to take an income of £50 per week from the business in the early stages. It has been established that the following costs will be incurred:

(a) Rent of lock-up shop premises – £3000 p.a. payable quarterly in advance.

(b) Refurbishment of these premises to suit her business needs – £1750.

(c) Fixtures and fittings will cost £3000, payable on installation. These will be depreciated at 10% p.a. on cost.

(d) Reprographics equipment – £6000. Finance will be needed for this. The depreciation rate will be 20% p.a. on cost.

(e) Stocks of materials – £500 to be replaced at the

rate of 10% of sales value for the month. No credit available until established for three months.

(f) Other occupancy costs will total £2000 p.a. payable in equal quarterly amounts in arrears. Because the service is primarily for business customers, it is expected to have to allow one month's credit. Sales are estimated at £500 in the first month, rising by £200 per month until the sixth month, after which no further increase is expected.

Estimate Linda's capital requirements and suggest methods of financing these requirements to her. You may offer alternatives, but let her know of any assumptions you have made so that she can make an informed decision on the financing of her business.

Task 4

Assume that Linda Thompson decides on a combination of bank loan and overdraft to finance her business capital requirements that cannot be provided from her own resources. Interest is to be 10% p.a. *flat rate*. Making allowances for any monthly loan repayment, draw up a Cash Budget for Linda's first six months.

Task 5

Linda Thompson realises that during the first six months of her business, she is unlikely to make a large profit. It is hoped that in a full year with sales having reached their normal level in Month 6, that a reasonable profit will be made.

Draw up a Statement for Linda to show what profit she can expect in the first year. Assume that all start-up expenses are written off in the first year.

(Remember to charge loan interest only as an expense. Capital repayments are *not* an expense.)

Task 6

Assuming all revenues and normal running expenses having reached their expected levels at the end of Year 1 remain the same for Year 2, draw up for Linda Thompson a Statement of estimated profit for Year 2 and calculate the sales revenue at which she will break even.

Task 7

(*See* Example in Chapter 19.)
David Mathews wishes to draw up a business plan for the second year of his business. The following information is available:

(a) The supplier's estimates of annual sales volume appear realistic for the second year.

(b) Assume that all normal operating expenses remain at the same level as for the first year.

Help David with the financial aspects of his business plans by drawing up:

(a) Cash Budget for Year 2 on a monthly basis;

(b) A Budgeted Income Statement for Year 2;

(c) A Budgeted Balance Sheet as at end of Year 2;

(d) An estimate of the annual sales required to break even.

Task 8

David does not believe his business will be without competition for long. He expects large manufacturing companies to copy the product he sells and become a major threat to the business after five years. His plan is therefore to remain in business for five years and then sell out to any large competitor who will buy his business. The following assumptions are made about the five years of David's business.

1 The level of profits achieved in the second year will be repeated in the third and fourth years. In the fifth year, the profit will be reduced by a third because of competitors taking David's market share.
2 The competitor will buy the business for the equivalent of 2½ times the average profit for the last two years at the end of the fifth year of operation.
3 The net cash inflow to the business for any given year is found by adding Net Profit and Depreciation charge for that year (remember depreciation is a non-cash expense).
4 The company's cost of capital is 20% p.a.

Calculate the Net Present Value of David's business investment for the five years under consideration and advise David if, in retrospect, his original investment in the business can be considered worthwhile under these expected circumstances.

Task 9

On leaving college, John Cooper wishes to set up in business selling needlecraft products to craft and gift shops. He has taken samples round to potential customers, who have placed orders worth £500 per month for delivery within the first three months of business. Indications are that repeat orders would be forthcoming from these customers and John estimates that by extending the geographical area to which he sells, the business turnover for the second quarter could be easily doubled with a further 50% in the third quarter. Capacity would then prevent further expansion of sales. John will purchase materials, deliver them to outworkers, then collect the completed products for distribution to the customers. As goods are only produced to order, finished goods stocks are not held.

Details of his business operations are given:

1 All goods are sold at a standard gross profit margin of 50% of sales value. One month's credit is given to customers.

2 Production expenses are:

Labour (outworkers)	50% of cost
Materials	20% of cost
Variable overheads	30% of cost
Total production cost	100%

With the exception of materials, for which one month's credit is available, all production expenses are paid in the month incurred. Materials are purchased in the month required for production. As far as possible, stocks are not held.

3 Fixed administration expenses of £180 per month will be incurred, payable in the month incurred.
4 Distribution is by way of contract parcel post and is a variable cost being based upon the weight of the goods being despatched. In his estimates, John has based the cost of packing and distribution on a figure equal to 10% of the cost of production, payable one month in arrears.
5 John will require sufficient profit to cover his need to withdraw a minimum of £360 per month for personal expenses during the first year.
5 Capital will be provided by the transfer of £1000 from John's savings to a business bank account and the transfer of his mini van, worth £600, to the business. Depreciation on the van at the rate of 20% p.a. on cost to the business is included in the fixed administration expenses. Any other requirement John hopes to obtain by way of an overdraft.

Prepare the financial aspects of a business plan for John, in particular:

(a) Estimate the minimum capital required to commence trading.

(b) Prepare a Cash Budget on a monthly basis for twelve months and forecast any overdraft requirements.

(c) Estimate the break even, in value of sales turnover, per month.

(d) In which month is the sales turnover sufficient to provide the profit necessary for John's required level of drawings.

(e) Draw up Budgeted Income Statements for the first six and twelve months.

(f) Draw up a Budgeted Balance Sheet as at the end of the first twelve months.

(g) Calculate suitable accounting ratios and, in so far as is possible without any given business for comparison, comment on what they reveal.

20 Integrative Assignments

ASSIGNMENT 1 'IT'S YOUR MONEY'

An integrative assignment having particular links with *People in Organisations 1*.

Objectives covered: elements of the indicative content for the following general objectives are covered in this assignment:

Finance A
People in Organisations 1 B,E,F
The Organisation in its Environment 1 A

Skill areas assessment – this assignment develops the following skill areas: numeracy, identifying and tackling problems, learning and studying, information gathering, communicating and working with others.

Situation
The Students Union at your college wish to provide new students with some information about personal finance. The assignment is in two parts:

1 the production of an information leaflet
2 the setting up of a 'It's your Money' Panel; a panel of students who have studied *Finance* and can answer questions on personal finance from Students Union members at a meeting arranged for the purpose.

NB The assignment provides material for a simulation of this situation, but running a 'real life' panel could prove to be a worthwhile activity.

Assignment material
The following letter is received by a representative of the students on the BTEC National course.

It is agreed to assist the Students Union. As a first step, each BTEC National Year 1 student is to produce a leaflet entitled 'Credit, a students guide' so that the best one can be selected for printing.

All course members have agreed to participate in the 'It's your Money' panel at a series of meetings provided advance notice of the general question areas is given. After inviting questions, the following letter, with details of questions, is sent to all participants.

Students Union Office
FE College
October 19

Student Representative
BTEC National Year 1

Dear Member

The Students Union committee has expressed concern about the lack of information available to new members about personal finance. We would be grateful if you and your fellow students would help by providing advice to students in this matter.

We would like to be able to provide new students with
a) a leaflet giving a students' guide to credit, say an A4 sheet folded in three, advising on types of credit and their suitability for different purposes, explanation of terminology, restrictions imposed, etc.,
b) a panel of experts who could answer questions at a student meeting.

Thank you for considering our proposals.

Yours sincerely
NUS Branch Committee

Student Union Office
FE College

BTEC National Course

Dear Course Member

Thank you for agreeing to be a member of our 'It's your Money' Panel, and we look forward to hearing your advice to our members.

The question areas are indicated by the sample questions attached to this letter. You will be asked one question by a member of the audience who may wish to raise an additional point. Other panel members will be invited to add to your answer if they wish after you have finished your reply.

Thank you again for your participation.

Yours sincerely
NUS Branch Committee

'It's your Money' questions

1 My fiance/fiancee and I wish to buy a house. How can we work out the amount that can be borrowed?
2 I have a tax code of 242, what does this mean?
3 What is the best way of financing a car purchase, bank loan or HP?
4 If I take out a mortgage of £40 000, can you explain how much, if any, tax relief I will get on the interest payments?
5 Can you explain how *net* pay is calculated? I contribute to an occupational pension scheme.
6 I have been told that it is very expensive to use a credit card, is this true?
7 Can you suggest a suitable investment of a £5000 inheritance I recently received? I wish to use it as a house deposit some time in the future.
8 I pay a lot of bank charges because my account is overdrawn four or five times a year, can you suggest a method of planning my finances to avoid this problem?
9 I hope to buy a stereo, it costs about £400. As I have no spare savings, can you suggest to me the cheapest source of finance?
10 From my part-time earnings of £30 per week, I have saved £500. This is still in my bank current account, should I move it to another account?
11 How much can I earn per week before paying tax and National Insurance?
12 I seem to have higher monthly deductions from my pay packet than my colleagues on the same salary. I am a married man with two children, my tax code is 242, do you think anything is wrong?
13 Can you explain the difference between a repayment and an endowment mortgage?
14 How do I go about selling the British Airways shares that I recently purchased?
15 Do I have to pay tax on my holiday earnings? I am a student on a full-time course.
16 Can you explain the difference between *not contracted out* and *contracted out*?
17 What is APR?
18 A friend of mine has told me about *revolving credit*, but I am not sure how it works. Can you explain this to me?
19 Why do most shops offering credit state that you must be over eighteen years old?
20 My dad says it is best to make sure that when I leave college I find a job with a company where I can stay until I retire or else my pension will not be very good. Is this true?

The meeting is now organised either as

(a) a real meeting in the Students Union room or

(b) a simulated meeting with course members taking turns at acting as the panel and asking questions as the audience.

ASSIGNMENT 2 'MAX DEACON'

An integrative assignment having particular links with *People in Organisations 1*.

Objectives covered: elements of the indicative content for the following general objectives are covered in this assignment:

Finance B,C,D
People in Organisations 1 B,C,E,F
The Organisation in its Environment 1 E

Skill areas assessment – this assignment develops the following skills areas: numeracy, learning and studying, identifying and tackling problems and communicating.

Situation

Max Deacon was a pilot for an air taxi company, flying executive aircraft in Europe and the Middle East. Unfortunately, he was made redundant and, as he had only worked for the company for a short time, received no redundancy payment. Because of his relatively little experience he found it impossible to obtain new employment as a pilot.

Max did not deliberately plan to start his own business, it grew out of odd jobs done for friends and recommendation by them to others. The business he is engaged in is minor domestic building maintenance and alterations. Max identified his market as the wives of DIY enthusiasts who never quite finish the project, and jobs too small for normal tradespeople. Small advertisements were placed in the local paper aimed at these people. Most of his work was simple jobs, like fixing dripping taps or finishing kitchen tiling, but customers were prepared to pay well and in cash.

After some months Max decided that his financial records needed sorting out and the business monies kept separate from his own.

Task 1

Design a simple book-keeping system suitable for Max. You should include written instructions on how to use the system.

Task 2

Like a lot of small traders Max will probably need convincing of the merits of book-keeping. Write a short letter to Max explaining the benefits of maintaining good records.

On 1 May 19X5, Max had the following assets: £1200 in his bank account, £500 of which he considered to be business funds to be deposited in a business bank account; various items of equipment, like ladders and power tools, which he valued, taking their condition into consideration, at £300. When made redundant Max had sold his BMW and bought a Mini Van, this he also considered was for business use. He had been quoted a part-exchange price of £450 for the Mini Van when looking at a newer model recently. He did not hold stocks of materials, buying what was necessary to complete a job when his quotation was accepted. However, this policy is likely to change as Max found that he was having to make repetitive purchases of small quantities.

Task 3

Calculate the capital Max has invested in his business, in preparation for opening a set of double-entry books.

Task 4

To help Max understand what is to be recorded in the business accounts write a short note to him explaining:

(a) the business entity (or separate entity) concept;
(b) the money measurement concept.

On 1 May 19X5 Max made a number of changes in the way he conducted his business, these included setting up a double entry book-keeping system and operating from business premises rather than from home.

At the end of the first six months trading under the new system you assist Max in the preparation of a trial balance.

Task 5

The following accounts are complete except for the last days' transactions. You are required to enter the transactions listed below into the accounts and then extract a Trial Balance.

(a) cash received for work finished that day, i.e. £25;

(b) cheque for £76 received from Mrs Grant in respect of account presented last month;

(c) postage £3 cash;

(d) petrol, £24 on account, at Central Garages;

(e) materials for tomorrow's work, £10 cash.

After extracting the Trial Balance you find an error that was not revealed by the Trial Balance.

Nominal Ledger

		Debit	Credit	Balance	
		£	£	£	
	Cash Account				
Oct 29	Balance brought forward			1257	DR
	Bank Account				
Oct 29	Balance brought forward			521	DR
	Equipment		154	367	DR
	Capital Account				
Oct 29	Balance brought forward				
	Rent Account				
Oct 29	Balance brought forward			644	DR
	Insurance Account				
Oct 29	Balance brought forward			120	DR
	Sales Account				
Oct 29	Balance brought forward			8246	CR
	Drawings Accounts				
Oct 29	Balance brought forward			4000	DR
	Postage & Stationery Account				
Oct 29	Balance brought forward			116	DR
	General Expenses Account				
Oct 29	Balance brought forward			258	DR
	Motor Expenses Account				
Oct 29	Balance brought forward			806	DR
	Equipment Account				
Oct 29	Balance brought forward			300	DR
	Motor Van Account				
Oct 29	Balance brought forward			450	DR
	Purchases Account				
Oct 29	Balance brought forward			1032	DR
	Bank	154		1186	DR

Sales Ledger

		Debit	Credit	Balance	
		£	£	£	
	Mrs Grant Account				
Oct 29	Balance brought forward			76	DR
	J A Contracts Ltd Account				
Oct 29	Balance brought forward			110	DR

Purchases Ledger

	Central Garages Ltd Account		
Oct 29	Balance brought forward	74	CR
	Hants Timber Co Ltd Account		
Oct 29	Balance brought forward	120	CR

Task 6

Explain to Max what the error he has made is and give him a list (with examples) of the errors not revealed by the Trial Balance.

ASSIGNMENT 3 PREPARING JANET FARMER'S FINAL ACCOUNTS

An integrative assignment with particular links with *The Organisation in its Environment*.

Objectives covered: elements of the indicative content for the following general objectives are covered in this assignment:

Finance B,D,E
People in Organisations B,C,E
The Organisation in its Environment A,C,J,O

Skill area assessment – this assignment develops aspects of the following skill areas: numeracy, identifying and tackling problems, learning and studying, information gathering and communication.

Situation

The 30th September 19X8 was the end of the first financial year for the business owned and run by Janet Farmer. The business supplies patchwork quilt kits; the sales are mainly through mail orders from customers who have seen advertisements, but there is some seasonal trade with retailers developing.

You have been given the job of preparing the final accounts of the business by a partner in the firm of accountants you work for. Janet keeps a Cash Book, totals from which are for the year ended 30th September 19X8.

1 Receipts sheet totals

Capital invested in business	£3000
Receipts from debtors, for goods sold	£3200
Cash received from customers	£16 300

2 Payments sheet totals

Payments to suppliers for materials	£5100
Packing and postage expenses	£2400
Advertising	£1000
Wages for casual packing labour	£3800
Bank charges	£200
General administration expenses	£700
Cutting equipment at cost	£3000
Printing of kit instruction sheets	£400
Cash withdrawn for private use	£5400

Balance at bank on 30th September 19X8 is £500, this has been verified against a bank statement.

Janet provides the following additional information:

(a) stocks of materials held on 30th September 19X8 were valued at £300, cost price;

(b) the equipment purchased is to be depreciated at 20% per annum using the straight line method (i.e. 20% of cost p.a.);

(c) the business is run from Janet's home and its estimated share of household expenses for the year to 30 September 1988 is:

Telephone	£200
Heat and light	£100
Rates	£100

This liability of the business was not settled until after 30th September 19X8.

Task 1

Prepare a draft of Final Accounts for the first year of Janet Farmer's business (Trading and Profit and Loss Account for year ended 30th September 19X8).

After preparing the draft final accounts, you visit Janet Farmer to discuss the accounts and discover that she has not provided you with all of the relevant information. There are outstanding amounts from customers, debtors, for goods sold during year ended 30th September 19X8 amounting to £1300. Stock of packing materials were held at the end of the year, in total worth £200 and the figure given for administration expenses did not include your firm's fees for the year; Janet can expect a bill for £400 to cover these.

Task 2

Redraft the Final Accounts taking the extra items detailed above into consideration.

Janet is pleased to see that the new Final Accounts show an increased profit, but she cannot understand why an increase in profit does not result in an increase in cash in the bank, and why if she put £3000 into the business is there only £500 left even though the business has made a profit?

Task 3

Write to Janet answering the above questions.

During the first year, Janet set her selling price by adding an average of 300% to the cost of goods sold in order to cover overheads, packing and profit margin. At the price charged, she has found that the demand for the kits has exceeded her capacity to supply. In fact, some retail trade orders have been turned down in order to satisfy the mail order side of the business.

Janet reasons that in these market conditions she can raise her prices and hence increase her profit without there being any effect on her output. Therefore during the next year she proposes to add an average of 400% on to the cost of goods sold. Janet is planning to make sufficient money to be able to withdraw a total of £10 000 from the business for her personal use during the next year.

Task 4

Write to Janet and comment on her assessment of the market conditions. You should also enclose a budgeted set of Final Accounts for the year ending 30th September 19X9, based upon her plans.

Assume that cost of sales and business expenses remain the same as for the first year. For the purpose of the budget you may further assume that there will not be any outstanding debtors or creditors, prepayments or accruals on 30th September 19X9, but you will need to calculate the balance at bank.

Janet Farmer believes that demand for her product will remain strong in spite of the increased price, but she recognises that it will be necessary to increase production if the market is to be exploited to the full.

To increase production capacity will require financial resources that Janet does not personally have and therefore outside finance would be required. She requires information and advice on the finance available.

Task 5

The senior partner asks you to write a short report on the sources of finance available to businesses in similar situations to Janet Farmer's, making particular reference to any organisation's structural changes that could be required to obtain certain types of finance.

The report will be for the use of the firm when advising any client, not specifically Janet Farmer.

When the report is finished, send Janet a copy and enclose any literature on suitable finance, available from local sources, that you can find.

ASSIGNMENT 4 CHILTERN BODGERS

An integrative assignment drawing on some aspects of *People in Organisations* and *Organisations in their Environment*.

General objectives: elements of the indicative content for the following general objectives are covered in this assignment.

Finance F
People in Organisations I
Organisations in their Environment E

Skill area assessment – this assignment develops the following skill areas: numeracy, identifying and tackling problems, learning and studying, information gathering and communicating.

Situation

Chiltern Bodgers is a business set up by Ian Davids to make reproduction joinery for the house restoration market. He currently produces two products, i.e. Victorian style skirting board and turned banister spindles. Ian has asked you to look at his business and establish just how much it costs him to produce his products and to help him with financial management decisions.

The first steps are seen as establishing the direct and indirect costs for the business and allocating the indirect costs on an equitable basis to each product, so that a production cost for the finished goods may be found.

During the quarter year ended on 30th June 19X8, the following information was accumulated.

Stocks on 1st April 19X8

(a) 307 metres of planks for skirting board production, cost £0.25 per metre;

(b) 300 metres of square section for spindle production, cost £0.10 per metre.

Stocks on 30th June 19X8

(a) 100 metres of planks for skirting board production cost £0.25 per metre;

(b) 200 metres of square section for spindle production, cost £0.10 per metre;

(c) 35 metres of finished skirting board, value?

(d) 85 spindles in finished condition, value?

During the period 1st April to 30th June 19X8 the following production costs were incurred.

(a) timber for skirting boards, 1500 metres at £0.25 per m;

(b) timber for spindles, 3000 metres at £0.10 per m;

(c) wage costs for three machine operators, £5150, to be charged equally between the products;

(d) wage costs for one general labourer, £1500, to be charged equally between the products;

(e) factory rent and rates £1000, to be charged equally between the products;

(f) consumable stores £43 for skirting board production, £225 for spindle production;

(g) factory electricity consumption £1100, charged 70% to spindles, 30% to skirting boards;

(h) depreciation on the production machinery is provided for on the basis of 20% per annum on cost (straight line method). The machines were acquired for £32 000. Sixty per cent of depreciation is charged to skirting boards production, forty per cent to spindles.

Output for the period was:

(a) finished skirting board, 1435 metres;
(b) finished spindles, 2885.

These figures *include* the finished goods stocks listed above.

Selling prices for the period were:

(a) skirting board, £6.50 per metre;
(b) spindles; £3.00 each.

Task 1

Produce two separate manufacturing accounts for the products and establish the cost per metre of finished skirting board, and the cost of a finished spindle. Using these figures, value the stock of finished goods at 30th June 19X8.

During the period 1st April 19X8 to 30th June 19X8, the following non production expenses were incurred.

Administration	£1120
Selling and distribution	£1680
Total	£2800

As there was no discernible bias towards one or the other of the products in the way these costs were incurred, it was decided that if necessary these costs would be allocated to the products equally. All of these expenses, and the factory overheads, are considered to be fixed in the period under consideration, and for the capacity of the factory during this quarter, which was estimated as 2000 metres of skirting board and 3000 spindles.

Task 2

Draw up break-even charts for both products taking into consideration the allocation of costs between them, and establish for both products:

(a) break-even point;
(b) margin of safety at current production levels;
(c) profit at the level of sales for the period;
(d) profit if maximum output achieved.

What would be the effect of an increase in the price of spindles by £0.25 each, on (a) to (d) above. Assuming all other factors remain constant.

Which product would you suggest to Ian that he concentrates his sales efforts on?

On 30th June 19X8 one of the machine operators gives in his notice. This means that production of one product will have to be concentrated on, at the expense of the other, until a replacement operator can be employed. **NB** The price of spindles is to be increased from 1st July 19X8 by 0.25 each.

Task 3

Advise Ian which product to concentrate on while the labour shortage lasts.

As a result of his sales efforts, Ian has received a special order for 100 metres of skirting board, but as this is a bulk order for a trade customer, the price offered is only £3.90 per metre.

However, he has found a small machine shop which does sub-contract work for other wood machining firms. They have quoted a price of £3.00 per metre to produce the skirting board. This price seems too good to be true, so Ian proposes giving them the special order as a test batch to check their quality. Ian reasons that even if their work is not up to his usual standard, it will be good enough for the special order and he will simply take the 90p difference between the prices as profit.

Task 4

Advise Ian on:

(a) the advisability of accepting the special order, wherever it is produced;

(b) whether sub-contracting is the most profitable way of producing the special contract.

ASSIGNMENT 5 T BREAKS LTD

An integrative assignment with particular emphasis on the *Information Processing* skills area.

This assignment assumes that students have access to appropriate applications software packages.

Objectives covered: elements of the indicative content for the following general objectives are covered in this assignment.

Finance B,C,E,F
People in Organisations 1 A,B,C,E
The Organisation in its Environment 1 H,J,K

Skills area assessment – this assignment develops the following skills areas: numeracy, identifying and tackling problems, learning and studying, information gathering, information processing and communicating.

Situation

T Breaks Ltd have negotiated the sole rights to manufacture and distribute a crispy snack bar which has recently been successfully launched in Scandinavia.

Market research has indicated that sales could reach 1/4 million bars per month by the end of the first year on the UK market. The research also indicated that the bar was likely to be viewed as an upmarket product which would command a premium price, 40 pence per bar would appear to be the optimum sum.

The equipment to manufacture the product will cost £250 000 installed and commissioned; an injection of working capital will be required at the start of the project. T Breaks have allocated £40 000 to working capital for this project, any extra will have to be borrowed, but all of the finance for equipment will have to come from external sources. The finance packages offered have been:

(a) the manufacturer of the equipment is prepared to lease it to T Breaks Ltd under the following terms:

- a five-year lease with option to purchase at the end of this time;
- six payments of £62 500, the first on delivery and commissioning of the equipment, followed by a payment at the end of the first year and at the end of the following four years. The last payment must be increased by £1000 if the option to purchase is exercised.

(b) T Breaks Ltd's bank are prepared to provide finance which will be over four years with repayments of £85 000 being made at the end of each of the four years.

(c) Financial assistance from the Scandinavian inventor and manufacturer of the bar has been offered. It comprises an interest free loan repayable over just two years, with repayments of £125 000 at the end of each year.

Task 1

Evaluate the alternative methods of financing the equipment and recommend to the management of T Breaks Ltd the option you consider best. The company considers its average cost of capital to be 18% p.a.

The departmental managers of T Breaks Ltd have been asked to provide estimates of their revenues, costs, activity levels and any restrictions on these activities envisaged. Their responses are given below.

Sales Manager

Sales will be 150 000 bars in the first month on sale, 175 000 bars in the second month on sale, 200 000 bars in the third month on sale and 225 000 bars per month for the rest of the first year.

Customers will require two months' credit. Selling and distribution expenses will be £4000 per month, payable in the month incurred.

Production Manager

Production will have to start one month before sale and will be at the following rates per month:
1 to 6 inclusive – 200 000 bars
month 7 onwards – 225 000 bars

Supervision costs will be £5000 per month payable in the month incurred.

Energy costs will be £60 000 per quarter payable in arrears, commencing month 3.

General production expenses will be £5000 per month payable in the month incurred.

Production labour cost is calculated at 10p per bar, payable in the month incurred.

Purchasing and Stores Manager

The raw materials will be imported from Scandinavia at a cost equivalent to 10p per bar, delivered to T Breaks warehouse.

These raw materials will be delivered during the month for which they will be required for production, but in the first month twice the required quantity will be needed in order to obtain a buffer stock. No credit terms have been negotiated.

Accountant

Depreciation of the equipment will be over five years using the straight line method.

Rent and rates for this project will be £12 000 per half year, payable in advance, commencing month 1.

Heating and lighting charges will be £1500 per quarter payable in arrears, commencing month 3.

Administration expenses will be £1500 per month payable in the month incurred, from month 1.

Task 2

Draw up the Cash Budget for the first twelve months of operation, to show the amount of any overdraft required.

Note Remember to include any loan and loan repayments you are recommending, along with capital expenditure.

Ignore interest on any overdraft required.

The bank have set the maximum overdraft for T Breaks Ltd at £150 000. In response the company have found it possible to allocate further cash for the projects working capital. After some negotiation, it is agreed that T Breaks Ltd would allocate extra working capital to the project, sufficient to ensure that the overdraft does not exceed £200 000 during the first six months of operation, and that the £150 000 limit will apply for the second six months. The maximum additional funds available for T Breaks to use in this project are £20 000.

Task 3

Rework the Cash Budget to take into consideration the agreement made above. If it is necessary to change your previous advice on anything, write a memorandum to the Managing Director explaining why these changes are necessary.

Task 4

Draw up a budgeted income statement for the first twelve months of operation, for presentation to the management and supplement it with a diagram to show the profit or loss expected during the next twelve months, when the average monthly sales are expected to be 250 000 bars.

Note Any interest payments on borrowings may be charged as if arising on a flat rate basis.

Index